ROBERT WHALEN

The Poetry of Immanence: Sacrament in Donne and Herbert

UNIVERSITY OF TORONTO PRESS
Toronto Buffalo London

© University of Toronto Press Incorporated 2002
Toronto Buffalo London
Printed in Canada

ISBN 0-8020-3659-7

Printed on acid-free paper

National Library of Canada Cataloguing in Publication

Whalen, Robert, 1963–
    The poetry of immanence : sacrament in Donne and Herbert /
    Robert Whalen.

    Includes bibliographical references and index.
    ISBN 0-8020-3659-7

    1. Donne, John, 1572–1631 – Criticism and interpretation.   2. Herbert,
    George, 1593–1633 – Criticism and interpretation.   3. Christian poetry,
    English – Early modern, 1500–1700 – History and criticism.   4. Lord's
    Supper in literature.   I. Title.

PR2248.W47 2002   821'.30938234163   C2002-902241-x

University of Toronto Press acknowledges the financial assistance to
its publishing program of the Canada Council for the Arts and the
Ontario Arts Council.

This book has been published with the help of a grant from the Humanities
and Social Sciences Federation of Canada, using funds provided by the
Social Sciences and Humanities Research Council of Canada.

University of Toronto Press acknowledges the financial support for
its publishing activities of the Government of Canada through the
Book Publishing Industry Development Program (BPIDP).

For Joel and Michael

Contents

Acknowledgments

Turning an idea into a book is an arduous task made worthwhile by the discovery that my otherwise peculiar interests are supported by a dedicated community of scholars. Heather Ross and William Halewood listened patiently as I struggled through my earliest encounters with the poetry of immanence, and I am grateful to Michael Dixon and David Galbraith for their challenging questions and advice as the project began to take shape. Patricia Vicari has been throughout a mentor, valued colleague, and friend whose enthusiasm has helped in good measure to sustain my own. Michael Schoenfeldt, Nancy Lindheim, and Alexandra Johnston read drafts of the manuscript at various stages, offering both valuable suggestions and encouragement. Ray Siemens, David Shore, Michael Allen, and Richard Todd read earlier versions of chapters 4 and 5 and contributed generously to what finally emerged. For extensive and thoughtful commentary on what became chapter 3, I am indebted to Daniel Doerksen and Christopher Hodgkins. I would like also to thank Annabel Patterson and Jeanne Shami for reading a final draft of the same and for reminding me, toiling in the editorial slough of despond, why we do what we do. Barbara Porter and Miriam Skey skilfully piloted the book through the Press.

My deepest gratitude I owe to Eva, whose generosity and wisdom are inestimable.

Earlier versions of material from the introduction and chapters 4 and 5 appeared under the following titles: '"How shall I measure out thy bloud" or "Weening is not measure": TACT, Herbert and Sacramental Devotion in the Electronic Temple,' *Early Modern Literary Studies* 5.3 / Special Issue 4 (2000): 7.1–37, jointly published in a special issue of *Text*

Technology 9.3 (1999): 27–65; 'George Herbert's Sacramental Puritanism,' *Renaissance Quarterly* 54.4 (2001): 1273–1307. I am grateful to the editors and presses involved for permission to reprint these materials here.

Prologue

James Joyce once asked his brother Stanislaus whether there might be 'a certain resemblance between the mystery of the Mass' and what happens in *Dubliners*. 'I mean that I am trying,' wrote Joyce, 'to give people some kind of intellectual pleasure or spiritual enjoyment by converting the bread of everyday life into something that has a permanent artistic life of its own ... for their moral, and spiritual uplift.' Though Joyce's literary Mass differs in meaning and scope from the Holy Communion experienced by the Renaissance devotional writer, the idea that such ordinary daily life as that portrayed in *Dubliners* is imbued with sacramental significance would have been familiar to John Donne, George Herbert, and their religious contemporaries. Joyce's profane transubstantiation and devotional poets' deployment of sacramental topoi serve different purposes, but implicit in Joyce's remarks, however ironic, is a spiritual nostalgia suggesting his affinity with these earlier writers. The author of *Ulysses* – which opens with a burlesque of the old Latin Mass, *Introibo ad altare Dei*[1] – would have recovered for modern human life, love, and desire something like religious significance, albeit *nec ecclesia ritualis*. Seventeenth-century Christian poets such as Donne and Herbert, on the other hand, observed in their quotidian worlds evidence of that which would have been inconceivable apart from the rites and ceremonies of the English church: St John's proclamation of the Word become flesh.

But just how did Herbert, Donne, and their contemporaries understand the sacramental dimension of this central Christian kerygma? Combining current historiography with close reading of verse and sermon, *The Poetry of Immanence* examines the role of sacrament in early modern understandings of the relationship between the sacred and the profane, and the Eucharist in particular as the institutional convergence of ceremonial and psychological dimensions of religious experience. Fundamental to both concerns is that most scandalous of doctrinal notions, the Incarnation.

Louis L. Martz recognized long ago that while continental meditative practices had always had a strong psychological component, it was 'the inward surge of Puritanism' combined with these older techniques that gave rise to the unique devotional poetry of the seventeenth century.[2] Stopping short of Martz's Anglo-Catholic ideal as an accurate description of early Stuart mainstream divinity, this study nevertheless builds on his provocative but insufficiently developed observations about the puritan aspects of the English *via media*. His investigation of Ignatian spirituality as providing the formal and tonal materials of devotional literature in the English Renaissance allowed Martz to coin a wonderful phrase overlooked by both his champions and detractors. 'Catholic Puritanism,' Martz's remarkable description of one continental meditative's tendency to condemn external forms and exercises, complements the observation that in Herbert it is 'the weapon of *mental communion* which makes the sacraments flow from Christ's side.' Martz was reluctant, however, to recognize the extent to which early seventeenth-century moderate Calvinism accommodated and was accommodated by this sacramental impulse. The 'new stage' of English puritanism versed in 'that union of the powers of the soul' hitherto the province of 'Anglo-Catholics,' he writes, did not emerge until fully mid-way through the century of revolution, most notably in Richard Baxter. Nor did Martz allow that the puritan emphases on 'special grace,' 'inward researches,' and 'mistrust of the senses' had any formative influence on the so-called Anglican divines.[4]

Inspired by Martz's illuminating study but reluctant to endorse its implicit denial of predestinarian Calvinism as a significant factor in mainstream divinity, 'sacramental puritanism' is my own critical shorthand for an important aspect of the complex devotional literature and confessional identity of the early Stuart church. It emerged as a result of establishment divines' efforts to reconcile the potentially contrary imperatives of sacrament and devotion, an eirenic strategy that allowed for the cultivation of puritan devotional enthusiasm through an internalized yet fully sacramental and sacerdotal apparatus. Religious inwardness was certainly not exclusive to Protestantism. But in the late Reformation English church, as recent historiography has shown, an ideological conflict intensified between two styles of divinity: that for which external forms and ceremonies were paramount, and another that placed relatively greater value on preaching, doctrine, and the development of a keen devotional interiority. It is in this context that metaphysical wit was much more than a stylistic feature of Donne's and Herbert's poetic and homiletic methods. A rhetorical invention born as much of polemical necessity as of genuine spiritual need, sacramental puritanism played a crucial role in these divines' contribution to the pre-Civil War *via media*, that volatile fusion of Reform doctrine and Roman Catholic ecclesiology. If the centrality of ceremonial forms was a feature of what Peter Lake has called 'avant-garde conformity,'[5] establishment clergy such as Donne and Herbert were concerned nonetheless that sacrament reify and be subsumed by the otherwise ephemeral motions of the soul's progress. Private devotion for them necessarily reflected the creeds and traditions of the broader Christian community, while these in turn, embodied in ceremony and ritual, witnessed the application of a grace which ultimately exceeds ritual's grasp. The Pauline admonition to examine oneself when receiving Holy Communion suggests the mutual relevance of ritual act and psychological reflection, of external and internal aspects of religious devotion. Sacrament, then, and particularly the Eucharist, occupied a liminal position in the formation of Christian subjectivity, for in bringing the materials of ceremony within close proximity of the devotional psyche, they provided a highly stylized, even theatrical, means of integrating the private and institutional dimensions of religious life. This intersection of private and public spheres, moreover, is analogous to the incarnational features of sacramental doctrine. As religious community and ceremony are material counterparts to the spiritual body of the church, so do the elements of bread and wine flesh out the promise contained in the words of institution, 'This is my body.' Ceremony provides material and visible sustenance to the otherwise invisible operations of Christian salvation.

The political dimension of this psycho-ceremonial dichotomy is informed by centuries of extensive theological discussion about the relationships among spirit, matter, psyche, the body, and language. The Introduction reviews this complex history up to and including the religious scene of the Elizabethan and early Stuart eras, arguing that the same issues dissected in Reformation debates over the nature of the Eucharist long had been a feature of theological discourse and that the reformers by and large were as concerned as their Roman Catholic enemies to maintain a doctrine of 'real presence' even while jettisoning the traditional scholastic logic that had supported it. Misunderstanding of this crucial issue among literary historians, critics, and scholars has contributed to a confessionally based rift in Donne and Herbert studies between, on the one hand, Anglo-Catholic Martzians and, on the other, those whose *via media* readings veer in the direction of a 'Protestant poetics.' Thus in his early *Poetry and Dogma* – until very recently the only book-length treatment of the Eucharist in seventeenth-century English poetry – Malcolm Ross derided the disintegration of psyche and sacrament, aligning the former with the fluid instability of the conceit – the 'metaphysics of process, in which symbolic belief and practice exist only to be annihilated in a metaphorical holocaust.' In recent years, however, critical assessment of the English *via media* has veered in a decidedly Genevan direction, a view that has been particularly influential among Herbert scholars. In *Love Known*, for example, a sophisticated development of the Protestant poetics first advanced by William Halewood and Barbara Lewalski, Richard Strier avers that eucharistic terminology in *The Temple* is for the most part metaphorical.[7] Gene Veith, similarly, while allowing external ceremonial forms 'closest to Herbert's experience,' emphasizes the poet's discussion of the sacraments 'in the more guarded terms of Reformed, Calvinist theology.'[8] Christopher Hodgkins is more emphatic in identifying Herbert's *via media* as 'very nearly Calvinist. Very, very nearly.'[9] Hodgkins, like Veith, rightly points out the significant roles sacrament and ceremony played in Reform theology and ecclesiology, and his analysis of *The Temple* persuasively challenges Louis Martz's influential view of Herbert as exemplary Anglo-Catholic. In his discussion of the church's and Herbert's indebtedness to Reform theology for their sacramental views, Hodgkins thus compares key passages from the *Institutes of the Christian Religion*, the Elizabethan Articles, and selected lines from several *Temple* lyrics.[10] Perhaps the foremost champion of a Calvinist Herbert, Daniel Doerksen concurs with Hodgkins by seeing in the Jacobean and early Caroline church a middle road that runs directly *through* Geneva – between not Rome and Calvin's Swiss church, but rather between Rome and the more radical separatists or 'those considered heterodox in theology.'[11] But this only restates rather than answers the question of the church's confessional identity: 'considered' by whom? Indeed, what is the standard by which anyone in the pre–Civil War religious establishment is to be considered heterodox, particularly with respect to sacraments and their role in the spiritual life of the church? Doerksen tells us that the eucharistic element in Herbert's poetry is 'overrated' by those who neglect to notice that even the most sacramental of the lyrics is about the speaker's heart. His observation that Herbert's religion (and Donne's) is 'personal and biblical rather than institutional,'[12] however, is based on a false dichotomy, as though the focus on inwardness and scripture were not compatible with the contemporary religious hegemony. Indeed, Doerksen's study itself characterizes the conformist mainstream of the early Stuart church as predominantly and therefore *institutionally* Calvinist.

The relationship between doctrine and discipline – between, that is, formal theological belief and outward matters including church governance, polity, and ceremonial practice[13] – is important for our understanding of Donne's and Herbert's sacramental poetics. Theories of eucharistic presence emphasizing its material aspects tended to support a style of divinity in which priest, ceremony, and outward conformity are key features. Belief in the centrality of inward spiritual life, on the other hand, was reinforced by a theology in which the external elements are less effectual instruments than mere signs of a strictly invisible grace. Though these binarisms are problematic in so far as they reflect more the polarizing rhetoric of Stuart religious polemic than any stable and readily identifiable groups, they are useful if understood as framing a continuum traversed by contemporary divines in their struggles over the church's confessional identity. Such polarizations, then, are meant not to indicate precise confessional categories but rather ideological tendencies, so that while there were those whose theological itineraries suggest the desire for a stable middle road embracing both puritan and ceremonialist inclinations, these Anglo-Catholics, or puritan moderates, or Calvinist conformists were not immune to the controversies that preoccupied their more openly polemical contemporaries. This critical flexibility is necessary in considering Donne and Herbert, who clearly valued both external and internal dimensions of religious piety. Achsah Guibbory demonstrates such sensitivity in suggesting that when Herbert's lyrics are personal and introspective they tend to 'spiritualise the church festivals and ceremonies ... in a way that deemphasizes the material, ceremonial, and outward aspects of worship.'[14] Another way of looking at this, however, is to see sacrament and ceremony as penetrating the inner devotional realm and claiming its otherwise insular space as contiguous with the trappings that are its institutional surface. In Elizabeth Clarke's attractive formulation, for example, Herbert's poems externalize 'the inward spiritual holiness which is the essence of Reformed piety.' In her study of the relationship between the public and private dimensions of prayer in Elizabethan and Stuart England, Ramie Targoff similarly has shown that 'there is absolutely no opposition for Herbert between liturgy and inwardness.'[15] Internal and external components of religious experience converge on eucharistic topoi, devotional and ceremonial pieties vying for the identity of Christian grace and the location of its authority, just as competing sacramental theories focus on the manner in which the eucharistic elements communicate their holy referents. A style of divinity emphasizing devotion as integral with ceremonial forms and ritual tends toward more sensualist eucharistic formulae. Obversely, the extent to which the Eucharist was thought to contain or otherwise effectually to communicate grace is an index of its importance in promoting the church's social and confessional cohesion. The Pauline admonition to examine oneself when receiving the Eucharist was important for early Stuart divines of all stripes, whether moderate puritan, conforming Calvinist, or proto-Laudian. But just as Jesus' words of institution were the site of exegetical conflict, so were the relative emphases placed on private devotion and ceremony potentially divisive.

In an important recent study, R.V. Young endorses Malcolm Ross's neglected thesis – that 'the attack upon the traditional Catholic doctrine of the Eucharist played a major, if inadvertant, rôle in the secularization of Western culture.' Against Ross, however, Young avers that the devotional poets of the seventeenth century did not succumb to this process, despite the pressures of Reformation theology.[16] In the spirit of Louis Martz, then, Young's study is a long-overdue rebuttal to the Protestant poetics reviewed above. It is also an attack on both the postmodern poetics of absence advanced by Stanley Fish and of new historicist reductions. But in blaming the reformers for inaugurating a process that led to postmodern nominalism – 'splitting apart the tenors and vehicles of metaphors' is 'the contemporary [critical] equivalent of Puritan iconoclasm'![17] – Young, like Ross, does not allow that Reform theology was concerned precisely with the effective realization and communication of sacramental presence. This notion that the Reformation was a watershed event leading inevitably to late twentieth-century relativism becomes untenable when it is observed that the postmodern critique of presence is just as easily appropriated by Young's critical allies. Seeking to maintain for Herbert a distinctively Anglican sacramentalism that avoids the declension of the sacramental symbol into mere rhetorical figure and devotional subjectivism identified by Ross, Heather Asals is also suspicious of Reformation formulae. Rather than Young's emphasis on analogy, however, it is equivocation – the Aristotelian notion that individual words have multiple significations – that is the basis of a poetics which allows the brokenness of language to constitute a fragmentary indeterminacy parallel to the breaking of bread in the Eucharist. In Herbert, writes Asals, 'All things and all words, as well as the relation between

things and words, are made to "spell" God, whose name *is* (*I AM*).'[18]
Suspicious of this Derrida-inflected theology, Young is relieved to observe that in her actual readings of Herbert what Asals calls equivocation
is really Thomist analogy. Young and Asals thus share a concern to find
in Herbert an important feature of sacramental metaphysics, whatever
the confessional context: the idea that the sign is somehow joined to its
referent, really and not merely figuratively. In Young's words, analogy is
'inclusive of meaning,' allowing for a 'multi-layered density of reality
where the symbols that man devises, like the creatures of nature, are
both manifestations of, and incitements to, his spiritual experience.'[19]
This is not very far from Asals after all. I would add, however, that while
there are significant differences between Roman Catholic and Reformation theories of the sacrament, even Calvin himself held that it is by
'analogy' that the human mind comprehends spiritual significance in
the physical domain.[20] Now, a Thomist might object that Calvin's idea of
analogy was very different from that of Aquinas. But if the reformers
twisted scholastic ideas beyond recognition, St Thomas was criticized for
his dubious reading of the Aristotelian philosophy of matter. The difference between Thomism and the reformers' theories is at once slight and
highly significant, for if in the former, as Young argues, the sacramental
signs are related to their substances by virtue of an analogy of proportion,[21] a similar analogy, I argue in my introduction, is suggested by
Calvinist and other Reformation formulae, only now the analogous relationship inheres not between the metaphysical components of the sacramental species, but rather between the species and the invisible soul of
the communicant. As Judith H. Anderson so persuasively has demonstrated, it was the English reformers who, anxious to maintain a real if
non-corporeal presence in the sacrament, devised formulae in which
sacramental signs derive substantive power from their referents without
actually embodying them.[22] If ostensibly metaphorical and symbolic,
such understandings of sacramental presence were neither simply nor
merely so. Moreover, if the reformers' oxymoronic solution – a non-
corporeal 'real presence' – suggests merely that they wanted it both ways,
so did the doctrine of transubstantiation assert the reality of a corporeal
substance which, strictly speaking, is inaccessible to the senses.

At issue in all such efforts to understand the relationship between the
internal and external domains of eucharistic experience are the affective
powers and referential limits of signs, both sacramental and linguistic:
their capacity to communicate spirit, to penetrate and to articulate the
innermost workings of the soul, and, in the case of the Eucharist, to

manifest their otherwise transcendent objects. Because linguistic and sacramental affectivities are so closely aligned in Reformation theology, it is not surprising to discover in the English devotional writers an interest in the Eucharist as the supreme expression of a Word made flesh.

Donne's and Herbert's explorations of sacrament were motivated by overlapping and divergent concerns. While both poets provide ample evidence of ideological struggle over the English church's confessional identity, Donne in addition has left a startling record of the relevance of sacrament for the profane aspects of his poetic experience. Interest in sacramental ideas is most evident, surprisingly, not in the religious poems and sermons but rather in the 'secular' love lyrics, elegies, satires, and verse epistles. In his witty combining of eucharistic with a variety of analogous but ostensibly nonreligious concerns Donne, I argue in chapter 1, tests the limits of an incarnational poetics for his unique understanding of the relationship between the sacred and the profane. The residue of a medieval, Roman Catholic world view allowed him to invest a surprising range of interests with eucharistic significance, the poems' sacred profanities at once analogous to and an extreme manifestation of the Incarnation. Such poems are an extension into the long English Reformation of what Miri Rubin has described as the medieval impulse to find in eucharistic language the 'means and rules for [the] construction' of a manifold religious discourse. Her observation that in medieval culture the 'rituals within which [the Eucharist] unfolded offered ideas of further and analogous uses in other spheres of life'[23] is highly applicable to the alchemical wizardry of Donne's secular verse. And yet his sacramental poetics suggests also something of the Protestant reformers' emphasis on the word as the primary communicator of divine grace wherein the linguistic sign, like the bread and wine, was a quasi-sacrament both instrumental and efficacious.

Donne's secular-sacramental wit, a collision of medieval sensibility and post-Reformation logocentrism, evinces a confidence in the incarnational power of language that in the sacred verse, I argue in chapter 2, yields to a nervousness about the psychological and therefore transitory status of devotional experience. However we care to date the earlier lyrics, their secular audience allowed Donne to draw on his Roman Catholic heritage in ways and to an extent that in an explicitly devotional context would have been controversial – or downright dangerous if the execution of the Jesuit poet, Robert Southwell, is any indication. Nevertheless, though written for two different audiences,

Donne's secular and sacred poems instantiate specifically a divergence in *religious* sensibility, one that reflects on a personal level that which troubled the English people from the Reformation through to the Civil War. The difference is between a faith in which sacred and profane are mutually reinforcing aspects of human experience and one in which concern with the sacred dimension of the world and the flesh yields almost entirely to the inward deliberations of the Christian soul and, for Donne, a more than passing interest in the predestinarian aspects of English Calvinism. The sacred verse, however, though largely eschewing ceremonial for more exclusively devotional concerns, yet retains considerable vestiges of Donne's imaginative commitment to the religion of his noble Catholic ancestors.[24] No longer merely the subject of a playful though profound theological wit, sacrament now is the speaker's devotional lifeline, the external, ceremonial, and objective escape from a Calvinist interiority with which it is held in dialectical tension. This conflicted relationship in the divine poems between sacramental means of grace and the predestinarian anxieties they relieve is dealt with most effectively in the Christmas sermon of 1626, the subject of chapter 3. There Donne manages to advance a potentially controversial formula for 'real presence' in the Eucharist while at the same time cultivating in his auditory a meditative attitude that is subtly predestinarian in tone and content, this in the context of an intensification of anti-Calvinism and avant-garde policies among the religious establishment.

George Herbert's verse, though highly self-conscious and introspective, is fully immersed in the affective somatic imagery of sacrament and ceremony, perfecting the integration of external and internal aspects of religious experience only partially realized by Donne. Chapters 4 and 5 examine Herbert's sacramental puritanism as combining more successfully than his elder the potentially contrary imperatives of ceremony and devotion, a success which consists not only in a harmonization of these modes of religious experience but also in the drama resulting from the ideological conflict the poems trace. Herbert much more than Donne would commune with Christ through sacramental means. *The Temple*, not unlike Robert Grosseteste's thirteenth-century *Templum Dei* in which confessional and Eucharist are central features, is at once a spiritual-architectural edifice and a linguistic medium on which converge both divine love and the human longing for transcendence. The tension between word- and sacrament-oriented pieties so much at issue throughout the English Reformation is ameliorated by the affective intensity of Herbert's poems – scripturally and typologically inflected linguistic constructions, yet earthen vessels redolent of both religious desire and its object. Close reading of such celebrated sacramental lyrics as 'The H. Communion' and 'The Banquet' is expanded to include those, not often considered in this context, in which a sacramental apparatus inevitably is called upon to alleviate the speaker's spiritual impasse and thereby to facilitate a communion with the divine that is simultaneously psychological and ceremonial.

It is this sacramental convergence of private prayer and ritual in *The Temple*, finally, that provides Herbert with a way of thinking about the relationship between poetic *dévote* and God – between maker and Maker, the artist's words and the Word that is All. Chapter 6 explores Herbert's sacramental conception of artistic identity and agency, his struggle to arrive at a positive understanding of the nature and value of human art while recognizing the full extent of human depravity. Though Herbert, unlike Donne, rarely was troubled by the implications of predestinarian Calvinism, he was keenly aware of the Augustinian conception of depravity from which it was derived. His solution to the problem is a sacramentalization of the devotional sphere, a writing of the self whose centre is not the autonomous ego but something like what William Blake was to call the human form divine, though Herbert was no Romantic mystic. It is in sacrament and ceremony that divine and human initiatives coincide, both poetic and sacramental media conducive to the fullest possible realization of divinity in the world. Fusion in the sacrament of sensible and non-corporeal aspects of religious experience sanctions Herbert's art as the necessary manifestation of devotional realities, his words the linguistic elements of a poetic Eucharist transformed by the presence they would evoke. If the Donne chapters document both the decline and persistence of a Roman Catholic religious sensibility, *The Poetry of Immanence* finds in Herbert a *via media* that runs neither between Rome and Geneva, nor, as Daniel Doerksen would have it, *through* Geneva between Rome and radically Protestant Amsterdam. Herbert's middle road, rather – the one that, though not less-travelled, proved for Donne considerably more difficult – is a sacramental *via romana* that runs straight through the English Protestant heart.

The Poetry of Immanence would restore to sacrament the attention it deserves in the critical literature surrounding two of the seventeenth century's most celebrated poets. The book elucidates a sacramental poetics and contextualizes it amid both theological debate and the broader ideological tension between ostensibly non-corporeal and corporeal dimensions of religious life: private piety and ceremonial form, differentiated ego and community, soul and body, devotion and art, sacred and secular. Eucharistic topoi became for Donne and Herbert powerful conceptual tools with which to explore both the intersection of the somatic with the psychological domains and their respective claims to Christianity. Sacrament in early modern culture is shown thus to have played a crucial role in the formation of religious subjectivity and in imaginative understandings of the sacred and profane as intersecting spheres of human experience.

The Poetry of Immanence

The Eucharist and the English Reformation

Hoc meum corpus est. Thought to be instituted by Jesus and therefore of powerful ritual appeal, the Eucharist in the Renaissance long had held a central place in Christian life and worship. As is true of any important aspect of the faith, interest in and controversy over the precise nature of the sacrament are not exclusive to the tumultuous Reformation. Indeed, the various positions staked out and defended by the magisterial reformers derived from a centuries-old debate.

The febrile theological discussions of the English Reformation tended to pit reformed or 'true' piety against 'popish' idolatry – or, to attenuate that implicit value judgment, innovative against traditional or conservative religion. The ideological divide separating Roman Catholic and Protestant sensibilities is evident, for example, when we compare two sixteenth-century contemporaries, Robert Southwell and Edmund Spenser. Heavenly bliss in Southwell's 'Seek Flowers of Heaven' is conceived in sensual terms, flowers whose 'leaves are stain'd in beauty's dye' (9) and whose 'sug'red veins' are filled with 'Life-giving juice of living love' (13–14). That sacramental hint of Christ's blood gives off a 'sovereign scent, surpassing sense' that 'ravisheth the mind' (21–2). Clearly Southwell, a martyred Roman Catholic, recognized the affective power of verse to take the Christian psyche beyond itself and its 'loathsome load' (2). But the poem is a rather reluctant *contemptus mundi*, very different in tone and diction from Spenser's comparatively anaemic and Neoplatonic 'Hymn of Heavenly Love' where the motion from 'this base world' to 'heauens hight' (2) is toward such rarefied objects as 'rolling Spheres' (26), 'lamps of burning light' (59), and 'gemmes of shyning gold' (60), which in turn are attended by the abstractions 'high eternall powre' (27) and even 'trinal triplicities' (64). It is in the same poem that the Incarnation is characterized as a rather unfortunate necessity: 'In flesh at first the guilt committed was / Therefore in flesh it must be satisfyde' (141–2), original sin being 'that infected cryme ... enrooted in all fleshly slyme' (167–8). It is thus not surprising to discover that 'the food of life,' Christ's 'deare sacrament,' feeds but 'our hungry soules vnto us lent' (194–6).

Despite the evidence of such disparate sensibilities, however, it would be misleading simply to align carnal understandings of the Eucharist with Roman Catholicism and symbolic or metaphorical understandings with the reformers. To do so is to allow the polemical dimension of the debate to distort our understanding of the actual positions involved.

Long before the advent of the Latin church in the Middle Ages, and before Aquinas immersed Christian theology in Aristotelian thought, the Greek fathers were accustomed to thinking of sacramental presence as a changing of the ritual elements into the body and blood of Christ, a process, according to E. Schillebeeckx, similar to but not exactly the same as that indicated by the later *transubstantiatio.* Just as for the patristic authority, Irenaeus, Christian conversion was a taking possession of the convert by the spirit of God, so the eucharistic elements or 'species' of bread and wine were thought to be appropriated or assumed by God, the deity descending and possessing them. An early example of carnal attitudes to Christ's words of institution, writes Schillebeeckx, is Theodore of Mopsuestia's claim, 'Christ did not say, "This is the symbolum of my blood," but "This is my blood," a change of the wine takes place.'[1] As Theodore's assertion implies, opposition to a literal reading of the words of institution had always been a feature of sacramental theology. In his *De corpore et sanguine domini,* notes Miri Rubin, Paschasius Radbert (ca. 785–ca. 860) insisted that Jesus' words of institution intend the very flesh and blood born of the Virgin, an emphasis on *veritas* to which his monastic colleague, Ratramnus (d. 868), responded by asserting Augustinian *figura* as best describing the nature of the sacrament. Paschasius insisted that Ratramnus was a heretic even though the latter agreed on a fundamental change or *conversio* for the elements. The first major challenge to Paschasius's realist position came only in the eleventh century when Berengar of Tours (ca. 999–1088) asserted a symbolic function for the species as signs of a conversion that takes place principally and solely within the believer. The inside/outside dialectic formerly referring to the elements themselves and concerned with positing a real though veiled conversion became for Berengar a question of the sacrament's role in signifying or representing a primarily spiritual transformation located in the soul. Berengar insisted, anticipating Calvin's own anxiety some five-hundred years later, that Christ's body is incorruptible, dwelling always at the right hand of God in heaven rather than on the altar.[2]

Sharing this distaste for an ultra-sensualism, yet wanting to maintain and comprehend a doctrine of 'real presence,' thirteenth-century scholastics adopted Aristotelian categories to explain the continuing appearance of material bread and wine after they supposedly had been transformed into the body and blood of Christ. In the *Summa*, Aquinas argued that the species communicate Christ's physical presence but in a way not perceived by the senses. Communicants experience in eating the sensations associated with mere bread; in reality, however, it is Christ's physical body that is present:

> Our bodily eye is unable, because of the sacramental species, to see the body of Christ which is underneath them; it is not just that they are a sort of covering, preventing us from seeing him in the way a bodily veil hides what it veils; it is rather because Christ's body has no connection with the ambient of the sacrament [circumstat hoc sacramentum] through its own proper accidents, but only by means of the sacramental species.[3]

It is important to understand that Reformation attacks on the doctrine of transubstantiation and Roman Catholic practices that emphasized the carnality of the 'real presence' both derived from a misunderstanding of the metaphysical underpinnings on which the doctrine was based. St Thomas was influenced by his understanding of the Aristotelian philosophy of matter in which it is held that bodies consist of matter and form, form being an extension of matter governing its particular appearance. The substance or essence of a body inheres in both aspects or principles – both its matter and form. For Aquinas, it was possible that the matter or substance of Christ's body be present under the form of bread even while still in heaven. The conversion of the bread, then, is not a formal or accidental but rather a substantial one only. The body of Christ, moreover, is present not as a 'body in place,' but in a 'special way that is proper to this sacrament [sed quodum speciali modo, qui est proprius huic sacramento].'[4] It is present not locally, as an extended body is, but rather as 'purely and simply substance.'[5] Just as the substance of bread is never present as an extended body, neither is the substance of the body of Christ. In the doctrine of transubstantiation was thus developed the idea that while the substance of the elements is wholly changed, the 'accidents' or the elements' appearance remains,[6] a view which was to persist through to and beyond later Tridentine reform. True Aristotelianism, however, would not have tolerated such a division, and so the Thomist doctrine was perhaps responsible for misunderstanding after all. For Aristotle, substance is a complex of matter, 'which in itself is not a "this,"' and form, 'which is that precisely in virtue of which a thing is called a "this."' Therefore it is absurd to separate, except conceptually, 'the matter of a thing and that of which it is the matter.'[7] That Thomas was very much aware of this is evident in his observation that in the sacrament the accidents of the body of Christ are present *because the substance is*.[8] According to Rubin, however, Duns Scotus (1264–1308), William Ockham (1300–47), and John Wycliffe (1335–84) all were to recognize in Thomas the implied separation of substance and accident and thus a departure from Aristotle's model in which the categories can be separated only conceptually. But while all three were avowed Aristotelians, Wycliffe's realism differed both from the nominalism of Scotus (who went so far as to argue for the total annihilation of the elements of wine and bread, which Aquinas denied) and from Ockham, who pursued sensualist understandings. Wycliffe was adamant that the substances of bread and wine remain after the consecration. His solution was a kind of consubstantiation whereby the sacrament is both bread and God simultaneously, a sacramental theology, writes Rubin, that allowed for a 'spiritual and yet *real* presence.' Officials at the Council of Constance, however, emphatically thought otherwise, formally endorsing the Thomist separation of substance and accident and condemning those, such as Wycliffe's fellow objector, Jon Huss, for opposing the doctrine and the clerical privilege it supported.[9]

Long before the Reformation, then, the Roman church struggled to reconcile corporeal and spiritual understandings of the Eucharist. It is difficult on this side of the sixteenth century to see the sacramental views of the principle reformers as anything but diametrically opposed to those of the Roman church. But if Luther, Zwingli, and Calvin were convinced of the primacy of word and spirit over matter and the ceremonial aspects of the faith, they were also reluctant, to varying degrees, to abandon an instrumental role for sacraments in Christian soteriology and even the carnal understandings it suggested.

Though vehemently opposed to the Roman doctrine, Luther gradually assimilated a doctrine of 'real presence' in his sacramental thought. That this was the chief impediment to his getting along with the Swiss reformers Zwingli and Oecolampadius and their ally Martin Bucer is evident in the *Marberg Articles* drawn up by Luther following the 1529

Colloquy and endorsed by all the Swiss delegates. Agreement was reached on fourteen of the fifteen articles; of the fifteenth's six points dealing with the doctrine of the Lord's Supper, only the sixth, which addressed the question of presence, was left unresolved. Here Luther insists, against Zwingli's figurative reading of the words of institution, that 'the mouth receives the body of Christ, the soul believes the words when eating the body,' that 'Christ is in heaven and in the Supper' even though this appears to be contrary to nature, and that the figure of synecdoche best characterizes the nature of presence, rather than metaphor which 'abolishes the content altogether.' Thus, the 'body is in the bread as the sword is in the sheath.'[10] Zwingli's preference at Marberg, on the other hand, is for the primarily memorial function of the sacrament – 'a byname,' not unlike Ascension Day or other names in the church calendar recalling biblical events.[11] Perhaps to facilitate greater Protestant unity, Luther gestured in *Admonition Concerning the Sacrament of the Body and Blood of Our Lord* (1530) toward the Swiss emphasis on the memorialist aspect of the sacrament derived from Jesus' words, 'Do this in remembrance of me.' Nevertheless, Luther here warns against the 'enthusiasts' who 'make mere bread and wine of the sacrament, peel out the kernel, and give them [the recipients] the husk'; he maintains instead that the Lord's Supper 'is a gracious, efficacious sacrament.'[12] Fearful, perhaps, that public opinion as to the putative agreement eventually reached between the Wittenberg and Swiss camps saw a compromise in favour of the Zwinglians, Luther sought to clarify his position in *Brief Confession Concerning the Holy Sacrament* (1544), which affirmed with renewed zeal a doctrine of sacramental presence. It is here that Luther bases the consubstantiation of body and bread in the sacrament on the hypostatic union, the 'humanity and divinity of Christ in one person.'[13] More controversial, however, was Luther's claim that the body consumed in the rite is a pre-ascension body, that of the earthly Christ who instituted the sacrament beforehand, thus clarifying his Marberg claim – that 'Christ is in heaven and in the Supper.'[14]

Against Luther's affirmations of presence and full integration of Christ's sustained divine and human attributes, Huldreich Zwingli sharply distinguished between Christ's two natures and insisted, as Calvin later would, that the ascended Christ is the divine Christ to which alone the sacrament refers. To 'feed on Christ's body,' writes Zwingli, is simply 'to believe in him.'[15] With respect to the words of institution, Zwingli avers that there are numerous instances in the Bible where 'is' means 'signifies' – a figurative, not literal, signification.[16] Zwingli was capable, however, of allowing the species a quasi-instrumental role: 'one and the same Spirit works all these things, sometimes without, sometimes with, the external instrument, and in inspiring draws where, as much, and whom he wills.'[17] In his later years, moreover, he affirmed sacramental presence: 'We believe Christ to be truly present in the Supper, indeed we do not believe that it is the Lord's Supper unless Christ is present.' However, the scripture Zwingli uses in support of this claim – 'Where two or three are gathered together in my name, there am I in the midst of them' – emphasizes corporate reception rather than the sacramental species.[18]

Calvin sought a *via media* that avoids, on the one hand, 'too little regard for the signs' to which the mysteries are 'so to speak attached,' and, on the other, an immoderate attention to the same signs, which might 'obscure somewhat the mysteries themselves.' Allowing that there is in fact 'no unanimity as to the mode of partaking,' he dismissed those who say faith is all that is required, or that 'to eat is only to believe.' Calvin preferred the formula, 'we eat Christ's flesh in believing, because it is made ours by faith.' Faith is no substitute for receiving the sacrament, for God instituted the rite and intends that his church exercise it. Eating, rather, follows from faith, the result being that the communicant feels within the 'remarkable effect of [a] faith' which, presumably, is there apart from any material ritual.[19] Apparently recognizing the difficulty of articulating the presence of a body that remains in heaven and cannot be in two places at once, Calvin's intellectual rigour occasionally yields to an *O altitudo*:

> And although my mind can think beyond what my tongue can utter, yet even my mind is conquered and overwhelmed by the greatnes of the thing. Therefore, nothing remains but to break forth in wonder at this mystery, which plainly neither the mind is able to conceive nor the tongue to express.[20]

This agnostic attitude toward the *modus* of sacramental presence, however, is uncharacteristic of Calvin's analytical and deeply curious intellect. To maintain significance for the elements as set apart from ordinary wine and bread while avoiding what he would have regarded as a contamination of the resurrected Christ by merely material being, Calvin settles on an *arcana virtus*, the doctrine of 'virtualism' that is his singular contribution to sacramental theology: Christ's flesh, though 'separated from us by such great distance,' nevertheless 'penetrates to us, so that it becomes our food'; the Spirit 'truly unites things separated in space.' Though the breaking of bread is a 'symbol' and not 'the thing itself,' nevertheless, 'by the showing of the symbol the thing itself is also shown.'[21] Elsewhere, notes Kilian McDonnell, he writes:

> Christ is not visibly present, and is not beheld with our eyes, as the symbols are which excite our remembrance by representing him. In short, in order that he may be present to us, he does not change his place, but communicates to us from heaven the virtue of his flesh as though it were present.[22]

This is in keeping with Calvin's general definition of a sacrament as 'an outward sign by which the Lord seals on our consciences the promises of his good will toward us in order to sustain the weakness of our faith.'[23] The 'outward sign,' rather than an 'accident' veiling an inward 'substance' (the traditional Roman Catholic formula) or, as for Luther, a manifestation of the hypostatic union, is instead an Augustinian 'seal' ratifying a sacramental reality which takes place in the heart or soul of the communicant. The material elements are important insofar as they are the means by which God chooses to indicate his gifts, serving to mitigate communicants' inability to comprehend spiritual truths without material aids. Our 'small capacity' and the 'dullest minds' are led by 'analogy' from physical to spiritual things.[24]

Denying the doctrine of transubstantiation, Calvin accepted the conversion of the species to 'something else' but rejected the idea that the substance of the outward sign is 'wiped out.' Indeed, 'the signification would have no fitness if the truth there represented had no living image in the outward sign.' By insisting that the 'analogy' would be impossible with 'only the empty appearance of bread' rather than true bread, Calvin ironically suggests that his doctrine is not less but more affirmative of 'real presence' than is transubstantiation.[25] It is a satanic error, however, to believe 'that Christ's body, enclosed in the bread, is transmitted by the mouth of the body into the stomach.'[26] Calvin repeatedly resists any such suggestion. His opponents 'think they only communicate with [the body of Christ] if it descends into bread; they do not understand the manner of descent by which he lifts us up to himself.'[27] That the communicant is raised to Christ in the Eucharist rather than receives an incarnated Christ, an idea directly opposed to Luther's and Wycliffe's consubstantiation but fully compatible with Zwingli's doctrine, is articulated through the complementary notion that at the Ascension Christ forever left behind his carnal existence. We are joined to Christ in the Lord's

Supper because we are lifted to him – a human ascent rather than divine descent: 'there is no need to draw Christ to earth that he may be joined to us.'[28] Calvin's insistence on Christ's permanent removal from the earthly or material sphere corroborates his concern to maintain a deity whose sovereignty and power would be compromised by any suggestion of carnal immanence.

In an important recent study Judith H. Anderson finds in the arguments advanced by the early English reformers against their conservative opponents a kind of 'logical derivation' for the sacrament not unlike Calvin's virtualist position, but which nevertheless was an attempt to go beyond the Genevan reformer's symbolic understanding. While not containing the substance of the body of Christ, the sacramental sign nonetheless is involved in 'a systematic connection between the virtual, figurative substance and divinity.' The sacramental referent, the body, is, 'in a sign and by grace and in spirit, effect, and faith, virtually and derivatively present.'[29] In addition to those passages discussed by Anderson, there are in Nicholas Ridley and Archbishop Cranmer moments in which their own sacramental theories appropriate the letter if not the spirit of their Catholic opponents' formulae. In the *Examination* of 1555 as recorded in Foxe's *Acts and Monuments*, for example, Ridley dismissed what he perceived to be his conservative examiners' understanding of 'a lively and moveable body under the forms of bread and wine.' A moment later, however, he applies 'lively' to his own positive formulation:

> In the sacrament is a certain change, in that that bread, which was before common bread, is now made a lively presentation of Christ's body, and not only a figure, but effectuously representeth his body; that even as the mortal body is nourished by that visible bread, so is the internal soul fed with the heavenly food of Christ's body, which the eyes of faith see, as the bodily eyes see only bread.[30]

That the inward soul of the recipient is the place of 'a certain change' is made clear enough; but the application of 'lively' both to the opposed and to the accepted formula demonstrates the degree to which Ridley sought to accommodate his interlocutors while refusing to cross the line to a corporeal understanding. He might also have known that the concern about 'moveability' was not exclusive to the reformers. Aquinas, as we have seen, maintained that the body of Christ is present in the sacrament not as an extended body in space, but rather as a substance in the non-extended Aristotelian sense. Ridley's 'eyes of faith' and 'bodily eyes,' moreover, echo St Thomas's similar distinction between intelligential and mere bodily 'seeing.' Other applications of Catholic-sounding language to decidedly innovative formulae include Ridley's observation earlier in his career that 'as the bread which we receive is turned into our substance, so are we turned into Christ's body,'[31] and his surprising assertion in the 1555 Marian *Disputations at Oxford* (offered, perhaps, under considerable pressure) that in the sacrament is received 'the virtue of the very flesh of Christ, life and grace of his body' and 'grace flowing into a sacrifice.'[32]

Ridley and Cranmer shared with Calvin a fondness for the sun analogy often used by the reformers to explain their understanding of 'real presence' (a phrase positively endorsed by both divines, albeit with significant caveats).[33] Cranmer, for example, writes:

> We say that as the sun corporally is ever in heaven, and no where else, and yet by his operation and virtue the sun is here in earth, by whose influence and virtue all things in the world be corporally regenerated, increased, and grow to their perfect state; so likewise our Saviour Christ bodily and corporally is in heaven, sitting at the right hand of his Father, although spiritually he hath promised to be present with us upon earth unto the world's end.[34]

Whereas Ridley perhaps inadvertently applies 'lively' to both his own and his opponents' formulae, Cranmer is careful not to transfer the phrase 'corporally regenerated' to the solar virtue's divine analog. In a much more interesting analogy, however, Cranmer assigns sacramental change to the naming operation. In opposition to the conservative Bishop of Winchester, Stephen Gardiner, Cranmer argues that as the body of Christ 'is all one in nature' both before and after the Resurrection, yet 'for the dignity of his exaltation' after 'is called a heavenly, a godly, an immortal, and the Lord's body,' just so is the bread after the consecration 'called with addition, heavenly bread.'[35] Is Cranmer saying that the resurrected body is no different, that only the name is changed, not the body itself? Is he saying, furthermore, that the power that raised Christ never actually resides *in* Christ's risen body? In order to maintain for the bread as much affective power as possible without allowing a carnal understanding, Cranmer approaches a position from which he might be accused of nominalism. His emphasis on naming suggests that the linguistic element, being applied both to the heavenly referent, Christ's body, and to the bread, is the locus of the sacrament's true power. When Cranmer allows 'a certain kind of worshipping the signs, the reverent esteeming of them above other common and profane things,' the worship he means consists in the act of naming, the name sliding ineluctably over the material sign of bread and attaching itself to the heavenly body; the name, that is, is 'principally to be referred to the celestial things represented by the signs.'[36] The bread is an objective sign raised above ordinary bread by the communicants' effectively referring the name evoked by that sign, 'the body,' to its heavenly reality. And yet, as Anderson points out, there is in Cranmer's denominative attributions a measure of 'substantiality.'[37] The power of worship among the laity is not unlike that of the traditional priest who, in Aquinas's formulation, speaks the words of consecration in such a way that they 'derive from Christ an instrumental power.'[38] In emphasizing the linguistic and psychological dimensions of sacramental experience, then, the English reformers, like Luther and Calvin, were concerned nevertheless to maintain an efficacious and instrumental role both for the species and for the words of institution.

Though Christ's 'humane substance in it selfe is naturallie absent from the earth, his soule and bodie not on earth but in heaven onlie,' Richard Hooker was to write in *The Laws of Ecclesiastical Polity*, yet 'because this substance is inseperablie joyned to that personall worde which by his verie divine essence is present in all thinges, the nature which cannot have in it selfe universall presence hath it *after a sorte* by beinge *no where severed* from that which everie where is present ... preasence *by waie of conjunction* is in some sorte presence.'[39] The phrases 'after a sort' and 'in some sort' recall Ridley's 'certain change' and complement also Hooker's own thoroughly Reform appropriation of a traditionally Roman Catholic doctrinal phrase: 'The reall presence of Christes most blessed bodie and bloode is not therefore to be sought for in the sacrament, but in the worthie receiver of the sacrament.' Despite this and other similar assertions, however, Hooker on the whole advanced an adiaphoric view that could be said to accommodate rather than to dismiss outright the theological positions he opposed. He allows, for example, that whether the sacrament be communicated 'with change or without alteration of the element such as [proponents of con- and transubstantiation] imagine' is something about which 'wee neede not greatlie to care nor inquire.'[40] Having described the Lutheran and Roman Catholic understandings, Hooker avers that his own 'instrumental' position, whereby the elements '*through concurrence of divine power*' are '*a cause of that mysticall participation*,' is one which 'hath in it nothing but what the rest doe all approve and acknowledg to be most true.'[41] Hooker thus goes slightly further than Cranmer and Ridley toward rapprochement with the Lutheran and even Roman churches in his desire to maintain for English sacramental policy the affective power of their more explicitly carnal understandings. Such desire becomes most evident in a passage uncharacteristic of the *Polity*'s largely forensic tone, one that might as easily be ascribed to Richard Crashaw as to the celebrated founder of Anglican theology:

> Christ giveth plaine securitie that these mysteries doe as nailes fasten us to his verie crosse, that by them wee draw out, as touchinge efficacie, force and vertue, even the blood of his goared side, in the woundes of our redemer wee there dip our tongues, wee are died redd both within and without, our hunger is satisfied and our thirst for ever quenched.[42]

The conceptual and ideological divide separating corporeal from symbolic understandings of the sacrament in the Reformation is the same difficulty that troubled the Roman church through the Middle Ages and beyond. But the issue was far more than intellectual. Formally enshrined at the Council of Constance in 1415, the Eucharist had been widely accepted and firmly established by the end of the thirteenth century. The social dimension of sacramental thought therefore cannot be underestimated. In her monumental study *Corpus Christi*, Miri Rubin documents the Eucharist's centrality in medieval culture as a ritual that allowed for direct encounter with Christ and reception of very real benefits, both spiritual and physical. And while most people received Communion only once a year, at Easter, they frequently encountered the Eucharist in the elevation of the Host during Mass and in related rituals such as the distribution of *eulogia* or blessed (though not formally consecrated) bread and the kissing or touching of the pax, a small Hostlike object on which was inscribed a cross or scene from the Crucifixion.[43] The Eucharist was also a significant feature in the *cultus* of Mary in which it was thought that the body born of the womb of the Virgin was reborn on the altar at the Mass. Indeed, Rubin points out that as early as the ninth century Paschasius Radbert held that 'just as real flesh was created from a virgin by the Spirit, without coition, thus from the substance of bread and wine, that same body and blood of Christ is miraculously consecrated.' Perhaps this latter belief had some influence on the association of the Eucharist with the erotic dimension of the mystical tradition, particularly by women who longed to incorporate Christ into their bodies.[44] Such beliefs and practices derived from what might be described as a sacramental cosmology, a conception of the world in which the Word become flesh was an ever-present reality rather than the religious abstraction it was to become. The most remarkable feature of the Corpus Christi pageants and plays of the fifteenth and sixteenth centuries, for example, was their combination of the sacred and the profane, a fusion which derived arguably from the pre-dramatic liturgy of the celebration that asserted a corporeal view of real presence in the Eucharist despite (or because of) the growing influence of merely figurative understandings.[45] Thus might the Christ child in the homely Nativity scene of the Towneley *Second Shepherd's Pageant* receive as a gift 'a bob of cherries' (718) and be referred to affectionately as 'little tiny mop' (724). Rubin, moreover, notes that Corpus Christi homilies were numerous and, in addition to the plays proper, a dramatic feature of the feast. They provided the doctrinal framework linking Old and New Testaments, a typological organization centred around the Eucharist and permeating the festivities.[46]

The central element of English sacramental experience throughout the Middle Ages and into the sixteenth century was the elevation of the Host, a simultaneously communal and deeply personal moment. In addition to the 'high' Masses on Sundays, informal 'low' Masses held on weekdays provided the laity with frequent access. These minor Masses were often celebrated at simple altars with no rood screens or other separating devices and thereby allowed a degree of intimacy not usually associated with so ceremonial an occasion. The large veil introduced during Lent to deny the laity their view of the celebrant and the sacring was, according to Eamon Duffy, a temporary deprivation in a dynamic ceremonial rhythm designed to augment the sacrament's emotional power.[47] The stages of the Mass together with the priest's actions formed an allegory of the Passion so that the all-important moment of elevation was anticipated and followed by gestures weighted with religious meaning.[48] The elevation, then, was a highly affective moment in the service, a point at which individuals in prayer, hearing the sacring bell, would raise their heads and hands toward the Host in rapt adoration and expectation of both bodily and spiritual blessing. Indeed, the elevation itself could be quasi-sacramental; merely gazing upon the Host, Rubin observes, might be a kind of spiritual communion and even substitute for the ritual proper.[49] Crucial to the concerns of the present study is Duffy's observation that offical liturgy did not preclude extended moments of private devotion during the Mass. The ceremony consisted, rather, of an alternating rhythm of private prayer and, at key moments such as the elevation, uniform corporate response. 'Everyone at Mass was expected to participate in two quite different modes – private prayer, focusing on the relation between the Host and the Passion of Christ, and ritual action, geared to the community.' We must be careful, therefore, to avoid 'any assumption that the religion of ritual, relic, and miracle is somehow at odds with the religion of meditation, reading, and the quasi-monastic devotion of the mystics and spiritual guides, as filtered into the devotional handbooks of the later Middle Ages.'[50]

While this observation might be true of pre-Reformation England, the stripping of the altars in the sixteenth century was to compromise severely the alternating rhythm of external ritual and private devotion, the affective bond uniting individual, community, and cosmos. The decline of this sacramental order, however, was not without ambiguity and ambivalence. Duffy notes that the first official documentation of Church of England doctrine and policy, the Ten Articles of 1536, confined treatment of sacrament to Baptism, Penance, and the Eucharist, even if they endorsed traditional practices such as the veneration of images and prayer for the dead (though even this included caveats against idolatry). However supportive of reform policies with respect to saints and images, Henry VIII was a staunch traditionalist when it came to the Mass.[51] Prior to his conflict with Rome Henry had been awarded the title *Defensor Fidei* by Pope Leo X, supposedly for defending the Roman sacramental system in *Assertio Septum Sacramentorum* (1521).[52] Nevertheless, numerous measures in the years following facilitated a rapid decline of the old religion. Duffy writes, for example, of the protection of radicals by the archbishop of Canterbury and by Thomas Cromwell – the latter a powerful member of the Privy Council and later earl of Essex – and of the reformer Hugh Latimer's 1534 appointment as Lenten preacher.[53] There was the Act, introduced just a week after the 1536 Articles, outlawing 'certain holydays' and effectively destroying the ritual calendar with its numerous feasts, festivals, and saints' days; then there was the dissolution of monasteries and religious houses from 1536 to 1538. The 1538 Injunctions called outright for the abolition of images and other 'works devised by men's phantasies,' while the denunciation of such 'idolatry and superstition' was complemented in the same year by a royal proclamation that sharply distinguished between mere 'rites and ceremonies' and 'the things commanded by God' in the scriptures, even though the latter document was meant to appease conservatives distraught by previous policies.[54] A 1541 decree reified the emerging ideology by ordering the bishops and lower clergy to see to the removal of all shrines and monuments from both cathedral and parish. The 1545 *King's Primer*, finally, was designed to replace all other primers so that now there would be 'one uniforme ordre of al suche bokes throughout our dominions,' and it excluded the prayers offered to the sacrament of the altar, a mainstay of the traditional books.[55]

Duffy's survey of the period makes clear, however, that the decline was not without resistance. Both the archbishop of York and Richard Sampson, bishop of Chichester, for example, made known their opposition to the 1536 Act attacking the traditional ritual calendar. The offical record, moreover, includes among the program for reform more than occasional concession to conservative pieties. Unrest stemming from the Ten Articles and subsequent Act and Injunctions prompted Henry, not for the first time, to admonish his bishops not to tolerate radical preaching nor anyone openly opposed to 'honest ceremonies of the church.' In an attempt to prevent further disquiet, the *Bishops' Book* of 1537 contained a set of instructions for the proper teaching of the Articles and restored sacraments missing from the earlier document.[56] Moreover, the above-mentioned 1538 proclamation was, as Duffy observes, unmistakably conservative in its attack against the 'contentious and sinister opinions' of Protestant primers, its reaffirmation of support for traditional ceremonies, including the distribution of such sacramentals as holy bread and holy water, and its forbidding of debate on the Eucharist.[57] The most contentious gesture toward the maintenance of the old religion, however, was the 1539 Act of Six Articles which resurrected traditional piety sufficiently as to cause the reformer Hugh Latimer to resign his see rather than enforce them.[58] Included among the decrees, notes Peter Whiting, was the imposition of the death penalty for anyone openly critical of traditional sacramental doctrine.[59] Other favourable gestures toward the old religion included the *Rationale of Ceremonial*, established by the same conservative commission that oversaw the formulation of the Six Articles and which, though emphasizing the symbolic rather than carnal dimension of ceremonies and the need to avoid superstition by 'taking them for good tokens and signs,' nevertheless affirmed their value along with 'the Right use of Images.' Also pleasing to conservatives was the 1543 Act 'for the advancement of true religion,' which indicted the spread of unauthorized Bibles, such as the Tyndale New Testament, and, like a never-issued proclamation of 1539, condemned unrestrained lay Bible-reading, both public and private.[60] But, as Duffy points out, it was the *King's Book* of 1543, a reworking of the earlier *Bishop's Book*, that most fully developed the conservative policies first set out in the *Rationale of Ceremony*. Included in this new version was greater attention to the seven sacraments and especially to the Eucharist, while the earlier book's outright denunciation of images is replaced by moderate endorsement.[61]

The conservatives' hopes were short-lived. The ambiguities and alternating fortunes of opposed camps inscribed in offical documents during the Henrician era gave way under Edward VI to an overwhelming tide of Protestant reform. Under the influence of Cranmer and Protector Somerset, and beginning with a nationwide visitation in the summer following Henry's death in 1547, England was subjected to a wholesale purging of 'popish' superstition. A new set of Injunctions renewed attacks on relics, pilgrimages, the rosary, and censing, and ordered unequivocally the destruction of images throughout the realm. Also condemned was the magical or quasi-occult use of such sacramentals as holy bread and water.[62]

The 1549 Prayer Book was Cranmer's supreme contribution to Edwardine reform, particularly as regards the Eucharist. Duffy observes that the elevation of the Host at the sacring bell, the pax, and holy bread were now removed from the official Church of England liturgy. Now absent from the calendar were most of the traditional feast days, and eliminated also were the very popular and widespread Jesus Masses. And yet as tenacious a traditionalist as the bishop of Winchester, Stephen Gardiner, could find in the Prayer Book the teaching of the Mass to which he was accustomed, despite the obvious abrogation in its pages of essential features of English religious tradition.[63] But if the Edwardine Prayer Book of 1549 was largely an adaptation of the Roman Missal, that of 1552 constituted dramatic Protestant revision, evident especially in the notorious Black Rubric, hastily added in response to the influential John Knox and his disdain for popish ceremonies. It is perhaps one of the chief reasons the staunchly Roman Catholic Mary Tudor repealed the book upon her accession in 1553, for in addition to refusing the notion that kneeling in any way implies adoration, the Black Rubric was boldly Calvinist in its denial of 'any real and essential presence there being of Christ's natural flesh and blood. For as concerning the sacramental bread and wine, they remain still in their very natural substances ... And as concerning the natural body and blood of Our Saviour Christ, they are in heaven and not here.'[64] To the elimination of the elevation of the Host in the 1549 version, notes Duffy, the new book added the removal of the prayer of consecration at Communion and eliminated as well the signing of the cross over the elements and the stone altar, the latter to be replaced by a simple table in the body of the church.[65] Under Mary, of course, the religious centrality of sacrament and ceremony was restored. Though advocating a balance of scriptural and ceremonial emphases, Cardinal Reginald Pole stressed that 'the observatyon of ceremonyes, for obedyence sake, wyll gyve more light than all the readynge of Scrypture can doe.' Though 'the thynge that gyveth us the veraye light, ys none of them both,' neither ceremonies nor scripture, yet 'they are most apte to receyve light, that are more obeyent to follow ceremonyes, than to reade.'[66] Marian primers did go some way to restore the pre-Reformation character totally absent from the Edwardine primer of 1553. Indeed, later editions include a didactic treatise on the Mass that explicates and defends the doctrine of transubstantiation and the Sacrifice. According to Duffy, however, elaborate affective prayers on the Virgin Mary, the saints, and the Blessed Sacrament, staples of the conservative books, are almost entirely absent.[67]

When the Book of Common Prayer was restored under Elizabeth in 1559, the controversial Black Rubric was removed, never to reappear. The final version is a hybrid of the relatively conservative Edwardine book of 1549 and the more radically Protestant version of 1552. It allows communicants to 'eat of the flesh of thy dear Son Jesus Christ, and to drink his blood, that our sinful bodies may be made clean by his body, and our souls washed through his most precious blood.'[68] That both 'body and soul' are fed is repeated in the minister's prayer of thanksgiving, but the added phrase insisting that all is done 'in thy heart by faith' severely attenuates any suggestion of a physiological reception. In 1559 the Act of Uniformity made adherence to the ceremonies of the Church of England legally binding. But the ambiguities already apparent in the wording of the Prayer Book took on even greater significance with the closing words of the Act:

> If there shall happen any contempt or irreverence to be used in the ceremonies or rites of the church by the misusing of the orders appointed in [the Prayer Book], the queen's majesty may, by the like advice of the said commissioners or metropolitan, ordain and publish such further ceremonies or rites as may be most for the advancement of God's glory, the edifying of his church, and the due reverence of Christ's holy mysteries and sacraments.[69]

If 'contempt' and 'irreverence' target antisacramental disdain, the same phrase might be said to refer to an excessive or popish regard (as opposed to the 'due reverence' of the passage's final clause) and thereby offer consolation to those churchmen hopeful of further reform.

The theological counterpart to the liturgy is the Thirty Nine Articles, which, in their final form of 1571, are also not without ambiguity. According to Article 28, the sacrament is 'not only a sign'; the reception of the bread and wine, rather, is a 'partaking' of the body and blood of Christ for those 'such as rightly, worthily, and with faith, receive the same.' 'Transubstantiation' is 'repugnant to the plain words of scripture, overthroweth the nature of a sacrament, and hath given occasion to many superstitions.' Nevertheless, the 'body of Christ is given, taken, and eaten,' though again, 'only after an heavenly and spiritual manner,' while 'the means whereby the body of Christ is received and eaten in the supper is faith.'[70] This careful balance affirming the physical act while subordinating it to spiritual mystery recalls Calvin's own reluctance to stress externals any more than is absolutely necessary. Article 29, moreover, recalls Calvin's characterization (quoting Augustine) of the wicked as he who 'presses with the teeth' rather than 'eats with the heart.'[71] The article states that those 'void of a lively faith, although they do carnally and visibly press with their teeth (as St. Augustine saith) the sacrament of the body and blood of Christ, yet in no wise are they partakers of Christ: but rather, to their condemnation, do eat and drink the sign or sacrament of so great a thing.' That the Articles' most sensual language is applied to the wicked is perhaps a deliberate irony, but there is also the suggestion that the faithless, because they receive only in a carnal manner, do not attain to the edification of either soul or body, whereas for those who receive 'worthily' and by 'faith' the sacrament is of both spiritual and bodily benefit, what Article 25 describes as 'a wholesome effect or operation.'[72]

Despite echoes of Reform theology, however, both liturgical and doctrinal ambiguities contributed to continuing dissatisfaction among those for whom the Elizabethan Settlement was decidedly less than sufficient. Conrad Russell points out that the Prayer Book and Settlement were constructed prior to the naming of bishops who thus bitterly complained of not being consulted. Formation of the Articles, however, because doctrinal in focus, had to wait until the first Protestant convocation in 1562-3. The church's discipline and doctrine 'came out of different minds, and therefore represented ideals of the church which were at least potentially divergent.'[73] Those divines eager for further reform set their sights not only on the Prayer Book, however, but on the Articles as well. The 'View of Popish Abuses' appended to the puritan *Admonition to the Parliament,* itself following hot on the heels of the Articles in 1572, recognized both there and in the liturgy remnants of such popish practices as idolatrous kneeling and 'breadengod' worship. This latter is described further as a 'half communion, which is yet appointed like to the commemoration of the mass.'[74] That such outrage was provoked by sacramental passages in the Articles is evidence against Christopher Hodgkins's claim that they are unambiguously Calvinist and that Rome, from a doctrinal perspective, 'is off the map – dismissed with the kind of stinging language [Cardinal] Newman was to find so intractable.'[75] If Elizabethan Catholics smarted under the language of the Articles, their enemies apparently thought papists had no small cause for celebration.

The confessional broils of the English Reformation derived from a complex ecclesiastical history of which a crucial feature was debate over sacramental theories and practices, a debate comprised of two distinct though related issues: the material extent of divinity in the eucharistic species, and the role of religious subjectivity in the communication of grace. Though presumably one might have doubted the 'real presence' of the Eucharist as equally as the indwelling presence of the Spirit, the availability of an external means of grace, whatever the vicissitudes of mood and psychological make-up, would have been reinforced by a doctrine which insisted not only on the efficaciousness of those means, but on the divine character of the instruments themselves. The reasons why Reformation *religieux* were so deeply divided over whether sacrament was more an internal than external matter is beyond the scope of this study. A simple answer is that the notions *sola fidei* and *sola scriptura* displaced the ceremonial from its previously central position in Christian worship. Anxiety about the carnal dimension of the rite, however, was as much a feature of prescholastic and medieval theologies as of polemical battles in the sixteenth and seventeenth centuries. Indeed, it is a problem that troubled not only the church fathers but at least one gospel writer for whom Jesus' disciples, shocked at his insisting that unless they eat of his flesh and drink of his blood they have no life, are perplexed yet again at the caveat that only the spirit gives life while the flesh profits nothing (Jn. 6.53–66). With scriptural authority so deeply vexing, it is not surprising that exegetes and other ecclesiastics subsequently struggled as fiercely as they did.

At issue here are the meaning, extent, and scope of the Incarnation, the profanation of the sacred, the Word become flesh. More than any of his literary contemporaries John Donne realized the radical potential both of an incarnational world view and for the language of theology to inform a surprising range of interests and curiosities. Before continuing in succeeding chapters with the primarily religious dimension of sacramental discourse, then, this study begins by addressing Donne's unique and very often surprising application of sacrament to ostensibly secular concerns. I hope to demonstrate that the poet's capacity for discerning the resemblances and analogies that permeate his myriad world is of particular poignancy with respect to eucharistic topoi, and that the resulting conceits test both the limits of an incarnational poetics and its ability to recall a pre-Reformation sacramentality. In starting here, moreover, I hope in the end to have shown that the sacramental features of devotional verse manifest desires concomitant with the need to rediscover among seemingly disparate spheres of human experience the underlying 'cohærence,' 'just supply,' and 'Relation' (213–14) whose passing is mourned in the first *Anniversary*.

CHAPTER ONE

Secular Verse of the Religious Man: Donne and Sacrament at Play

Donne applies sacrament both analogically and formatively to a wider area of concern than has been adequately recognized. Theresa M. DiPasquale's is the first book-length study of sacrament in Donne and is particularly valuable for its treatment of the secular verse. Her examination of the relationship between sacred and profane concerns, however, is limited in scope, focusing almost exclusively on Donne's response to the Petrarchan tradition. Perhaps because she begins by examining the sacred poems, DiPasquale tends to read her conclusions about the vexing issue of Donne's confessional identity back into the earlier work. That she attenuates the expansiveness of his sacramental wit is apparent, for example, when DiPasquale implies a link between Donne's Protestantism and the speaker's rejection in 'Aire and Angels' of the 'narcissistic Petrarchan poetics' that Donne was 'conscious of and uncomfortable with.' The speaker longs 'to escape the solipsism of his own imagination,' an escape analogous to Donne's religious conversion, so that Petrarchan poetics is deliberately and disparagingly associated with 'Catholicism and the sacraments of the Roman Church.' The 'attitudes and utterances of unrequited lovers,' writes DiPasquale, 'are often reminiscent of specifically Roman piety.' But surely this need to overcome the insufficiency of the love lyric, what DiPasquale calls 'the poetics of unconsummated desire,' is itself a fully Petrarchan gesture suggesting, if anything, the poet's awareness of his speaker's experience as comically inferior to the sacred discourse invoked.[1] If there is a marked disparity between his speakers' experience and the sacramental language they appropriate, it is less a deliberate slight on Roman Catholicism than part of the satirical dimension of a poetry that would celebrate human love even while light-heartedly recognizing both its limitations and pretensions. Donne is always fully conscious of what he is doing, yes – but uncomfortable? DiPasquale's otherwise illuminating readings thus fall prey to a historiographical fallacy in which Donne's thought is defined according primarily to later developments, and which implies that the earlier inevitably led to that later stage. More important, however, is a failure to observe the great variety and largely non-polemical contexts of the profane poet's sacramental conceits.

The issue of Donne's confessional identity, his handling of the controversy surrounding sacramental theology, and the socio-religious importance of ceremony will be addressed more thoroughly in chapters 2 and 3. Here I wish to broaden DiPasquale's investigation of Donne's secular poems to examine not only his explorations of the sacred in the erotic, but also the analogies that obtain among sacramental, monetary, and courtly topoi. Frequent and very often surprising, these conflations of sacred and profane indicate that while Thomas Carew's 'true Gods Priest' was no pious submissive, neither was the 'universall Monarch of wit' devoid of genuine religious concern. Sacrament, far from the merely topical occasion for witty blasphemies (though these abound), played a significant role in Donne's poetic development. His deployment of eucharistic ideas in the primarily nonsacramental contexts of certain songs and sonnets, satires, elegies, and verse letters is analogous to the incarnational features of sacramental thought. For the radical bringing together of disparate elements in the Eucharist – body and bread, blood and wine, the Word become flesh that is the conceptual heart of Christianity – is not unlike the violations of decorum in which Donne allows sacramental topoi to inform and to be contaminated by profane contexts. In subjecting the sacred to the profane (and vice versa), Donne pushes the incarnational paradox beyond anything previously attempted in English verse, thereby radically extending the already expansive sacramental discourse described in Miri Rubin's study of the Eucharist in pre-Reformation culture:

We are tracing here uses of this eucharist which transcended the normative code, and are searching for their meanings in the life-worlds of their users. Be they heresies, abuses, manipulations, extensions or extrapolations, different eucharistic utterances were testing the language, exposing its capacities, filling its spaces and spelling out its possibilities. Divergent and wide-ranging as these utterances will appear, the eucharistic language of religion provided the means and rules for their construction.[2]

Reflecting the incarnational paradox, then, a conceptual aid to this investigation might appropriately consist of an analogy resembling the intersecting axes of the cross, that potentially scandalous symbol of the Atonement. The vertical dimension or axis of the Eucharist is the transcendent Word or divine body it mysteriously communicates, while the horizontal includes all material aspects of the ceremony – bread, wine, gesture, words of consecration. Similarly, sacramental topoi, to the extent they evoke a dimension of human experience rarefied and set apart from the quotidian, may be aligned with the vertical axis, while the complementary horizontal axis corresponds to the myriad of other topoi among which the sacramental are interpolated. These others include the monetary, courtly-political, and erotic topoi that comprise a good part of Donne's distinctive oeuvre. The point at which these axes intersect is the crux of an incarnational poetics, the most profound collision of sacred and profane, T.S. Eliot's 'still point of the turning world' where 'Garlic and sapphires in the mud / Clot the bedded axle-tree.'

The axes model thus adduced recalls Ferdinand De Saussure's distinction between *langue* and *parole*, between language as preverbal system and as individual utterance.[3] The vertical axis suggests the static correspondence of a single signifier and its signified, or a group of related topoi whose meanings derive from the group's internal relationships; the horizontal axis, on the other hand, indicates that expanding totality of signs or semiotic grid, with its exchanges and history, apart from which the vertical dimension of language does not obtain. By pushing sacraments' topological currency beyond purely sacred contexts, Donne subjects them to a semantic play that not only radically alters their own significance and meaning, but also alerts us to the sacred potential of the other topoi involved. The Incarnation, similarly, subjects the Logos to history, a body and death, while at the same time imbuing that horizontal plane with a significance it would not have otherwise. No doubt sensitive to the primarily sacred nature of sacrament, Donne forces its engagement with secular topoi to effect a poetic fleshing of the Word, thereby realizing afresh the imaginative power of the Incarnation.

Donne's sacramental wit is evident in his treatment of several recurring topical concerns: human love, the nature of monetary value, and the power and influence of the court. Just as the Eucharist addresses the gap between a transcendent deity and its material immanence, so sacramental topoi in the love poems participate in an interrogation of the relationships among platonic and sensory loves, inner virtue and external beauty, lovers' constancy and inconstancy, tumescence and detumescence. Similarly, as the eternal presence sacrament proclaims is inextricable from doctrinal formulae, controversy, and ecclesiastical politics, so are sacramental topoi conducive to Donne's explorations of monetary value, with its complex relationship between intrinsic and extrinsic worth – the magical glitter of precious metal and its commercial reputation and power as currency. Again, according to the Renaissance doctrine of the king's two bodies and the related anatomical trope of king as heart of the body politic, the relationship between court and realm is analogous to the notion of a God whose grace is materially disseminated by virtue of sacrament and ceremony. That 'presence' is a term shared by both courtly and eucharistic discourses is but one of the more salient features of their commonality.

Viewed primarily as symbol and ritual that according to varying doctrinal formulae communicate the gifts derived from the incarnation, death, and resurrection of Christ, the Eucharist is always in danger of diminishing these central Christian truths by failing adequately to sustain their vitality, by attenuating through ritual familiarity sacraments' otherwise unique capacity to bridge the human and the divine. Understood, on the other hand, as what Louis-Marie Chauvet has called the locus of a 'cultural pact' apart from which it has no identity at all, the sacramental sign endues with a sacred significance the unique and shared experiences of communicants who enjoy its benefits.[4] By extending the boundaries of such a pact beyond the traditional context of church, altar, ceremony, and received doctrine, Donne explodes traditional understandings of sacrament and challenges the propriety of official religious observance. 'Renaissance literature,' according to Elizabeth Mazzola's attractive formulation, 'teaches Protestant theology what it can do.' Sacred symbols such as the Eucharist continued throughout the long English Reformation – with its conflicted Protestant identity – 'to orient behaviour and arrange perceptions, and persisted in specifying to believers and nonbelievers alike the limits of the known world.'[5] This insight is nowhere more supported than by Donne's sacramental profanities – by poems, moreover, in which *theology* teaches Renaissance culture what *it* can do.

Eros

Donne's treatment of love and its proper object, like that of his Petrarchan antecedents, suggests the duality of Platonic or transcendent ideal and its experiential and sensory manifestations, the vertical dimension of transcendent beauty, virtue, and tumescent bliss intersecting the horizontal realm of bodies, desire, and detumescence. The still point of the axes model here articulates Donne's appreciation of love's eternal qualities as inextricable from their sublunary realizations. Whereas in 'The Undertaking,' for example, outward beauty is rejected for 'lovelinesse within' (13), and those who 'Vertue'attir'd in woman see' (18) are lauded over 'all the *Worthies*' (26), the love poems more often indicate a complex relationship between Petrarchan ideal and earthly loves analogous to the paradox of Incarnation.[6]

In 'Valediction to his booke,' the lovers' love is of sacramental status, their letters canonized as the sacred records of Love's grace, while the lovers 'for loves clergie only'are instruments' (22). There is thus a sense in which love is surpassed by a source for which the lovers merely act as stewards, so that even while the sacred book contains or reflects the 'Annals' (12) or record of their relationship, that relationship is itself but the manifestation or 'instrument' of 'Love [which] this grace to us affords' (17). But just as sacraments are sacred despite their material character, so 'This Booke' is 'as long-liv'd as the elements' (19). While maintaining for experience and ideal an ostensibly hierarchical relationship, the poet prefers to accommodate all who would receive from love's book, whether sensualist or Neoplatonist:

> Here Loves Divines, (since all Divinity
> Is love or wonder) may finde all they seeke,
> Whether abstract spirituall love they like,
> Their Soules exhal'd with what they do not see,
>   Or, loth so to amuze
>   Faiths infirmitie, they chuse
>   Something which they may see and use;
> For, though minde be the heaven, where love doth sit,
> Beauty a convenient type may be to figure it.   (28–36)

A weak or infirm faith is no barrier to receiving the benefits love offers; those dull sublunary lovers whose soul is sense are typologically incorporated into Love's vast design. There is some ambiguity, moreover, as to what in fact is infirm: a particularly weak faith, or the purely abstract love of souls exhaled? The latter are not unlike those souls in 'The Extasie' who must to bodies go, 'Else a great Prince in prison lies' (68). As Donne reminds us in 'Loves growth,' Love is 'no quintessence, /

But mixt of all stuffes, paining soule, or sense' (8–9):

> Love's not so pure, and abstract, as they use
> To say, which have no Mistresse but their Muse,
> But as all else, being elemented too,
> Love sometimes would contemplate, sometimes do.   (11–14)

Here, the implied antitheses of purity and impurity, abstraction and substance, together with the more explicit Mistresse/Muse, and the humanist dichotomy of contemplative and active service, are qualified by the realization that all things must be 'elemented,' composed of the world's material constituents, just as sacramental presence is somehow contiguous with the instruments or elements of bread and wine in which it is mysteriously made manifest.

Though justly celebrated as innovative, Donne's verse is far from immune to the alternating hot and cold flashes of the traditional courtly lover. Where poems such as 'To his booke' celebrate (and offer consolation for the loss of) connubial or coital bliss, others, like 'Twicknam Garden,' document the grief and sexual frustration of the spurned Petrarchan *amoureux*. Though sacramental topoi normally would suggest the eternal, transcendent ideal of Petrarchan love, here they comprise a diabolical Eucharist in a demonic parody of Eden, a 'True Paradise' complete with 'serpent' (9). Donne begins by playing on the Roman Catholic sacrament of Extreme Unction, his speaker coming

>   to seeke the spring,
> And at mine eyes, and at mine eares,
> Receive such balmes, as else cure every thing.   (2–4)

'Eyes' and 'eares' exploit the semantic duality of 'unction' as both religious rite and flattering speech, thus anticipating (with 'else') the plaint which follows. Reproaching his own gullibility, the speaker regrets having brought to the garden a 'spider love, which transubstantiates all, / And can convert Manna to gall' (6–7). Alluding to the tradition that sacraments ill-received are poisonous, the passage relies on both explicit eucharistic terminology and a typology which finds in the dew-changed-to-manna of Exodus 16 an anticipation of the Communion bread. This postlapsarian Eden is far from that of Milton's first parents, who 'thir fill of Love and Love's disport / Took largely, of thir mutual guilt the Seal, / The solace of thir sin' (9.1042–4). Whereas in *Paradise Lost* the Augustinian 'seal' becomes part of a demonic parody in which the archetypal transgression is ratified sexually, sacramental topoi in 'Twicknam Garden' torment a Petrarchan Adam cursed with an enforced abstinence. As DiPasquale points out, the poem is based on 'a sacrament of envious nonfulfillment.'[7] In the second stanza, finding that he occupies that no-place between transgression and its pleasures, moved to love but frustrated in his attempts, the lover nevertheless would be suspended inanimate, 'some senselesse peece of this place bee' (16) rather than see it blighted by winter's 'grave frost' (12). Tumescent suspension is both frustrating and titillating, alternately 'Manna' and 'gall,' the 'spider love' a poison sacrament drawing on the belief that spiders reproduced without sexual intercourse. If 'Valediction to his booke' celebrates lovers' erotic identification with the 'elements' of their vast 'Booke,' 'Twicknam Garden' dramatizes a frustrating communion of one. Spurned, petulant, and not a little angry, the speaker once again raises the notion of a false or ineffective sacrament and contrasts it with a true 'wine' in the image of the weeping fountain:

> Hither with christall vyals, lovers come,
>   And take my teares, which are loves wine,
>   And try your mistresse Teares at home,
> For all are false, that tast not just like mine.   (19–22)

In a moment of messianic self-oblation the speaker discards his status as fallen first Adam to become the second. 'Teares' are combined with 'loves wine' in a eucharistic-typological conflation, the first/second Adam allusion complemented by an implicit meeting of Edenic garden and Gethsemane, where Jesus, agonizing over the 'cup' he is about to receive, sweats blood-tears. Like the spider love transubstantiated into gall, so are false women's tears a poisonous sacrament for the unwary. DiPasquale likens the speaker's claim that 'all are false, that tast not just like mine' to that of 'a Roman dogmatist.' Surely Roman Catholics did not hold a monopoly on dogmatism. The sermon passage DiPasquale cites in support,[8] though admonishing controversialists to 'referre thy reason, and disputation to the Schoole,' is not directed at scholastics alone. Donne takes issue, rather, with *any* 'peremptory prejudice upon other mens opinions, that no opinion but thine can be true, in the doctrine of the Sacrament, and an uncharitable condemning of other men, or other Churches that may be of another perswasion then thou art' (*Sermons*, 7.291). Withdrawal from requited love into a self-absorbed and 'infinite superiority of feeling,' moreover, is as much the mark of a puritan sensibility – the assurance of grace as a private and invisible rather than corporate celebration – as of some haughty Roman priest.

Sacramental authenticity is also at issue in 'Loves diet.' The speaker seeks to prevent Love's nourishment, both by rendering his own weeping the product of 'scorne or shame' and by denying the sincerity of his mistress's pining:

> If he suck'd hers, I let him know
> 'Twas not a teare, which hee had got,
> His drink was counterfeit, as was his meat;
> For, eyes which rowle towards all, weepe not, but sweat.   (15–18)

Several decades later Richard Crashaw's 'Out of the Greek Cupid's Cryer' will offer a variation on the false tears topos. Rather than a dubious mistress, the antagonist is Eros himself:

> Pitty not him, but feare thy selfe
> Though thou see the crafty elfe,
> Tell down his Silver-drops unto thee,
> They'r counterfeit, and will undoe thee.   (59–62)

Whereas Crashaw's is a strictly pagan variation, however, the topos in Donne's poem is rendered explicitly sacramental by the telling 'meat' and 'drink.' These, the mistress's sighs and tears, are the means or 'feast' (11), moreover, by which her 'favour' (21) is conferred – or not, depending on who the beneficiary is – and thus analogous to a Calvinist sacrament which, depending on the elect/reprobate status of the communicant, is or is not an effective means of grace.[9] 'For, eyes which rowle ...' recalls Donne's ironic characterization of the whorish church in 'Show me deare Christ' as 'most trew ... When she'is embrac'd and open to most men' (13–14), or the Erastian Graccus of 'Satyre III' who 'loves all as one' (65). By contrast, sexual drink and meat distributed to all in 'Loves diet' lack that 'which love worst endures, *discretion*' (6), just as ecclesiastical policies supporting universal access to sacraments and thus a broad-based membership in the state church tended to subvert the predestinarian prerogative of a Calvinist deity. But even if the speaker's mistress were to exercise discretion and have her 'eyes ... rowle towards' him alone, he is not willing that Love should determine or govern his involvement with her. Though demanding fidelity, he is not satisfied with being among the few or even the only member – 'burdenous corpulence' (2) – and 'name' of his mistress's 'entaile' (24). He prefers, rather, total claim to the arbitrary whim hitherto Love's alone: 'Thus I reclaim'd my buzard love, to flye / At what, and when, and how, and where I chuse' (25–6). And yet just as the predestinarian psyche alternates between powerless anxiety and bold presumption, the speaker's final remarks are as suggestive of enslavement to a relentless cycle as they are assertive of his mastery and control:

> And now as other fawkners use,
> I spring a mistresse, sweare, write, sigh and weepe:
> And the game kill'd, or lost, goe talk, and sleepe.   (28–30)

The speaker of 'The Primrose,' rather than exhausted and indifferent, rationalizes female inconstancy in a wry sacramental celebration of polygamy – or, at least, serial monogamy. The typologically eucharistic dew of Israelite manna forms flowers radiant with the reflection of their heavenly source:

> Upon this Primrose hill,
>   Where, if Heav'n would distill
> A shoure of raine, each severall drop might goe
> To his owne primrose, and grow Manna so;
> And where their forme, and their infinitie
>   Make a terrestriall Galaxie,
>   As the small starres doe in the skie:
> I walke to finde a true Love; and I see
>   That'tis not a mere woman, that is shee,
> But must, or more, or lesse then woman bee.   (1–10)

The marriage of heavenly purity and earthly fecundity, particularly in the oxymoron 'terrestriall Galaxie,' reflects the sacramental paradox of Incarnation, where reconciliation of Word and flesh is not unlike the integration of celestial influence and sublunary matter in medieval cosmology. The distillation of a heavenly substance or quintessence into a typologically sacramental repository is here preparatory to interrogating the presence of 'true-Love' (13) in woman. Reasoning that four- or six-leaved flowers are 'monsters' or aberrations – that both she who is 'lesse than woman,' or promiscuous, and she who 'would get above / All thought of sexe, and think to move / My heart to study her, and not to love' are freaks of nature (13–18) – the speaker settles finally on the 'true number five' (22). Post-Petrarchan disdain for the conventions of courtly love is momentarily withheld as we are led to believe the number five is somehow indicative of a stable balance of sensuous beauty and chaste virtue. Such expectations, along with the whole discourse on love for which falsehood in woman is the only alternative to her status as paragon of chastity, 'by art' (20) are shattered in the final stanza where 'women may take us all' (30) celebrates the promiscuous side of the fairer sex's failure to adhere to the impossible mean. Donne thus advocates 'Falshood in woman' through an elaborate sacramental conceit in which the poet identifies with manna dew and thus becomes the quasi-messianic 'distill[ation]' or transubstantiation of one in search of an earthly bride – who, as it turns out, is most true when open to most men.[10]

That one sacrament, the Eucharist, implicitly rationalizes the undoing of another, monogamous Marriage, is certainly daring if not blasphemous. And yet for Donne this is but an exaggerated exploration of the intersecting axes of rarefied and carnal loves, one which satirizes the gap between them. Though distinctively his own, Donne's poem draws on a tradition, dating back to the twelfth-century troubadours, in which the erotic is subsumed by the mystical. Dante's Beatrice and Petrarch's Laura are only the most famous of mistresses whose beauty radiates a transcendent source. Characterizing the ladder of love as 'the energy and labour of creation,' Northrop Frye cites the opening lines from Chaucer's *Parliament of Fowles* to suggest that poetic endeavour and the *ars amore* are analogous spiritual pursuits:

> The lyf so short, the craft so long to lerne,
> Th'assay so hard, so sharp the conquerynge,
> The dredful joye, alwey that slit to yerne:
> Al this mene I by Love.   (1–4)[11]

For Donne, as for Chaucer, such yearning is perhaps never to be satisfied, even if he jokes about it, as in 'Negative Love':

> My love, though silly, is more brave,
> For may I misse, when ere I crave,
> If I know yet, what I would have.   (7–9)

Sacrament, particularly the Eucharist, is among the most profound expressions of human desire. Donne's use of such topoi demonstrates as much their importance in considering the mysteries of love as it does his poetic fancy or capacity for far-flung conceits. Sacrament in *Songs and Sonets* advances a very powerful analogy according to which secular and sacred lovers share a common desire for an ostensibly unattainable union with their respective beloveds. Sexual congress and ingestion of the eucharistic elements are thus parallel intimacies. The sacraments of Marriage and Holy Communion both derive from the bridegroom-bride relationship traditionally characterizing Christ's love for the church, an analogy complemented by Renaissance physiology and the notion that lovers were thought to exchange vital bodily fluids – the sighs and tears or 'drink' and 'meat' of 'Loves Diet.' The conventional identification of coitus and religious imagery is frequent in Donne's poetry. Even 'The Flea,' with its combination of cloister, marriage, Communion, and blood, suggests a sacramental twist to a literary commonplace.[12] Other poems include 'Elegie VIII: The Comparison,' in which lovers are as 'devoutly nice' as 'Priests in handling reverent sacrifice' (49–50); 'Epithalamion made at Lincoln's Inn,' where the bride is 'Like an appointed lambe, when tenderly / The priest comes on his knees t'embowell her' (89–90); and 'A Tale of a Citizen and his Wife,' where 'wine' and 'signe' (the wife's suggestive glance) comprise the rhyme of the final couplet (70–1).

If 'The Primrose' is a daring celebration of woman's inconstancy, 'The Funerall' applies sacrament to a much darker portrayal of jealousy and sexual revenge. A 'subtile wreath of haire' is the 'mystery, the sign you must not touch' (4) recalling the sexually prohibitive 'seales' of 'The Relique.' Messianic posturing is once again evident, if muted, this time supplemented by royal authority and thus suggesting the doctrine of the king's two bodies. The early Stuart kings also recognized in sacrament and ceremony the potential for promoting social cohesiveness and uniformity; in historian Patrick Collinson's phrase, sacraments were the 'theological cement' of the Jacobean and Caroline churches.[13] Here, the speaker's sacramental or 'outward Soule' (5), the 'mystery, the sign' which 'crowns' (3) his arm, is also

Viceroy to that, which unto heaven being gone,
 Will leave this to controule,
And keep these limbes, her Provinces, from dissolution.   (6–8)

DiPasquale's Protestant reading of the poem equates 'Viceroy' with the pope, so that just as Protestants 'detected in the doctrine of Eucharistic sacrifice a hubristic desire to control the Giver of the sign,' so does the speaker see in the beloved's 'sign of herself' a 'talisman' on which to wreak his revenge and 'love her to death.'[14] The relationship among crown, heaven's viceroy, limbs and provinces, however, might just as easily suggest the doctrine of the king's two bodies and thus a Roman Catholic recusant's or church papist's veiled critique of the Oath of Allegiance and James I's *iure divino* claims. Donne certainly is playing with sacramental ideas, but the poem is hardly a confessional polemic. If the wreath is the speaker's 'outward Soule,' it becomes in the second stanza that of 'a better braine' (13), the reminder of one absent 'she' who intends that he, by this token, should suffer pain, 'As prisoners then are manacled, when they'are / condemn'd to die' (14–16). Interpenetration is thus achieved symbolically, both souls converging on this somewhat dubious manifestation of their union. Exploiting the *petite mort* trope, the spurned lover will 'bury some of you' (24), an act of revenge which, because 'she,' like his soul to 'heaven,' is 'gone' (6), is comically autoerotic. The object of desire, though absent, is yet made present through the fetishization of a mysterious sign. But the relic which 'crowns' *this* king's arm, viceroy to his absent soul/lover, is the host of a private Mass – sacrament to a lone communicant's masturbatory devotion. The entire poem, then, is built on an irony not unlike that of a Chaucerian monologue, enjoyed by poet and reader at the expense of a speaker who fancies for himself the upper hand, so to speak. But because masturbation is neither something to be particularly ashamed nor proud of, the speaker is both *alazon* and *eiron*, aware of the phantasmal nature of his enterprise while nevertheless fashioning and playing the roles it suggests.

Turning on a similar conceit, 'The Relique' nevertheless abandons the jealousy and sexual frustration of 'The Funerall' for the liberating mysticism of 'The Primrose.' The poem begins by exploiting the Renaissance connection between coitus and death, Donne sanctifying as relic of his vaginal grave 'A bracelet of bright haire about the bone' (6). Having exercised in the second stanza his capacity for messianic posturing – 'Thou shalt be a Mary Magdalen, and I / A something else thereby' (17–18)[15] – and having granted the poem scriptural status as didactic 'paper' (21), thus providing these 'Reliques' (16) with a sanctifying text, Donne offers two subtle eucharistic allusions:

First, we lov'd well and faithfully,
Yet knew not what wee lov'd, nor why,
Difference of sex no more wee knew,

> Then our Guardian Angells doe,
>   Comming and going, wee,
> Perchance might kisse, but not between those meales.
>   Our hands ne'r toucht the seales,
> Which nature, injur'd by late law, sets free,
> These miracles wee did.   (23–31)

Like 'The Extasie,' this poem offers two versions of the same sexual union, here progressing in platonic fashion from the purely material realm commemorated by the bracelet/relic, to the miraculous domain of 'harmelesse lovers' (22). This latter falls outside human history, that framed by the two 'meales' of Christ's last supper and the marriage supper of the Lamb in Revelation, 'seales' sacramentally marking genitalia as the boundary of ordinary sexual experience. That such boundaries are by nature 'set free,' a freedom 'injur'd' only 'by late law,' alludes to the scriptural notion that there is no marriage in heaven (Mt. 22.30; Mk. 12.23). Because here interpenetration or union is total, there is no need for the relatively limited act of coitus; neither are sacraments necessary when their *raison d'être* has become obsolete. But again, just as in 'The Extasie' souls must 'descend / T'affections, and to faculties' (65–6), so the past tense of the final stanza here integrates the miraculous experience with that which it putatively has surpassed. The final lines are less Platonic celebration than carnal reluctance:

>   but now alas,
>   All measure, and all language, I should passe,
>   Should I tell what a miracle shee was.   (31–3)

The joke that 'measure' and 'language' – the poem that is 'The Relique' – *do* indeed 'tell' complements the implied notion that 'shee,' like the variously false/chaste mistress of Petrarchan convention, is associated as much with sensual 'mis-devotion' (13) as with the more rarefied mysteries to which 'seales' and 'those meales' can only gesture.

The idealized union of lovers, like that of communicant and God, relies on the sensory dimension apart from which it is in danger of becoming rarefied beyond the limits of human knowledge and experience. Such is the incarnational argument of 'Farewell to Love,' where 'Things not yet knowne [and] coveted by men' are comparable to the gingerbread man 'from late faire / His highnesse sitting in a golden Chaire' (8–12). For both, 'Our desires give them fashion, and so / As they waxe lesser, fall, as they sise, grow' (9–10). In a playful reversal, the inexperienced lover who thinks there to be 'some Deitie in love' (2) is compared with 'Atheists' who call 'at their dying houre ... what they cannot name, an unknowne power' (4–5). Donne's approbation of agnostics, possibly an allusion to St Paul's encounter with the Athenian philosophers (Acts 17.22–3), is less an assault on Love's acolytes than resignation to the finally insatiable condition of desire. The gingerbread man suggests religious idolatry – as in Ben Jonson's *Bartholomew Fair* where the puritan minister, Zeal-of-the-Land Busy, denounces dolls and gingerbread as pagan idols (3.6, 5.5) – and thus the tendency of ritual to become mechanical, emptied of significance, stale bread. Like religious ceremony, love is constantly in need of revitalization, otherwise 'What before pleas'd' will soon become a 'sorrowing dulnesse to the minde' (18–20). Yet it is not at all clear that an alternative to the cycle of worship, enjoyment, and decay is offered, for even celibacy – or atheism proper – is 'but applying worm-seede to the Taile' (40): sooner or later the cycle must resume its inexorable motion.

If the gingerbread man of 'Farewell to Love' and the cynicism of Donne's frustrated lovers suggest spiritual torpor and ennui, it is not so much due to the failure of sexual or religious experience to intimate adequately the mysteries they defer as it is a general failure to realize the dynamic quality of all meaningful experience, spiritual or otherwise. By implicating sacramental topoi in the collision of mystical experience with more palpable realities, Donne's exploration of human love suggests an incarnational poetic in which 'His highness' – whether Petrarchan ideal or divinity – must occasionally come down from its 'golden Chaire.'

Value

The integration of sacramental and more profane topoi suggests an immanence largely foreign to Reformation religious thought. The Yuletide scattering of nuts, once said, notes Patrick Collinson, to be symbolic of Christ's body,[16] is at odds with a religious culture whose deity, if theoretically nearer than ever – *sola scriptura, sola fide, sola gratia* – had become radically transcendent and thus less susceptible of apprehension through the senses and the material world. Despite his eventual 'apostasy,' a significant feature of Donne's poetry is the considerable extent to which he allows the sacred to be contaminated by less exalted aspects of human experience and thus to recall that homely aspect of medieval religiosity suggested by Yuletide ritual. Victor Shklovsky's concept of defamiliarization, in which our understanding of a thing is rejuvenated by being made strange, nicely describes Donne's incarnational poetics.[17] In associating sacramental topoi with the more profane elements of his experience, Donne forces a recognition of the immanence of divinity in the world. His elaborate conceits replicate linguistically the incarnational paradox sacrament embodies, the paradox wherein the divine character *changes*, is impossibly altered in order to recover some of the shimmer or *mysterium tremendum* lost to familiarity.[18] This notion of rebirth through estrangement is perhaps a feature of all poetry. That a flea may represent the bawdy union of lovers depends on an already established convention. That the same 'living walls of Jet' become a cloister so stretches signification that the student of Donne no longer can see a flea in the same way, just as the student of Eliot can never dissociate the concrete image of a house surrounded by low-lying fog from the notion of dream-dispersed consciousness – nor either from a sleeping cat.

Given its traditionally redemptive function, it is not surprising to find Donne combining sacrament with monetary topoi. As the intersection of heavenly and sublunary loves marks a point analogous to the Incarnation's integration of Word and flesh, so is the problem of monetary signification analogous to that of the sacramental sign's power to communicate its divine referent. For just as the manner in and extent to which a sacrament manifests presence is inextricable from the religious discourse which describes it as such, its symbolic power derived from this discursive reification of religious desire, so does the power of money to signify wealth derive from a complex relationship between its inherent value and its socially determined status as currency. Whereas Donne's erotic poetry concerns the relationship between constancy and change, spiritual and earthly loves, here the appropriate dichotomy comprising the vertical and horizontal components of our axes model may be said to consist, respectively, of Karl Marx's use value and exchange value: the value-sign as that which is derived from real human needs and that which is ontologically self-possessing, reifying those needs as a fetishized object. According to Marx, money conceived as such is 'the power ... to change representation into reality and reality into mere representation.'[19] In his archaeology of wealth in early modern Europe, Michel Foucault observes the paradox that money derived its power as standard from 'the basis of its own material reality as wealth' even though 'the monetary sign cannot define its exchange value, and can be established as a mark only on a metallic mass which in turn defines its value in the scale of other commodities.'[20] This tension between 'money-as-sign' and 'money-as-commodity'[21] is explored by Richard Halpern in his analysis of More's *Utopia*. The Utopians' deliberate debasement of gold marks the ascendancy of use value over exchange value. Real human needs, that is, rather than the chimeras of Marx's fetishized 'commodity-form,' triumph over the irrational valorization of precious metals. Halpern notes, however, that the Utopian strategy of devaluing gold by using it to make chamber pots and the like is contradictory, for it is merely a reactionary strategy that only represses the 'innate desirability' it inadvertantly invests in the object it would debase. This 'commodity fetishism,' writes Halpern, 'causes the social origin of value to disappear from consciousness. What replaces it is, on the one hand, an innately valuable "thing" and, on the other hand, an equally mysterious valuation of it on the part of the subject.' The value sign is thus a 'hieroglyphic':

> on the surface, a figure or discourse of valuable objects and their relations and, beneath, an occulted figure or discourse of social relations, which becomes the unconscious of the system of commodity production, revealing itself only through the 'symptom' of mysterious value relations among objects.[22]

This convergence of use and exchange values, of desire and its objective reification, is analogous to a twofold tension in sacramental discourse. Politically, the sacrament is at once both the malleable site of evolving theological and ecclesiastical debate, and a static symbol of ecclesiastical unity. On a purely theological level, there is tension between, on the one hand, the sacrament as a representational sign, and, on the other, the sacrament-as-commodity on which the religious desire to commune with God is projected and reified. For English establishment divines eager to envision a 'real presence' which nevertheless remains unsullied by its material means, this tension is between a sacrament shimmering with the glow of the mystery it embodies, and one in which presence is recognized to be the absent referent of a representation, the ephemeral product of a cultural pact.

Preference for woman's 'Centrique part' (36) over woman's virtue in 'Elegie [XVIII]: Loves Progress' parallels preference both for pagan over civilized religious ceremony and for an interred metal apart from its supralunary counterpart: Love is 'an infernal god and underground ... where gold and fire abound,' the sacrifices due its godhead lying not 'on Altars' but rather in 'pits and holes'; and 'Although we see Celestial bodies move / Above the earth,' it is 'the earth we Till and love' (29–34). The occult correspondence of metals to their celestial counterparts is all but severed, the collapse of its vertical stability complemented both by the motion from 'Altars' to 'pits and holes' and by the phallic/agricultural plow of Donne's lover/husbandman. The glitter of precious metals, the carnal essence of woman, pagan sacrifice – these are the 'strange shapes' of a love 'oe'r lick[ed]' by one who fails to 'propose / The right true end of love' (2–5):

> I when I value gold, may think upon
> The ductilness, the application,
> The wholesomness, the ingenuitie,
> From rust, from soil, from fire ever free:
> But if I love it, 'tis because 'tis made
> By our new nature (Use) the soul of trade.   (11–16)

The opposition Donne draws here is as disingenuous as it is ingenious, for the qualities he ascribes to gold as intrinsic are surely part of the discourse or 'Use' which invests the metal with value in the first place. That the motions of trade could have a soul only augments the implicit and sly observation that whatever intrinsic value a thing may have is impossible finally to separate from the complex web of extrinsic qualities, notions, and desires which bring it to our attention as such – which unearth it, so to speak. Something of this complexity is evident in the Soul's answer to Pleasure's temptation of 'minted gold' in Marvell's 'Dialogue, between the Resolved Soul and Created Pleasure,' the only answer in the poem given in the form of a question: 'Were't not a price, who'd value gold?' (58–62).

Recognizing the fluid and transitory nature of desire, Donne knew that excessive veneration or fetishization may devalue an object, whether sacrament, coin, or woman's 'Centrique part': the value of a currency may drop proportional to the abundance of its circulation, just as formulaic and repetitive aspects of sacramental ritual threaten to render ordinary that which it celebrates as extraordinary. The objective reification of sacramental, sexual, and acquisitive desires thus ironically hastens their obsolescence. Something of this is evident in 'Elegie II: The Anagram,' where 'Women are all like Angels; the faire be / Like those which fell to worse' (29–30). The pun on 'Angels' suggests a triple conceit: beautiful women are more in demand and thus cheapened through sexual use, not unlike the pride or over-estimated worth of the heavenly host which fell with Satan, nor again the devaluation of coinage resulting from its increased circulation and abundance. The less admired of women may prove in the end a better investment:

Oh what a soveraigne Plaister will shee bee
If thy past sinnes have taught thee jealousie!   (37–8)

Flavia's 'Anagram of a good face,' like a sacrament, acts as a medicinal for 'past sinnes,' while the pun on 'soveraigne' (king and coin) establishes both the royal status of courtly presence (in this case the king's touch as cure for 'jealousie' – where scrofula might be expected!) and the anagram's currency as acceptable substitute for 'good Angels.' It is the surface arrangement of that face or coin – its accidental appearance or currency rather than its substance (to invoke the Aristotelian categories of transubstantiation) – that solicits admiration, envy, or worship. Just as the intrinsic value of a sacrament is inextricable from the institution which valorizes it; just as the value of a currency is the unstable product of need, trade, and the circulation of wealth; so too woman's beauty is best viewed as the fortuitous and fashionable arrangement of common materials, the same 'leane dearth of words' put 'but one way' (17–18).

The economics of inside/outside or intrinsic versus extrinsic value are concentrated on the poetic endeavour itself in 'To the Countess of Bedford, On New-yeares day,' where the doctrine of transubstantiation is implicitly analogous to the dangers inherent in the art of praise. The poet's verse, like a sick body, is enlivened by 'strong agents' and 'extracts' (18–20) that also have the capacity to obliterate that body:

So, my verse built of your just praise, might want
    Reason and likelihood, the firmest Base,
And made of miracle, now faith is scant,
    Will vanish soone, and so possesse no place,
    And you, and it, too much grace might disgrace.   (21–5)

Reformation controversy surfaces with the observation that the multiplication of miracles – of which the Roman Mass was the most notorious example – is a poor substitute for faith, just as excessive flattery undermines its own ends. But the sense here is not so much a fear of excess or undue praise as an inability to contain that which exceeds the boundaries of poetic encomium, much as an excessive fondness for the carnal features of sacrament neglects sufficiently to revere what finally is ineffable. Just as in 'Crucifying' from the *La Corona* sequence Donne is disdainful of those who would reduce Christ, 'selfe-lifes infinity to'a span, / Nay to an inch' (7–8), so here he wonders:

> how I
> One corne of one low anthills dust, and lesse,
> Should name, know, or expresse a thing so high,
> And not an inch, measure infinity.   (27–30)

Praise is sacrificial and, not unlike communicants' offering of self at Holy Communion, it always falls short of that due its object; or like the eucharistic species, it embodies that which surely must exceed its grasp. Like a sacrament, praise must avoid both excessive show, which draws more attention to itself than its referent, and despair at total inadequacy, which would render the ritual pointless. The solution is to turn all over to God, who 'useth oft, when such a heart mis-sayes, / To make it good, for, such a praiser prayes' (34–5).

Thus far we have seen Donne demystify sacraments by drawing them from their vertical dimension into the horizontal flux of profane topoi. Here, because both poem and poet receive their grace from patron and deity respectively, it would appear that it is the horizontal axis that is rotated upward into alignment with its vertical counterpart. On the other hand, though the instructions which follow are assumed to be of divine authority – 'I cannot tell them' (31) – it is nevertheless the speaker who confidently corroborates God's decrees with the ten-times repeated 'He will' (36–53). This appropriation of the divine voice to sanction his admonishing of Lucy's conduct at court ends by invoking a predestinarian-inflected Baptism complete with penitential tears and heavenly register:

> From need of teares he will defend your soule,
>   Or make a rebaptizing of one teare;
> Hee cannot, (that's, he will not) dis-inroule
>   Your name; and when with active joy we heare
>   This private Ghospell, then'tis our New Yeare.   (61–5)

The parenthetical qualification questions this external will's sovereignty. In hindsight, then, the cipher which in the opening stanza the speaker fancies himself to be reverberates with the paradox of a presence that is conspicuously absent: 'of stuffe and forme perplext, / Whose *what*, and *where*, in disputation is, / If I should call mee *any thing*, should misse' (3–5, my emphasis). What begins as an epideictic strategy disclaiming its own artifice in an effort to elevate the object of praise ends, willy nilly, by establishing the speaker himself as both officiating priest and stubborn (if deferred) presence.

The relationship between intrinsic and extrinsic value is interrogated in Donne's verse letter, 'To the Countesse of Huntingdon: Man to Gods image.' In reading the poem as alluding to Donne's status as 'recusant-turned-Protestant,' DiPasquale cites a passage from the prose letter to Goodyere in which the poem is contained: 'You shall seldom see a Coyne,' writes Donne, 'upon which the stamp were removed, though to imprint it better, but it looks awry and squint. And so, for the most part, do mindes which have received divers impressions' (*Letters*, 101–2).[23] In addition to its ironic echoes of Donne's conversion, however, the passage suggests a theory of monetary signification in which a currency's extrinsic value – its stamped authorization – becomes fused with its substantial being, so that subsequent impressions never wholly erase the former. Use in this case truly is the soul of trade. But if the passage suggests Donne's reluctance to abandon his Roman Catholic heritage, the theory of wealth it assumes anticipates the poem's interrogation of extrinsic and intrinsic value with respect to Elizabeth Stanley herself. Beginning with the conventional notion that woman's inferiority is sanctioned by scripture, Donne proceeds to make an exception of Egerton's stepdaughter by comparing her to the miraculous appearance of a star among others whose 'milde innocence' (9) is but that of 'vagrant transitory Comets' (5). Initially like the star that guided the Magi to the Nativity, the countess is then afforded a more boldly messianic status. Virtue, in falling 'so low as woman' and thus apparently 'neare her end' (20), is in fact

> not stoop'd, but rais'd; exil'd by men
>   She fled to heaven, that's heavenly things, that's you;
> She was in all men, thinly scatter'd then,
>   But now amass'd, contracted in a few.
> She guilded us: But you are gold, and Shee,
>   Us she inform'd, but transubstantiates you,
> Soft dispositions which ductile bee,
>   Elixarlike, she makes not cleane, but new.   (21–8)

Herself the incarnation of virtue, the countess is earthly host to virtue's otherwise transcendent being. Whereas 'ductilness' of gold in 'Loves

Progress' is subordinated to the lover's desire or 'use,' here the elasticity of the soft metal is subject to a more divine manipulation. Again, as with the New Year's letter to the countess of Bedford, the poet denies that his praise constitutes the subject's value; rather, 'my ill reaching you might there grow good, / But I remaine a poyson'd fountaine still' (53–4). The lines recall the poisoned sacrament and fountain of 'Twicknam Garden.' Allusion to the Roman doctrine (and alchemical change) in 'transubstantiation,' however, is here a celebration of immanence analogous to that of the Incarnation and Nativity. DiPasquale argues that favourable references later in the prose letter both to the Book of Common Prayer and to Donne's and Goodyere's membership in the reformed community of the English church 'undercut the quasi-Catholic Eucharist of the verse letter.'[24] But this assumes that the sacramental views of the English church in 1609 (when, according to Thomas Hester, the letter was written)[25] were undisputed, that among the 'reformed community' there would not be those who would endorse formulae similar to if not explicitly acknowledged as transubstantiation and thus 'quasi-Catholic.' Moreover, while DiPasquale is right to see that in the verse letter the countess falls short in the end of the divinity to which she is compared,[26] it is precisely because his praise is equivocal that Donne's gradual questioning of Stanley's worth depends on maintaining reverence for the Roman sacrament from which she is finally dissociated. On one level the countess is to virtue what the Magi's star is to the infant Jesus, or what the Virgin is to the same, or, again, what the Eucharist is to the presence it embodies; indeed, 'woman' is the nadir of Virtue's sunlike progress. And yet the 'low names' of wife and mother in which, 'for our sakes,' virtue 'abide[s]' (29, 36) are integral with 'The manger-cradled infant' in whom, also for our sakes, divinity dwells, 'God below' (14). It is that incarnational paradox that prevents Donne from separating the husk of woman-wife-mother from the kernel of an unsullied and transcendent virtue. But just as the doctrine of transubstantiation held that the species become God – and not the converse, as anti-Roman polemicists charged – so is Elizabeth Stanley redeemed insofar as she is 'soft' and 'ductile,' willing to have the substance of her being – woman-wife-mother – displaced by the elusive 'virtue' that is the true object of praise. Ben Jonson's disdain for 'An Anatomy of the World' – concerned that that poem's 'shee' receives praise more properly belonging to the Virgin Mary – might equally have applied here. But Donne's response that in The First Anniversary he intended the idea of a woman and not as Drury actually was finds parallel in this poem's reluctance to conflate the countess of Huntingdon and 'vertue' in a single 'shee.' As the final proviso clarifies, 'I was your Prophet in your yonger dayes, / And now your Chaplaine, *God in you to praise*' (69–70, my emphasis).

The money/sacrament analogy and Donne's interrogation of value are perhaps nowhere more explicit than in 'Elegie [XI]: The Bracelet.' The lover here bemoans not so much his loss of a love memento or 'silly old moralitie' (5) as that of the gold 'Angels' (9), the 'twelve innocents' (17) that he now must smelt to form the 'seavenfold chaine' (7) symbolizing lovers' union. Midway through this longest of the elegies we find the distraught speaker responding to his mistress's attempt to console him:

> Thou say'st (alas) the gold doth still remaine,
> Though it be chang'd, and put into a chaine,
> So in the first falne angels, resteth still
> Wisdome and knowledge; but'tis turn'd to ill:
> As these should doe good workes; and should provide
> Necessities; but now must nurse thy pride,
> And they are still bad angels; Mine are none,
> For, forme gives being, and their forme is gone.   (69–76)

Apparent again is the familiar conceit identifying deflated coinage with the Satanic rebels of Christian mythology. Denying, in effect, that angels so fallen retain their essential or substantial goodness, the speaker implicitly compares such error to the scholastic separation of matter and form, a misunderstanding of Aristotle that allowed the doctrine of transubstantiation to assert the presence of the body of Christ despite appearances. Donne knew his Aristotle. In 'Elegie on the untimely death of the incomparable Prince, Henry,' for example, he asserts that 'if all the Substances were spent, / 'Twere madnes to enquire of Accident' (67–8). A similar sophistication is evident in Marvell's 'Flecknoe, an English Priest at Rome,' where the speaker, negotiating with the priest's colleague on the narrow stairs, parodies his victims' scholastic education:

>   I, that was
> Delightful, said, 'There can no body pass
> Except by penetration hither, where
> Two make a crowd; nor can three persons here
> Consist but in one substance.'   (97–101)

The speaker in 'The Bracelet' is an equally astute metaphysician, knowing that substance does not reside under or prior to accident, but rather that matter and form together comprise any substance. Now a mere chain rather than the liquid asset ('angels') it once was, his gold no longer *is*, for 'forme gives being, and their forme is gone.' And yet, though seeming to have accepted his loss by asserting the sovereignty of mutability – substance subject to formal manifestation, gold to angels or bracelet – the speaker follows with an optimism tantamount to conceding the scholastic perversion of the Aristotelian scheme: 'Pitty these Angels yet; their dignities / Passe Vertues, Powers, and Principalities' (77–8). Obsession with a finally intrinsic, immutable value is particularly apparent in the sequence of dismissals opening the poem, where the bracelet's status as token reminder of both the beloved's hair and hand, and the lovers' union, is but 'leaven of vile soder' relative to the gold's 'first state of ... Creation' (10–12). On the other hand, the angels were never more nor less than the means to an end, 'To gaine new friends, t'appease great enemies' (15), though even here the power to gain and appease is derived from their intrinsic value.

Echoing the Augustinian doctrine of human depravity, the speaker refuses to accept as consolation the capacity of these now fallen (smelted) angels still to 'doe good works' and 'provide / Necessities' (73–4). As we have seen, however, their status is at the very least ambiguous: we should thus be wary of assigning much confessional or polemical value to the theological allusions. It would be erroneous, for example, to assume that Donne piously denounces reliance on the external means of grace. Indeed, in the following lines –

> But, thou art resolute; Thy will be done;
> Yet with such anguish, as her onely sonne
> The Mother in the hungry grave doth lay,
> Unto the fire these Martyrs I betray   (79–82)

– the speaker assigns his angels veiled messianic status while reserving for himself the role of the Virgin Mary. If sacramental efficacy is dismissed altogether – suggested by the speaker's assertion that the smelted angels, 'in the furnace throwne, / And punisht for offences not their owne ... save not me' nor 'doe not ease my paines, / When in that hell they'are burnt and tyed in chains' (19–22) – the dismissal's theology is subordinated to the poem's comic playfulness. The ironic and satirical elements allow various dogmas to be explored, rigorously assumed, confused, or abandoned, according to rhetorical expedience. This is not to say that theological matters are *merely* poetic accoutrements; that they are woven into the poem with such subtlety suggests that Donne had given them considerable thought. 'The Bracelet,' rather, reveals the doctrinal iconoclasm of a restless and complex religious sensibility, a Christian humanist possessing keen theological understanding and yet willing to subject such knowledge to a boundless creative impulse.

If sacramental topoi appear to provide but light amusement in a poem ostensibly indifferent to theological concerns, however, their very obscurity may contribute to what is in fact political-religious polemic after all. In a lengthy reference to Catholic/Protestant conflict on the continent, the speaker valorizes his angels above foreign currencies. Whereas French crowns are dismissed for their debased value – 'so pale, so lame, so leane, so ruinous' even if 'French Kings most Christian be' (26–7) – 'spanish Stamps' (29) are not so easily ignored. The former fall by 'their countreys naturall rot' (24), while the latter stubbornly maintain value despite their intrinsic vileness: 'unlickt beare-whelps, unfil'd pistolets' (31). Indeed, 'as Catholique as their King' (30), such coins carry substantial influence and power – but in the negative sense of false sacraments:

> Which, as the soule quickens head, feet and heart,
> As streames like veines, run through th'earth's every part,
> Visit all Countries, and have slily made
> Gorgeous *France*, ruin'd, ragged and decay'd,
> *Scotland*, which knew no State, proud in one day,
> And mangled seventeen-headed *Belgia*.   (37–42)

Whereas the speaker's pure gold when 'put into a chaine' does *not* 'still remaine,' Spanish gold, in keeping with the doctrine of transubstantiation, retains its inherent or substantial (and in this case harmful) value, whatever the fortunes – or accidents, so to speak – of political power. False or poisonous sacraments – or Spanish currency – are as gall to those whose spiritual or economic constitutions are suited to more worthy fare (like the speaker's English angels!), or potentially (and deceptively) beneficial to the disaffected who, like Scotland, might find them attractive because temporarily empowering. Later, in what is perhaps a further veiled jibe at what Marvell in the 'Horation Ode' was to call the 'parti-coloured mind' of the disloyal 'Pict' (105–6), the speaker includes in his litany against the finder of the bracelet the curse that he 'be with forraine gold brib'd to betray / Thy Countrey, and faile both of it and thy pay' (97–8). That the eventual undoing of the bribed is analogous to that of those receiving popish sacraments is suggested in the speaker's wish that 'the next thing thou stoop'st to reach, contain / Poyson, whose nimble fume rot thy moist braine' (99–100) and eventually prove a false and therefore ineffective rite – perhaps even a damning rather than saving Extreme Unction: 'at thy lives last moment, / May thy swolne sinnes themselves to thee present' (109–10). And though the final *volte-face* accommodates true grace, *this* messiah-madonna's sincerity remains somewhat ambivalent:

> But, I forgive; repent thee honest man:
> Gold is Restorative, restore it then:
> But if from it thou beest loath to depart,
> Because 'tis cordiall, would 'twere at thy heart.   (111–14)

The analogy of foreign influence and false sacraments is based on that ubiquitous anatomical trope, the body-politic. And though 'Catholique' Spain receives much blame for the contamination of otherwise godly states, both loathed 'finder' and bracelet (the latter signifying *formerly* English coin) suggest even greater contempt for domestic (Scottish) as opposed to continental communicants. As sacraments may be positively efficacious or not according to confessional context; as a currency's value is contingent upon economic and political factors external to its intrinsic worth (not the 'Kings reall' but rather 'his stamped face,' to cite 'The Canonization'); just so are domestic political bodies offered cordial or poison – invited to commune or be excommunicated – according to whether they bear the appropriate marks of national identity, for in the end it is 'forme [that] gives being.'

Donne's interest in the metaphysics of symbolic identity – of whether it is somehow innate or externally determined or both – has a personal as well as an intellectual dimension. The problem of self-determination and personal agency must have been crucial for one whose vocational fortunes were somewhat imposed. While his eventual Ordination hardly marks Donne's resistance against circumstances beyond his control, his later verse and sermons, as is well known, bear witness to a vibrant and idiosyncratic personality. That Donne was sensitive to the partly royal nature of those forces governing his destiny is evident in a verse letter, 'To Mr Tilman,' in which a sacramental-monetary analogy informs the poem's rumination on the nature and authority of the priestly office that the author himself had recently assumed. Responding to Edward Tilman's

1618 Ordination, Donne sympathizes with his friend's apparent reluctance. 'Thou art the same materials, as before,' he writes:

> Onely the stampe is changed; but no more.
> And as new crowned Kings alter the face,
> But not the monies substance; so hath grace
> Chang'd onely Gods old Image by Creation,
> To Christs new stampe, at this thy Coronation.   (14–18)[27]

The Aristotelian categories of substance and accident are evoked here in an analogy linking the authorities of Ordination and royal currency.[28] If 'face' and 'substance' echo the categories comprising a Roman Eucharist, however, the analogy in this case *denies* a transubstantive change. Just as currency has value by virtue of bearing the king's stamp while its material significance is unchanged, so has Tilman's Ordination the external mark of an authority which, though otherwise absent, continually informs his office. If the king is deposed or withdraws his authority, the coin may become worthless even though it bears his visage or mark; likewise, Donne implicitly cautions, Ordination does not confer power in such a way as to preclude its ever being withdrawn. It is 'Christs new stamp,' the *use* to which Tilman is put, the office with which he is charged, that ultimately carries its borrowed authority. Similarly, according to Reform theology, sacramental efficacy is never *ex opere operato*, never conferred on the species by virtue of priestly manipulation or in such a way as to grant them intrinsic value. The Thomist formula here is subverted insofar as its categories are appropriated to ensure that the conferral of power is limited, always in some way held back, and in such a way as to guarantee total return, just as the flow of sacramental 'virtue' in a Calvinist scheme never compromises the radically transcendent status of its divine source.

Viewed one way, the analogy reinforces the king's *iure divino* status, for his role is identified with the elusive source of both priestly and sacramental authority. Alternatively, however, the coin analogy's valorization of 'accidental' as opposed to 'substantial' change suggests a much more complex relationship among God, king, and priest. Contrary to anti-Roman polemic, the doctrine of transubstantiation may in fact *deny* certain powers to the priest inasmuch as it suggests an autonomous efficacy for the species once consecrated. The priest's sacerdotal authority in this respect may actually find more support in a Calvinist view of the Eucharist in which carnal presence is withheld. In privileging an

authority finally extrinsic to the elements that carry its mark, such doctrine ensures that presence is always deferred, never settling on one
identifiable locus, subject to ceaseless negotiation among recipient, God,
and priest. And yet the priest, according to the poem, stands as the
visible and audible mediator of that presence, even if he too, in Ordination, is but the substance over which presence slides without ever making
more than 'accidental' contact. Preachers, writes Donne, 'give kingdomes
to more / Than Kings give dignities' and 'As Angels out of clouds, from
Pulpits speake,' bringing 'man to heaven, and heaven againe to man'
(39–48). Thus the coin analogy also allows that while the substance of a
thing always remains, its malleable or 'accidental' surface (in this case
the priest's earthly authority) is of a significance that is in fact substantial
after all. If the preacher's second birth is but the stamp of an authority
never fully his own, it is nevertheless of a currency whose value threatens
to exceed that of the earthly crown. It is important to remember that the
Oath of Allegiance was initially James's response to the threat of papal
authority surpassing that of the secular ruler.[29] That Donne's poem
reinforces royal prerogative while yet elevating priestly access to the
divine a notch or two higher attests to the ambivalences of an ecclesiastical establishment traditional in its support of episcopacy *iure divino* while
sympathetic to the nationalist polemic in which it found itself implicated. An analogy in which Ordination corresponds to royal minting
may imply the priest's *sub*-ordination to that crown: as coin is to king
and priest to God, so therefore is priest to king. But analogy, of course, is
not identification. Donne's valorization of the pulpit allows that the
priestly conduit of divine virtue is invested with powers exceeding those
of God's secular viceroy. When divested of an unequivocal 'real presence' and instead assigned the status of metaphor or token symbol of
remote realities, the species are separated from their referent by a space
into which a host of theological formulae are then put into play, each
one vying to bridge the divide. Similarly, the minister's status as God's
representative, though 'accidental' in the Aristotelian sense, is nevertheless reinforced to the degree to which his ministry is effective – in
preaching as an angel and thereby bringing men to heaven. (The *ars
praedicandi*, writes the dean of St Paul's, makes 'absent and remote things
present to your understanding,' just as sacraments bring Christ 'nearer
... in visible and sensible things' [*Sermons*, 5.144].) This allows for considerable ambiguity as to the final extent of the minister's authority. Royal
power, obversely, is limited by the efficacy of its representations – by the
degree, that is, to which a minted visage manages to communicate the
king's real as much as his stamped face.

Court

The conceptual malleability of a sacrament or coin is an essential part of its power to signify, inseparable finally from any notion of intrinsic worth. Sacramental incarnation involves the intersection of a cultural pact with the mystery of a valorized symbol, whether the presence thought to resonate in, with, or through consecrated bread, or the magical glitter of gold. The letter to Tilman extends the interrogation of value to include a veiled comparison of royal and priestly powers, thereby addressing Donne's relationship with what proved to be the most elusive of social spheres, the Stuart court. If sacrament is analogous to the dichotomies of intrinsic/extrinsic value and rarefied/sublunary loves, Holy Communion, with its communicants and the presence they celebrate, suggests a royal analogy in the intersection of realm and court, the constituents and heart of the body politic – or, to recall the critique of power in 'Satyre III,' the 'rough streame' and its 'calme head' (104). The student of Shakespeare knows well the anatomical identification of king and nation as components of a vast body. *Richard II* investigates the idea that the king is quite literally the lifeblood of his realm; with its highly ritualized scenes dramatizing the transfer of royal power, together with Richard's hyperbolic notions of self-sacrifice, the play ceremonially documents and interrogates the issue of divine right. Similarly, Hamlet's speech comparing the effects of Claudius's drunken revels to the 'o'erleaven[ing]' of 'some vicious mole' that threatens national reputation is one of the more famous appeals to the intimate connection of royal and common weals (1.4.23–38). Contrary to the threat of a corrupted royal power within, 'The Bracelet,' we have seen, exploits the notion that a foreign currency may act as a false sacrament contaminating the body politic from without. If sacramental topoi may serve a xenophobic nationalism, however, Donne was also capable of deploying such imagery to address the more insular politics among court, king, and courtiers.

In 'Metempsycosis' or 'The Progresse of the Soule,' the 'deathlesse soule' of the poem's subtitle is at one point described as a 'Prince' who 'sends her faculties / To all her limbes, distant as Provinces' (334–5), the great fish in which she resides sucking in 'every thing / That passeth neare' (325–6). The whale has no need to hunt for its food: 'as an officer' it simply 'stayes in his court, at his owne net, and there / All suitors of all sorts themselves enthrall' (321–3). Eucharistic imagery is associated with this leviathan's court, both by way of the conspiring 'Thresher, and steel-beak'd Sword-fish' who are unable to do 'Good to themselves by his death (they did not eate / His flesh, nor suck those oyles, which thence outstreat)' (344–51), and by way of those who *do* benefit from this otherwise unfortunate death:

> a scoff, and prey, this tyran dyes,
> And (his owne dole) feeds with himself all companies.   (359–60)

That the soul's leviathan body and not the soul itself is the 'slaine king' allows for the latter's resurrection among the followers on whose behalf he is sacrificed and consumed. These now transfer their adoration to some palpable and powerful object, the new Prince, for 'h'is now dead, to whom they should show / Love' (363–8).

Sacramental topoi are of central importance in 'Satyre IV,' a poem whose contempt for the court's social extravagances is attenuated by the speaker's recognition of his own courtly aspirations. The tale of his encounter at the royal Presence Chamber is recalled from the perspective of one who has passed through a purgatory, 'such as fear'd hell is / A recreation, and scant map,' and is about to receive the Eucharist – or, more specifically, Extreme Unction. 'Well,' he begins, 'I may now receive, and die' (1–4), the line echoing Robert Southwell's 'I Die Alive': 'My feast is done, my soul would be at ease, / My grace is said – O death, come take away' (3–4). As James Baumlin has noted, the sacramental opening of 'Satyre IV' provides 'a structuring principle for the poem as a whole.'[30] Offering the requisite Confession – a rehearsal of his (mis)adventures – the speaker compares himself with one 'Glaze which did goe / To'a Masse in jest' (8–9), got caught, but was reluctant to pay the fine. Just so, says the speaker,

> it pleas'd my destinie
> (Guilty of my sin of going), to think me
> As prone to all ill, and of good as forget-
> full, as proud, as lustfull, and as much in debt,
> As vaine, as witlesse, and as false as they
> Which dwell at court, for once going that way.   (11–16)

On the verge of participating in a distinctly Roman Catholic ritual, the speaker nevertheless suggests an analogy between the court and the Roman Mass. His supposed aloofness – to go to court, like Glaze to Mass, only 'in jest' – is comically disingenuous. For if the Mass is demonized in its alignment with the nefarious court, the *present* context of Confession and Extreme Unction, together with the claim to have passed through a purgatorial remission, are themselves far from immune to charges of popery. The irony anticipates and underscores the speaker's reluctance to abandon the court he vociferously denounces, and, implicitly, the Roman Catholic church with which it is associated. The perspective of confident hindsight with which he begins his tale is thereby qualified, thus deliberately casting suspicion on the righteous indignation that follows.

The court-Mass analogy becomes more apparent when the satirist finds to his dismay that in opposing his *adversarius*, the boorish 'macaroon' encountered on his way to court, he succumbs to a *tête à tête* itself not unlike the sparring of court wits. The description of his naivety suggests the Roman sign of the cross: 'But as Itch / Scratch'd unto smart, and as blunt iron ground / Into an edge, hurts worse: So, I (foole) found, / Crossing hurt mee' (88–91). Just as the mention of purgatory and participation in auricular Confession prior to receiving the sacrament undermine his apparent antipopery, 'Crossing' here indicts the speaker as ceremonially complicit with Glaze's Mass. There is now little doubt that the 'jest' has become dangerously real.

Also telling is the reference to the court as 'our Presence' and 'the Presence.' Disdain for the shallow trappings of the court is complemented by contempt for gaudy Italian fashion which 'at London flouts our Presence' (171), where 'Presence' suggests not only the royal Presence Chamber, but also, given the poem's sacramental context, the 'real presence' of the Eucharist. That 'presence' is a term common to both courtly and sacramental discourses is significant in light of the architectural arrangement, examined by Peter McCullough, of the royal privy chambers at Whitehall and Hampton court. The public Presence Chamber and the innermost Privy Chamber, McCullough notes, were separated by the Privy Closet which included a small private chapel in which both Elizabeth and James would have kneeled for private devotions. This Privy Closet or 'Oratory' bordered directly on the Presence Chamber and was furnished with a Communion table, presumably for private use.[31] In 'Satyre IV,' the speaker's meditative 'space,' as it were, may be characterized similarly as a private sacramental present at once removed from and nervously bordering on the Presence Chamber of his not-too-distant courtly past. That chamber, according to the poem, is a mockery of the English court, a mere 'waxen garden' imported from Italy: 'Just such gay painted things, which no sappe, nor / Tast have in them, ours are' (169–73). 'Tast,' the absence of which emphasizes the aesthetic emptiness of English court ritual, is synonymous also with 'sappe,' the pun thus characterizing the courtier's experience at court as an ingestive one void of real substance – precisely the experience, according to anti-Catholic polemicists, of a communicant in the Roman Mass. The twenty-ninth of the Elizabethan Articles, we recall, states that those who but 'do carnally and visibly press [the bread] with their teeth ... to their condemnation, do eat and drink the sign or sacrament of so great a thing.'[32] That the 'gay painted things' contaminating this Presence Chamber no 'Tast have in them' thus expands the speaker's indictment of the Italianate English court to include a veiled condemnation of English Holy Communion as dangerously similar to the Roman Mass condemned by that same English court. The suggestion becomes more explicit when the third and final occurrence of the term 'Presence' coincides with a description of the vainly apparelled courtier, whose entrance at court is preceded by a kind of auricular Confession that unmistakably recalls the speaker's own but that here is become public spectacle:

> Would not Heraclitus laugh to see Macrine
> From hat, to shooe, himself at doore refine,
> As if the Presence were a Moschite, and lift
> His skirts and hose, and call his clothes to shrift,
> Making them confesse not only mortall
> Great staines and holes in them; but veniall
> Feathers and dust, wherewith they fornicate.   (197–203)

Appearance and dress are offered as formal evidence of the courtier's worthiness to proceed to the inner sanctum and royal presence, just as confession of both mortal and venial sins in a Roman Catholic context is the prerequisite for receiving the Eucharist. This particular bit of mockery underscores the irony of the speaker's status, for the poem itself is confessional, the final and personal revelation of one about to receive sacramental pardon and thereby to enter fully into a presence of quite another sort.

The confusion of identity charted by the speaker's ironic involvement in court practices he loathes is a duplicity incorporated into the poem's structural and rhetorical framework, figuratively identifying the court as the locus of popish ceremony and then subverting the speaker's pretended aloofness. The court-Mass analogy linking confessional and social identities becomes glaringly evident in the figure of the courtier compared to 'a young Preacher' (209) who both 'protests protests protests / So much as at Rome would serve to have throwne / Ten Cardinalls into the Inquisition' and who, conversely, 'whispered by Jesu, so often, that A / Pursevant would have ravish'd him away / For saying of our Ladies psalter' (212–17). The artful wit, then, whose chameleon-like deceptions allow him disingenuously to negotiate his social world, is perhaps not unlike the politic divine eager to appease both mainstream puritans and avant-garde conformists, those churchmen who, from as early as the 1590s, deliberately opposed to a preaching- and predestinarian-centred Calvinism their own sacramental vision of the church.[33] In the final lines of 'Satyre IV,' the speaker admonishes 'Preachers which are / Seas of Wits and Arts' to have recourse to a word-centred Baptism by which they might 'Drowne the sinnes of this place,' i.e., the court. The speaker, who is 'but a scarce brooke' – and perhaps himself a soon-to-be 'young Preacher'? – is content for now 'To wash the staines away' (237–41) by settling for a private Mass, thus to 'receive, and die.'

Thomas Hester has argued that the parody of the Roman Mass in the Presence Chamber of 'Satyre IV' is an ironic indictment of the English court but not of Catholic ceremony per se. 'The satirist's ironic and oblique reliance on the topoi of Anglican antipapist polemics,' he writes, 'indicts the hypocrisy and injustice of a system that persecutes and destroys sincere devotees of a politically illegal religion at the same time that it tolerates and even fosters perversities of the devotional stances for which any devout recusant would be imprisoned, tortured, or killed.' Though careful not to 'overstate the autobiographical impulse in Donne's poems,' Hester finds attractive a connection between the apparently recusant satirist and the author, both 'laugh[ing] wryly at how salacious libellers, blasphemous courtiers, and vulgar politicians are given social and legal liberty to travesty the rites, rituals, and devotional practices for which sincere believers might end up on Tyburn Hill.' The speaker's private or 'meditative "Masse,"' in other words, is the real thing, the Confession a sincere devotional gesture bravely scorning the misappropriation and distortion of a legitimate, if illegal, form of worship.[34] This is a brilliant reading of the poem. And yet the framing principle of 'Satyre IV,' a sacramental moment evocative not only of the Eucharist but also of Extreme Unction and Confession, contains what can only be described as its own parody. At one point the speaker recalls his response to the *adversarius*'s invitation to 'leave loneness' and come to court: 'I said, not alone / My lonenesse is, but Spartanes fashion' (67–9). And yet the speaker knew even then that 'No more can Princes courts, though there be few / Better pictures of vice, teach me vertue' (71–2).

There is here perhaps more of the spirit of Chaucerian monologue than Hester allows. *The Pardoner's Tale,* for example, is largely a confession of his own corruption. Indeed, the Pardoner insists that he 'bothe drinke and eten of a cake' (34) as he tells his story; his mock-Confession thus is accompanied by a mockery of the Eucharist. The satirist's ridiculing of barren Presence Chamber rituals, moreover, is not unlike the Pardoner's ironic condemnation of 'cookes' who 'stampe and straine and grinde, / And turnen substance into accident' to excite the culinary proclivities of gluttons (250–2). The Aristotelian categories imply here a titillating experience void of anything truly edifying, much as the Presence Chamber's otherwise 'gay painted things' no 'Tast have in them.' Now, the speaker of 'Satyre IV' is no Pardoner. And yet the latter's ruthless cynicism concealing the pain of a deeply wounded psyche is not unlike the satirist's professed aloofness from the court he nevertheless finds so fascinating. We are invited to apply his moral wisdom to the speaker's proposal to confess in the first place, his offer to rehearse for his Spartan audience his past experience as something like one of 'Aretines pictures' (71). Though eager now to 'receive' a 'real presence' that transcends the court, the speaker suggests that his 'loneness,' his 'private' Mass, is, after all – or has been by the end of the poem – 'but Spartanes fashion,' ironically implicated in what it would leave behind.

Given the poem's framing context of auricular Confession, finally, what are we to make of the appeal with which it concludes? 'Though I yet / With *Macabees* modestie, the knowne merit / Of my worke lessen,' says the speaker, 'yet some wise man shall, / I hope, esteeme my writs Canonicall' (241–4). The apocryphal '*Macabees*' suggests that the speaker appeals to a Protestant audience, asking, in effect, that his recusancy be pardoned at least so far as to allow his satire a fair hearing. But how can we be certain that the audience is in fact Protestant given, once again, the framing context? Is not his auditory, rather, the speaker's *confessor,* the priest from whom he 'may now receive, and die'? The poem, on this reading, is a variation on the analogy discerned by DiPasquale in Donne's sacramental poems. Rather than a 'quasi-divine maker or priestly minister,'[35] the speaker, I suggest, is the sacramental communicant and the reader none other than a Roman Catholic priest presiding over a ritual that contains its own parody. The speaker's duplicity as both recipient and critic of Catholic ritual is extended finally to the reader who, whether recusant, church papist, or 'Canonicall' Protestant, precariously enjoys the satire even while being quite possibly its target.

If sacrament in 'Satyre IV' frames the speaker's ambivalence toward Roman Catholic ritual and ceremony, Donne's 'Ecclogue' or 'Epithalamion at the Marriage of the Earl of Somerset' includes a court-sacrament analogy suggesting the author's sensitivity to the doctrinally Calvinist mainstream of his soon-to-be adoptive church. Celebrating the scandal-plagued nuptials of Robert Carr and Lady Frances Howard,[36] the poem contains a description of the nature and scope of royal power that echoes Calvin's doctrine of Holy Communion. Sometimes called 'virtualism,' this doctrine, we recall, holds that Christ's body, while really and truly present by virtue of the sacrament, nevertheless remains in heaven. Christ's flesh, writes Calvin, though 'separated from us by such great distance,' nevertheless 'penetrates to us, so that it becomes our food.'[37] At first rejecting Idios's insistence that 'As heaven, to men dispos'd, is every where, / So are those Courts, whose Princes animate, / Not onely all their house, but all their State' (40–2), Allophanes argues that closer contact is necessary, that metal buried in the earth has the value of gold only if 'heaven gild it with his eye' (64). In keeping with his name (which, as Annabel Patterson notes, suggests duplicity),[38] Allophanes then advances a description of the court not unlike Idios's own:

> As, for divine things, faith comes from above,
> So, for best civill use, all tinctures move
> From higher powers; From God religion springs,
> Wisdome, and honour from the use of Kings.
> Then unbeguile thy selfe, and know with mee,
> That Angels, though on earth employd they bee,
> Are still in heav'n, so is hee still at home
> That doth, abroad, to honest actions come.   (65–72)

Like a Calvinist sacrament, angels (and would-be courtiers) carry the royal 'tincture' by virtue of 'use' or, more accurately, 'honest actions.' As such they not only refer back to court as from a distance but in fact manifest that cynosure's central presence. But just as sacramental grace, like heaven, is 'every where' only 'to men dispos'd' – and, in a predestinarian scheme, such as are disposed by God alone – so does Idios's exclusion from court compromise the court's authority over him. This is ironically evident in a series of questions by which Allophanes celebrates the real court as implicitly superior to Idios's 'Country of Courts,' asking, for example, whether for the latter

there is no ambition, but to'obey,
Where men need whisper nothing, and yet may;
Where the Kings favours are so plac'd, that all
Find that the King therein is liberall
To them, in him, because his favours bend
To vertue, to the which they all pretend?   (79–84)

Allophanes implies that the real court does in fact possess such qualities, which, for Idios, is less praise for than criticism of a world from which he finds himself excluded: that obedience can equal ambition, together with both the ambiguous object of 'pretend' ('vertue' or 'favours'?) and its pun (aspire or dissimulate?), suggests that Allophanes' court is much less worthy of the celebration he advocates. Idios, Allophanes says, is a 'foole' who, if he had come to court just yesterday, 'Might'st have read more then all thy books bewray.' There is no 'history,' he goes on to assert, 'which doth present / A Court, where all affections do assent / Unto the Kings, and that, that Kings are just / And where it is no levity to trust' (73–8). That Idios cannot produce any such precedent is an ironic indictment of the realm Allophanes adores, a realm in which, implicitly, it *is* 'levity to trust' and where 'Kings' in fact are *not* just.

Idios finally confirms the irony of Allophanes' praise by citing its content as the very reason he left: 'To know and feele all this, and not to have / Words to expresse it, makes a man a grave / Of his own thoughts' (93–5). But is this really much different from the alternative, a 'reclus'd hermit,' even one who may 'know / More of heavens glory' (48–9) than the zealous at court? While Idios would rather not 'stay / At a great feast, having no grace to say' (95–6), and would render what he calls his 'sacrifice,' the Epithalamion proper, a burnt offering – 'I'll burn it,' he rashly insists (227) – his alter-ego Allophanes intercepts the otherwise obscure sacrifice in order to 'lay'it,' as he says, 'upon / Such Altars, as prize your devotion' (234–5).

If Allophanes and Idios differ as to who is better off, they agree on one essential point: that the influence of the court, like that of heaven, is far-reaching. Allophanes avers that only at court can one fully adore and appreciate the royal presence, while Idios maintains a less ceremonial, unadorned and private piety – in the 'heart,' he says, where 'man need no farther looke' (50–2). But their descriptions of royal sovereignty are almost identical, whether Idios's animating prince of states, or Allophanes' divine 'tinctures' that 'move / From higher powers' as 'from God religion springs.' Unlike opposed sacramental doctrines for which presence can be only a matter of theory and opinion, however, the presence at court is a palpable reality. Whereas Idios echoes Allophanes in promoting kings' ubiquity, he also acknowledges Allophanes' point that nothing compares to the real thing. Sacramental analogy may or may not in the end suffice to reinforce the vast reach of royal power. It is one thing to experience the externals of grace in company with one's fellow communicants, not knowing who, finally, will remain among the courtly chosen; it is quite another to trust and obey from afar when an elect above the rest is so near but out of reach. Idios's ambiguous assertion, 'I am not then from Court' (54), suggests both the contiguity of his world and Allophanes' – 'I am not *away* from Court' – and an ironic recognition that he is indeed far from 'that brest / Where the Kings Counsells and his secrets rest' (89–90) – 'I am not,' that is, '*of* the Court.' A term signifying for Renaissance writers little more than a particular formal structure, it is perhaps not insignificant that the etymological origin of 'eclogue' is a Greek verb (*eklegein*) meaning 'to choose.'

If 'Satyre IV' and the 'Ecclogue' are contemporary with a Donne on the brink of forever abandoning courtly aspirations, a much earlier poem suggests a prescient sensitivity to the vicissitudes of vocational fortune. A haunting vision of sacrificial voyagers cum Communion elements anticipates the cri de coeur of a young and anxious would-be courtier in 'The Calme':

> on the hatches as on Altars lyes
> Each one, his owne Priest, and owne Sacrifice.
> Who live, that miracle do multiply
> Where walkers in hot Ovens, doe not dye.   (25–8)

That self-oblation represents Donne's own weariness and uncertainty about his future prospects is suggested a few lines later:

> Whether a rotten state, and hope of gaine,
> Or to disuse mee from the queasie paine
> Of being belov'd, and loving, or the thirst
> Of honour, or faire death, out pusht mee first,
> I lose my end: for here as well as I
> A desperate may live, and a coward die.   (39–44)

Voyage becomes here a powerful metaphor of desire suggesting the frustrated aspirations of both lover and courtier, a frustration which might culminate in death if not for the sexual pun ('I lose my end') intimating that even death offers no relief from life's disappointments. The earlier image of bodies stretched out and totally vulnerable, possessing nothing but their own fragile existence, is appropriately associated with the Eucharist, for it recalls one who, in crying 'Eloi, Eloi, lama sabachthani,' endured, at least temporarily, alienation from the ultimate court and presence.

John Carey's seminal *Life, Mind and Art* celebrates the creative energies of the artist while making much of the 'apostasy' of his later years, by which Carey ironically intends Donne's acquiescence to English religious orthodoxy. Fascinated with the stubborn persistence of an earlier Donne contaminating the pious integrity of the mature divine, Carey does not allow for the possibility that the reverse might also be true; rather, he sees the presence of 'theological niceties' in the earlier poems solely as evidence of the young Donne's blasphemous proclivities. In thus allowing a partial secularization of the dean of St Paul's devotional personae while not permitting a genuine religious complexity for the would-be courtier, Carey's attempt to integrate multiple Donnes ironically has the opposite effect – an inadvertant resurrection of the Jack/ John dichotomy first advanced by Izaak Walton. It is difficult to see how Donne's religious beliefs, as elusive as they may be, are based merely on what Carey has called 'arbitrary preferences' while yet providing insight into the presumably less elusive 'workings of his fancy.'[39] Arthur Marotti supports Carey's implicit denial of a genuine religious impulse in Donne, reducing the devotional lyrics to 'the conversion of secular into religious values,' a mere 'attempt to reaffirm self-worth and regain a measure of control in the most unfavourable of social circumstances.'[40] It is as if the human desire for power or the anxiety over personal self worth have never been eminently religious issues, inclusive of the social and artistic spheres that for Marotti and Carey dominate the spiritual. Marotti elsewhere finds that Donne's reputation as pious dean was largely 'fabricated' by Donne himself and by the print culture that aimed to celebrate that aspect of his career.[41] But this merely infers that the notorious Jack was the 'true' Donne, as if the 'private' sphere of coterie verse was not involved in its own brand of self-fashioning. Courtly concerns, the quest for preferment – these constitute but a limited, not exhaustive, set of historical coordinates relevant for the contextualizing of Donne's work. That he was able to invest his secular lyrics with religious concerns and vice versa challenges those who would separate a complex integration of realities into wholly separate domains. Unlike some of his post-Victorian critics, Donne was very much conscious of and comfortable with the points of contact and shared vocabularies among otherwise disparate areas of his experience. The allegorical habits of thought informing medieval theology, cosmology, and philosophy remained powerful factors in his apprehension of a world that a much later poet would insist is 'charged with the grandeur of God.'

Sacrament in Donne's secular verse permeates his perception and poetic experience. Applicable through analogy to a surprising range of concerns, sacrament suggested an appropriate topos through which to exercise his uniquely alchemical intellect, that penetrating capacity to discern among the world's constituents an intricate web of correspondences. That they share with erotic, monetary, and courtly topoi a tension between relatively static and fluid realities – whether spiritual and sensual experience, intrinsic and extrinsic values, idealized cynosure and court politics, or deified and carnal bodies – suggests sacraments' appropriateness for exploring otherwise disparate domains of Renaissance culture, a culture that for Donne's idiosyncratic wit retains traces of the medieval doctrine of the analogy of Being. In allowing the sacred thus to be contaminated, these poems are exemplary of the Incarnation's claim not only to imbue creation with divinity, to invest sublunary realities with celestial significance, but also obversely to subject the Logos to a body, mutability, and death. The semantic and referential play to which Donne submits sacramental topoi becomes thereby a secular extension of that which otherwise is disclosed in strictly devotional and ceremonial contexts. His sacramental profanities are witness to the rhetorical power of a religious idea.

This contiguity of sacred and profane in Donne's secular verse raises several predominantly religious issues to be explored in the remainder of this study. In so far as they deal with desire and consummation, with rarefied Petrarchan ideal and carnal experience, and with the mythical dimension of sublunary lovers' loves, the erotic lyrics appropriately utilize sacramental topoi whose own concerns include the related paradoxes of life in death and of Word become flesh, and the delicate relationship between devotion and ceremony. Similarly, as in several poems monetary and sacramental topoi converge in an interrogation of the relationship between extrinsic and intrinsic values, just so do these poems anticipate succeeding chapters' concern not only with sacramental theories of 'real presence' but also the discursive dimensions of such doctrine – social, ecclesiastical, and political. The court-sacrament analogy in such poems as 'Satyre IV' and the 'Ecclogue,' finally, suggests Donne's recognition of the profoundly religious features of Renaissance courtship. These poems' speakers contemplate the court with an ambivalence not unlike that of Donne's holy sonneteer and Herbert's *Temple* communicant, sacramental images and allusion appropriately circumscribing their approach to the royal/divine cynosure. The variously divine and courtly contexts of Donne's and Herbert's verse suggest a diminution of personal identity and agency at once threatening and oddly liberating, both poets finding in sacrament the means whereby to grasp if not fully to understand the place of self and art in relation to the world and to the Word.

CHAPTER TWO

Sacrament and Grace

It is reasonable to expect that an investigation of sacramental topoi in Donne's poetry would find the sacred verse more yielding of relevant material than the profane. Donne proves that assumption to be errone-ous. The abundance of sacramental imagery and allusion in the secular verse relative to that of the divine poems is startling. How are we to account for this? Perhaps the secular poet, because concerned ostensibly with matters nonreligious, can be more cavalier in his handling of sacred ideas than can the devotional poet. Donne's secular audience, more-over, may have been but a small circle of friends and acquaintances, the intelligentsia of a cultured coterie, to use Arthur Marotti's term. Sacra-mental discourse in a religious context, on the other hand, is a grave matter and not to be treated lightly. Herbert's Country Parson, for example, 'being to administer the Sacraments, is at a stand with himself, how or what behaviour to assume for so holy things.'[1] Though like the secular verse Donne's divine poems saw limited circulation and were published only posthumously, they suggest a more public, official role for the speaker, that of the Christian Everyman whose audience is both Christendom and God. The difference, however, in no way obviates the very real *religious* significance of sacrament in Donne's secular poems. As we have seen, his formidable knowledge of the intricacies of sacramental thought allowed him to advance a vision of the sacred in the profane at once idiosyncratic yet rooted conceptually in a traditional understand-ing of the Incarnation.

Donne's sacred verse, I argue, marks his confessional identification with the doctrinally Calvinist mainstream of the English church. His capacity for perceiving the sacred in the profane documented in chapter 1 belongs to a medieval world view that had been carried into the early modern era in large part by Roman Catholic sacramentalism. The relevance of eucharistic topoi for otherwise profane concerns is suggested, according to Donnean logic, by a tradition that in the Mass proclaimed the paradoxical reality of the Word become flesh. The moderate Calvinism of Donne's adoptive English church, on the other hand, promoted a sacramental theology primarily psychological rather than carnal in orientation and thus for him comparatively less susceptible of the conceptual wit that endues the secular poems. Donne's fascination with the sacramental relationship between sacred and profane yields in the religious verse to a preoccupation with the inner workings of the spirit and with the predestinarian aspects of English Calvinism. And yet the sacred poetry never jettisons entirely Donne's Roman Catholic heritage nor the affectivity a sensual understanding of sacrament allowed him to indulge. The relationship between sacramental and devotional impulses in the sacred verse is thus one of both complementarity and conflict, evident in Donne's variously veiled, reluctant, confident, and desperate gestures toward sacramental means of grace as escape from the Calvinist interiority he otherwise so effectively cultivates.

Calvin's sacramental views reveal that the conflict suggested above was to some degree his own. The magisterial reformer, not unlike such English Protestants as Cranmer and Ridley, was deeply concerned to maintain an instrumental, efficacious role for the sacramental species in the communication of grace. His and theirs was a doctrine of 'real presence,' though Calvin denied absolutely any carnal manifestation of Christ's body and blood. His emphasis, rather, is almost exclusively on the spiritual effects of the sacrament as they unfold within the soul of the individual believer. Calvin believed that the sacramental signs have an affective power equal to that of the transubstantiated species in a Roman Catholic scheme, but that idolatry could be avoided by maintaining that the elements derive power from their divine referents without actually embodying them.

Though he did not articulate explicitly the connection between sacrament and predestination, it is apparent in Calvin's *Institutes* that receiving the elements in an attitude of genuine repentence is alone no guarantee that grace is conferred. Sacraments are 'poison' to the evil man who receives them in an evil manner, that is, he who concentrates on the visible sign and eats only outwardly, who 'presses with the teeth' rather than 'eats with the heart.'[2] Eating worthily as a criterion for receiving grace is certainly not exclusive to Calvin, nor to Augustine whom he quotes here. The Elizabethan Articles, as we have seen, contain warnings very similar to Calvin's own. Luther too allowed that sacraments are poison to the unworthy, even going as far as to suggest his opponent Zwingli as one such communicant![3] As early as the twelfth century it was thought that the real body of Christ was received by both worthy and unworthy communicants, but with damning effects by the latter.[4] And it is the sixteenth-century English Catholic, Robert Southwell, who writes in his didactic poem 'A holy Hymme':

> Both the good and bad receive him,
> But effectes are divers in them,
> True life, or dewe destruction,
> Life to the good, death to the wicked:
> Marke how both alike received
> With farre unlike conclusion.   (49–54)

In 'Of the Blessed Sacrament of the Aulter,' however, Southwell is very careful to nuance the predestinarian dimension of sacramental grace so as both to allow for the importance of the human will and, obversely, to make sin entirely man's and not God's responsibility. In the Eucharist, he writes, 'to delight the witt trewe wisdome is, / To wooe the will of every good the choise ... And if to all all this it do not bringe, / The fault is in the men, not in the thinge' (37–42). For Calvin, on the other hand, the sacrament 'is turned into a deadly poison for all those whose faith it does not nourish and strengthen, and whom it does not arouse to thanksgiving and to love.'[5] The syntax here is highly revealing. That the sacrament may or may not nourish and arouse depends not simply on whether one is faithful, thankful, and loving; rather, one is faithful, thankful, and loving to the extent one is in fact nourished and aroused. Sacramental grace in this scheme is starkly indifferent to human volition. Receiving the sacrament is not only no guarantee of its efficacy; it may prove poisonous regardless of one's intentions.

Though the intense debates over doctrinal Calvinism which plagued the final decades of the Elizabethan era abated somewhat with the Stuart succession, Reform theology was to have lasting impact on the church and especially on its handling of ceremonies. Calvinism was thought by some to threaten the integrity of sacramental ministry, a fact which becomes increasingly apparent during the years prior to the publication of Donne's and Herbert's poems. Nicholas Tyacke notes, for example, that Dean Francis White of Carlisle, in supporting the Arminian John Buckeridge's dispute with Thomas Morton over the doctrinal legitimacy of the ostensibly Calvinist Dortrecht articles of 1618, asked whether predestinarians in Holy Communion could 'say to all communicants whatsoever, "The Body of Our Lord which was given for thee," as we are bound to say? Let the opinion of the Dortists be admitted, and the tenth person in the Church shall not have been redeemed.'[6] And Samuel Ward, according to Peter Lake, had complained to then Archbishop James Ussher that some of the English delegates to the Synod of Dort were accused of being 'half Remonstrants for extending the oblation made to the father to all and for holding sundry effects thereof offered *serio* and some really communicated to the reprobate.'[7] It is highly instructive, Lake argues, to compare Ward's comments here with the eirenic advice offered some ten years later to friend and fellow Dort delegate John Davenant. Ward advises Davenant to refrain from asserting that grace is conferred by Baptism, fearing 'this time when the Arminians cleave so close one to another.'[8] Once indignant at the accusation that he was a 'half Remonstrant' for opposing the Calvinist doctrine of limited atonement, Ward now finds it necessary to protect his other half, so to speak. This caution against adding fuel to the fire is indicative of the subtlety of theological opinion among establishment divines during the decade following the 1618 Synod. Ward's advice was offered in 1629, the advent of Charles's personal rule – a period that would see a long-standing moderate, episcopalian, and Calvinist unity yield to an Arminian/puritan schism, each faction radicalizing the other. As Tyacke notes, however, it was some sixteen years earlier that the recusant-to-be Benjamin Carier advised James I that Calvinist predestination renders the sacraments meaningless and thus undermines episcopacy.[9] White's and Ward's remarks only reinforce what Carier so presciently realized – that doctrinal issues are of profound significance for the sacramental life of the church, the relationship between doctrine and ceremony crucial to the struggle over its confessional identity.

Essentially an alternative to the second-generation Calvinism of Theodore Beza, the views of Jacobus Arminius are distinct from Calvin's own in one important way. While he shared Calvin's conviction that Christ died for all even if not everyone is saved in the end, the implication for Arminius was a greater emphasis on human autonomy.[10] Whereas the Remonstrant controversy on the continent was concerned almost exclusively with doctrine, English Arminianism included an emphasis on sacramental ministry as an important feature of its own distinctive character. Not having experienced the same degree of ecclesiastical reform as its continental Protestant counterparts, the English religious establishment had retained not only episcopacy but also a liturgy which, in its inception at least, retained the spirit if not the letter of its Roman Catholic model. In rejecting an arbitrary, predestinarian decree impervious to human will, English Arminians advanced the universalist doctrine of a grace freely offered in the sacraments and available to anyone who chose to receive them. Lake has located the origins of this English Arminianism in Richard Hooker, who was among the first of English Protestants to emphasize the importance of ritual and ceremony as integral aspects of Christian communal experience rather than as matters to be regarded with indifference or, worse yet, merely tolerated.[11] Hooker's 'vision of the sacrament really offering Christ's body and blood to all who received it in good faith,' moreover, dispensed with the tendency to distinguish between the godly and ungodly as suggested by a style of divinity more predestinarian in emphasis. But as Lake also points out, Hooker nowhere in the *Polity* explicitly attacks Calvinist thought, even if the doctrinal implications of his episcopalian and ceremonialist biases conflict with Reform orthodoxy.[12] Indeed, Lake might have observed in Hooker a more positive rather than merely tacit endorsement of such theology. If the eucharistic elements, for example, are not to be taken merely 'for bare *resemblances* or memorialls of thinges absent, neither for *naked signes* and testimonies assuringe us of grace received before, but (as they are in deed and in veritie) for meanes efectuall,' it is also true that 'all receyve not the grace of God which receive the sacramentes of his grace.'[13] This conflict between the visible and invisible communication of grace is not exclusive to Hooker, of course, but it does become for him an issue connected with his erastian tendencies: 'It must be confest that of Christ, workinge as a creator, and a governor of the world by providence, all are partakers; not all partakers of that grace whereby he inhabiteth whome he saveth.'[14] If orthodox Calvinism was, in Patrick Collinson's phrase, 'the theological cement' of the early Stuart church,[15] some careful nuancing was required to reconcile its predestinarian and sacramental elements.

That Calvin can direct *everyone* to the Communion while knowing that the reprobate very likely are among those who receive depends on what R.T. Kendall has identified as that aspect of the reformer's doctrine of grace that distinguishes him not only from Arminius but also from such second-generation Calvinists as Theodore Beza and the English divines Kendall calls 'experimental predestinarians.' These latter actively sought evidence of election through inward examination and reflection, a practice Calvin explicitly forbade and to be distinguished from 'credal predestinarianism,' which Kendall defines as a purely doctrinal assent rather than the active encouragement of the sort of reflection endorsed by William Perkins and others.[16] Arminianism and experimental predestination represent opposite sides of the same coin, for both in effect are forms of voluntarism which, whether implicitly or explicitly, advance what in his discussion of Richard Sibbes Kendall calls an 'anthropocentric doctrine of faith.'[17] By encouraging a search for the marks of election, the Bezaean predestinarians inadvertantly seduced a theoretically depraved human will into playing a more active role than the Reform tradition, strictly speaking, would allow. 'The debate between Perkins and Arminius,' writes Kendall, 'is a case of two forms of voluntarism in opposition to each other.' Both the Perkins school and the Arminian believed that a person who falls away from grace is shown to be non-elect. The difference between the two positions is that whereas Perkins, like Calvin, would explain falling away with a doctrine of temporary faith – the general rather than saving faith of the non-elect in the visible church – Arminius held that the reprobate are simply those whom God foresees would not persevere. Arminius insisted that Beza's and Perkins's two-faiths theory – the idea that the initial desire to be saved is proven an authentic sign of election only if followed by other marks of grace – effectively allows the human will a significant role in the soteriological process. Indeed, notes Kendall, Arminius had his own version of the theory of two graces, 'the one sufficient, the other efficacious.' The first enables one to believe, while the second is evident when one actually 'wills, believes, and is converted.'[18] To argue that the assurance of grace that comes with inward examination and other such spiritual works proves that the first grace, the desire to be saved, was not the temporary grace bestowed by Beza's trickster God is *in effect* no different from the Arminian position, which is that those who persevere are in fact the elect. Arminius simply dispenses with the Calvin/Beza/Perkins doctrine of temporary faith, arguing that if faith is temporary it is because the faithful choose no longer to believe, not because their faith was never genuine in the first place. The *via media* between these two extremes which led logically to an identical conclusion is to be found, according to Kendall, in the theology of Calvin. Arminius agrees with Calvin that Christ died for all. But whereas for Arminius the application of the authentic grace issuing from the Atonement depends to a significant degree on the human decision to accept it, Calvin argues that conversion derives solely from Christ's intercession on behalf of the elect. Conversely, whereas the experimental predestinarians retain Calvin's emphasis on the absolute sovereignty of God, their doctrine of election is based on a doctrine of limited atonement: Christ died for the elect only. 'Only Calvin,' writes Kendall, 'holds that election may be enjoyed by looking directly at Christ. His view of the relation of Christ's intercession to His death seems never to have been considered' by either Arminius or the Beza/Perkins school.[19] What this means is that by maintaining that Christ died for all, Calvin can argue that there is no need for anyone to despair even while recognizing that the benefits of Christ's death will be applied actually only to those on whose behalf he intercedes. What Kendall fails to appreciate, however, is the precariousness of Calvin's position, that *in effect* Christ's death is of benefit only to the elect and that Beza and Perkins, in explicitly endorsing a doctrine of limited atonement, merely clarify what in Calvin is (perhaps deliberately) obscure.

The ritual of Holy Communion for Calvin is subject to the same anxiety attending reflection on the terrible decree that is double predestination, the idea that God not only predestines the elect but also damns the reprobate who, though 'justly charged against the malice and depravity of their hearts,' have, 'at the same time ... been given over to this depravity because they have been raised up by the just but inscrutable judgment of God to show forth his glory in their condemnation.'[20] As this passage from the *Institutes* suggests, double predestination was no Bezaean innovation. Though Calvin warned against indulging curiosity with respect to the divine decrees, he also knew that the temptation to do so 'is all the deadlier, since almost all of us are more inclined to it than any other.' Moreover, predestinarian curiosity is far from forbidden. One is free to feel that the daily benefits of grace originate in 'that secret adoption' and one can count oneself 'numbered among his flock if we hear his voice.' It is difficult to imagine, however, how one can ever arrive at a finally positive conclusion when it is allowed that the reprobate may 'have signs of a call that are similar to those of the elect' but do not in fact have 'that sure establishment of election' the gospels proclaim.[21] As Kendall asks in his discussion of Calvin, 'If the reprobate may believe that God is merciful towards them, how can *we* be sure our believing the same thing is any different from theirs? How can we be so sure that our "beginning of faith" is saving and is not the "beginning of faith" which the reprobate seem to have?'[22] The Pauline practice of indulging an introspective mea culpa prior to receiving the Lord's Supper is for such poor souls susceptible of devolving into the despair attending too curious a consideration of God's hidden decrees. It is thus not difficult to see how emphasizing an instrumental role for sacraments and an affective grasp of divine presence might counter the burden of recognizing that participation alone is no guarantee for actually receiving the benefits offered in the rite.

An experimental predestinarian psyche at Holy Communion is likely to stress St Paul's call to self-examination not merely as prerequisite for receiving the sacrament but rather as an obligation to find within the marks or signs of election. Unlike the Roman Catholic at auricular Confession, the experimental Calvinist goes beyond acknowledging sin to indulge an inquiry into the authenticity of his penitence, which, technically, depends less on his or her own efforts than on whether or not grace is in fact operative. Greater emphasis on the external and communal aspects of sacraments, though never precluding penitential obligation, nevertheless tends to extricate the workings of God's grace from the subjective anxieties of religious introspection.

P.M. Oliver criticizes the proponents of Protestant poetics for failing to recognize in *Holy Sonnets* Donne's dissatisfaction with Calvinism.[23] David Aers and Gunther Kress similarly argue that the shifting emotional state of Donne's speaker in *Holy Sonnets* precludes the 'introspective analysis' characteristic of a Calvinist devotional framework.[24] Resistance to Reform theology, however, may in fact be a feature of the devotional sphere it circumscribes. It is precisely in his sensitivity to and anxiety over an inconsistent and changing self that Donne's devotee can be said actively to resist and thereby to accentuate all the more the importance of Calvinism for his religious sensibility. The most salient feature of 'What if this present were the world's last night,' for example, is precisely the sort of experimental voluntarism described above:

> And can that tongue adjudge thee unto hell,
> Which pray'd forgivenesse for his foes fierce spight?
> No, no ...   (7–9)

It is doubtful that this is a clear refutation of Calvinist predestination, for it would mean that the speaker, rather than meditating, is engaged in a polemical argument with some imagined opponent. But this is first and foremost a devotional lyric, the silent interlocutor a component of the penitent's divided psyche. That the colloquy is reassuring – 'This beauteous forme assumes a pitious minde' (14) – indicates that the speaker has passed through predestinarian anxiety and *wilfully* discovered the signs of a grace over which, strictly speaking, he has no control.

Both the supporters of and those opposed to Calvinist readings of

Donne, however, fail to recognize the degree to which sacramental topoi in the poems register their speakers' desire to transcend the subjective anxieties they deliberately evince. The Eucharist in *La Corona* and *Holy Sonnets* signals escape from the manic-depressive turns of a lover/devotee who variously embraces and resists a radically transcendent deity. Whereas Donne's profane and usually absent mistresses rarely, if ever, are allowed the upper hand, absence here is God's tactical advantage, the speakers' submissive anguish occasioned and governed by the lack of divine response. The Renaissance English sonnet, with its Petrarchan combination of intense lyrical reflection and dialogue and an ostensibly absent interlocutor, is thus an ideal poetic medium for exploring this Calvinist interiority. But the 'experimental' thrust of Donne's dramatizations more often than not is attenuated by gestures toward the sacramental means of grace, by the application of external, universal symbols to his penitents' anguished plight. The devotional stance of the divine poems, then, neither rejects Calvinism, even the experimental variety, nor does it succumb wholly to the anxieties such inward searches inevitably foster. Whereas for Perkins ecclesiology and discipline are not nearly as important as understanding and applying the Gospel inwardly, for Donne the link between ceremony and doctrine is crucial. Patrick Collinson's observation that Calvinism did not extend its word-centred iconoclasm to the religious imagination is not entirely accurate, but it does suggest the resilience of the somatic aspects of religious experience among even the most inward of devotional sensibilities.[25]

The fifth sonnet in the *La Corona* series, 'Crucifying' assumes an important connection between predestinarian and sacramental doctrine.[26] Whereas the closing line of the fourth sonnet, 'Temple,' refers to the advent of the young Jesus' earthly ministry, its meaning as the first line in 'Crucifying' is expanded to accommodate that poem's predestinarian orientation. 'By miracles exceeding power of man' describes Christ's earthly ministry; but varied reaction to these same miracles is indicative of God's sovereignty which 'faith in some, envie in some begat' (1–2). It is impossible to see the poem merely as recalling events in Judea or to ignore its controversial potential when it is recognized that God himself is said to be the cause of people's response to Jesus' deeds. The 'worst' who are also 'most,' the reprobate multitude, are held responsible not only for Christ's death but for daring to usurp divine prerogative by prescribing 'a Fate' to 'the immaculate / Whose creature Fate is' and thus 'Measuring selfe-lifes infinity to'a span, / Nay to an inch' (4–9). This misguided attempt to subvert the divine will, moreover, ıs ımplicitly associated with the Roman Mass, said here to reduce Christ 'to an inch,' and which for some suggested *ex opere operato*, the idea that grace is obtained merely by virtue of receiving the consecrated species. In hindsight, then, the association of 'Miracles' with the mystery of divine election – 'Hee ... begat' – appropriates a term often pejoratively associated with transubstantiation. And though Donne pleads God's 'liberall dole,' the 'one drop of thy blood' is associated with his 'dry soule' (13–14) and thus sufficiently psychologized to avoid association with the heresy implicitly condemned a few lines earlier. The Atonement is thus reinforced as wholly God's – whose creature Fate is – both in act and efficacy, thus transcending any human effort to obtain its benefits. The final line's imperative – 'Moyst, with one drop of thy blood, my dry soule' (14) – is therefore somewhat of a surprise, even if consistent with the suppliant tone of the series. It identifies an unavoidable tension between Donne's need to act and his awareness that nothing he does can in the end make any difference apart from God's intervention. Theresa DiPasquale recognizes that those who are both 'the worst' and 'the most' are those whose 'will' is connected with the transubstantiators suggested by lines 7–8. In describing those who 'now prescribe a Fate' as 'wicked determinists,' however, DiPasquale neglects the previous phrase, 'Whose creature Fate is,' an admonitory reminder that if anyone it is God who is the poem's sole determinist. Donne's target is not determinism but rather the arrogance of the Pelagian 'worst' who are 'most' and their assumption that human will plays a role in sacramental grace. Thus while DiPasquale offers a sacramentally Calvinist gloss on the speaker's plea – 'Now thou art lifted up, draw me to thee' (12) – she elides the predestinarian aspects of both the poem's and Calvin's sacramental doctrine.[27] Donne's target may be those experimental predestinarians whose voluntarism, as we have seen, approaches Arminian heresy, but 'the worst are most' preserves the scriptural notion of an elect few in number. Here, perhaps, is an example of Kendall's 'credal' predestinarianism, the tacit acceptance of doctrine rather left in the shadows than stated explicitly.

The suppliant's dependence on prevenient grace is evident throughout the divine poems. In 'Thou hast made me' it is 'By thy leave' that he 'can looke' and 'rise again' (10); in 'Oh my black Soule!' he recognizes the need for genuine repentance but also the soul's utter inability to conjure it: 'But who shall give thee that grace to beginne?' (10); in 'I am a little world' the speaker cannot drown his sins unless God will 'powre new seas in mine eyes' (7); and, most famously, the speaker of 'Batter my heart' will never be 'chast, except you ravish mee' (14). Though not as pronounced, the psychological thrust of Reform piety is evident in *La Corona* as well, despite the series' formal and liturgical organization and ceremonial tone. Positive allusion to eucharistic grace in 'Crucifying' ('liberall dole' and 'blood') is circumscribed not only by the warning against a too presumptuous and, from a Protestant polemical perspective, Roman Catholic approach to sacramental grace, but also by a final emphasis on the essentially spiritual nature of the problem – the speaker's 'dry soule.' Similarly, in the following poem, 'Resurrection,' both the imperative construction of the reiterated 'Moyst, with one drop of thy blood, my dry soule' and its carnal tone are qualified:

> *Moyst with one drop of thy blood, my dry soule,*
> Shall (though she now be in extreme degree
> Too stony hard, and yet too fleshly,) bee
> Freed by that drop, from being starv'd, hard, or foule.   (1–4)

The altered punctuation in the first line (vis-à-vis the last of the previous sonnet) helps to establish the moistening as an accomplished fact (even though it 'shall ... bee' only in the future) and leads to the speaker's confidence in receiving an effectual remedy. In between, however, the soul's stony resistance accentuates the sole regenerative power of God's irresistible grace, the denigration of flesh complementing the primarily noncorporeal nature of both illness and cure.

The oscillation of carnal tone and (parenthetical) dismissal of flesh, together with the related conflict of personal agency versus divine prerogative, suggests the speaker's genuine perplexity and ambivalence. Neither Donne's tenacious autonomy nor his sacramental enthusiasm is easily quelled. 'Nor can by other meanes be glorified' (11) is ambiguous in reference: does it recall the expansive power of a single drop of God's blood, or rather his 'little booke' (8) – little because containing few names? And whereas 'If' in 'If in thy little booke my name thou enroule' (8) suggests that sacramental efficacy depends on whether the recipient is on the A-list, it may on the other hand imply that the speaker's exclusion would confirm the anti-Calvinist charge that a limited Atonement imputes the cause of sin to God.[28] John Stachniewski reads this sonnet as an example of Calvinist despair in so far as the speaker is dependent on his name being enrolled in God's 'little booke' and *thereby* receiving that one drop of blood.[29] It is precisely this atoning blood, however, that offers hope in the midst of despair, a universal and nonsubjective Christian claim to which any penitent might turn in his or her distress. Whether or not the speaker actually receives its benefits is perhaps another question, but the graphic invocation of blood in the context of a spiritual deliberation over election suggests sacramental escape from psychological anxiety. Moreover, the accentually activated blood pun of 'abléd' – 'by this death abled' (5) – playfully anticipates Donne's confident claim to the benefits of Christ's death and resurrection. The means of grace, then, involve a sort of proactive acquiescence, the speaker allowing God the triumph over death with the proviso that he, the speaker, be one of God's chosen. The penitent's 'Nor can by other means' is thus alternately submissive and a veiled but assertive reminder to God of his obligations. In contrast to the 'credal' quietism of 'Crucifying,' here Donne's penitent confronts a theoretically will-denying predestination with an 'experimental' voluntarism fuelled explicitly by the sacramental means of grace applied internally.

In 'Oh my black Soule,' one of several *Holy Sonnets* in which the speaker agonizes over man's total depravity as a result of original sin, Donne concentrates in bloody imagery the mutual relevance of penitence and grace, the speaker admonishing his soul to

> make thy selfe with holy mourning blacke,
> And red with blushing, as thou art with sinne;
> Or wash thee in Christ's blood, which has this might
> That being red, it dyes red soules to white.   (11–14)

Individual penitence and universal Atonement are nicely conflated in this 'blushing' soul. Similarly, in 'At the round earths imagin'd corners,' repentance is 'as good / As if thou'hadst seal'd my pardon, with thy blood' (13–14), where an Augustinian seal is the sacramental and efficacious guarantor of grace. This is more than merely a meditation on the *imago dei* or some other visual stimulus: rather, the speaker is concerned primarily with the sincerity of his repentance, just as in 'Oh my black Soule!' he is bent on ensuring that his soul's blushing matches the vermilion intensity of his saviour's blood. It is his utter helplessness and spiritual bankruptcy coupled with a determination to *make* himself acceptable to God that is an outstanding feature of Donne's devotional attitude. Just as the impossibility of looking into God's hidden decrees does not preclude, even in Calvin, encouragement to do just that, neither does recognition of his speaker's inability to merit salvation prevent Donne from indulging an experimental voluntarism. Comic awareness of this situation along with a once again subtle ploy are evident when he demands implicitly that God wait a little before inaugurating the final apocalypse. The imperative tone of 'blow' and 'goe' directed at 'Angells' and 'numberlesse infinities' (1–3) is maintained as the address shifts to God: 'let them sleepe, Lord, and mee mourne a space' (9). By aligning his penitential efforts with the blood of the Atonement, Donne invests what is otherwise ineffectual with sacramental power; joining his internal deliberations with his saviour's blood, he identifies with even as he would humbly defer to its divine source.

Such boldness borders on outright impudence in 'If poysonous mineralls.' The Calvinist potential for making God both author of evil and vindictive tyrant is broached by the frustrated speaker:

> Why should intent or reason, borne in mee,
> Make sinnes, else equall, in mee more heinous
> And mercy being easie, and glorious
> To God, in his sterne wrath, why threatens hee?
> But who am I, that dare dispute with thee?   (5–9)

The charge implies that because both reason and will are ultimately divine creations 'borne in mee,' man's freedom does not or should not limit the extent of God's mercy. If 'But who am I' (9) implies temporary delusion for what precedes, resolution is effected by the negotiated compromise of a sacramental 'Lethean flood' in which the penitent's tears are combined with 'thine onely worthy blood' (11) to abolish the memory of past sins – including, perhaps, that of excessive curiosity. 'Lethean flood' is typologically comprehensive of the Old Testament deluge and New Testament institution of Baptism (as it is in 'O might those sighs and teares' and 'I am a little world made cunningly'), while echoes of the chalice's water and blood, which flowed from the crucified Christ's pierced side, and Jesus' blood-tears at Gethsemane together suggest the Eucharist. This latter recalls the messianic conflation of the speaker's tears with 'loves wine' in 'Twicknam Garden,' but in 'If poysonous mineralls' such tears mark clearly the integration of private and ceremonial pieties, both inward devotional turmoil and the institutional means of grace. By combining penitential tears with the atoning blood of the sacrament Donne has a hand in expanding the scope of mercy thought lacking earlier, thus validating his initial challenge even though now assuming a submissive posture. Again, acquiescence in a devotional context is always in some sense a ploy, an agreement to play a prescribed role in exchange for spiritual assurance. As Anna K. Nardo has observed, Donne's devout persona 'push[es] mercy (he thinks) to the limit, and mak[es] God chase this slippery sinner down.'[30] According to Ronald Corthell, 'Intent or reason' is used against itself to produce a divided subjectivity.[31] Corthell fails to recognize, however, that Donne's (and not just the sophisticated critic's) *awareness* of his speaker's equivocating, divided self constitutes an artistic emancipation equal to the speaker's deliberate intention to be among those whom God alone chooses. By placing his penitential efforts within a wider ceremonial context, the speaker finds a solution to his predicament not unlike that of the poet in 'To the Countess of Bedford, On New-yeares day' whose sacramental art is imbued with the grace of a God who 'useth oft, when such a heart mis-sayes, / To make it good, for, such a praiser prayes' (34–5).

The application of sacrament to a devotional interiority facilitates escape from subjective doubt through identification with an ultimately stable, nontransitory power. This must be done with the greatest of subtlety, of course. Donne's speaker, in accordance with the conflicted logic of experimental predestination, must appear to be the unworthy beneficiary of an irresistible will and grace, even while actively advancing his favourable inclusion in God's scheme. The volta in this sonnet thus marks its division not into impudent rambling and contrary recognition of spiritual truth, but rather legitimate theological challenge and resolution in the sacramental mercy it calls forth. The speaker, after all, never does answer the question, 'who am I?' Just as the octave's interrogations are never requited, so the first line of the sestet, by anticipating the identification of 'my teares' and 'thine onely worthy blood,' in fact *does* 'dare dispute with thee,' self-determination thus vying with inscrutable judgment. This pattern of intense resistance followed by sudden resolution in sacramental mystery is perhaps appropriate for Donne's unceasingly sceptical mind, for it is a devotional strategy that allows alternation between the temporal limitations of thought, whose motions are the lifeblood of subjective identity, and momentary stabilization of that identity through association with a transcendent persona. Sacrament for Donne is the ideal mechanism in this process, for it rehearses and reiterates the paradox of the Incarnation – itself the supreme fusion of an otherwise coherent, stable identity with the obliterating flux of time and space, of God (in Christ) with history.

The sacramentalization of an ostensibly inward soteriological process is nowhere more evident than in 'The Crosse':

> Who can blot out the Crosse, which th'instrument
> Of God, dew'd on mee in the Sacrament?   (15–16)

The Atonement, sacramentally indicated by 'dew'd' (both the sign of the cross in infant Baptism and the bread of the Eucharist prefigured by the manna which fed the wandering Israelites), lends significance to the otherwise mundane 'Materiall Crosses' (25) of ship's mast, birds' wings, 'Meridians crossing Parallels,' etc. (19–24), on which is written the world's – and speaker's – redemption.[32] The man-as-microcosm trope and the medieval world view informing it – the organic web of correspondences, sympathies, and antipathies in early modern cosmologies – thus supplement and extend the poem's sacramental rhetoric. Though implicitly preferred over the preached word – 'From mee, no Pulpit, nor misgrounded law, / Nor scandall taken, shall this Crosse withdraw' (9–10) – this sacramental world is to be internalized as part of a spiritual exercise in which the recipient is actively involved, alternately 'crossing' both pride and excessive self-censure, 'those dejections, when it downeward tends, / And when it to forbidden heights pretends' (53–4). Experimental Calvinism, with its alternating diffidence and confidence, thus would render the wider cosmological and ceremonial contexts of the poem elements in its psychological machinery.

If elevating the word is evidence of a Protestant poetic, Donne nevertheless relies on older ideas in fashioning his 'spirituall' cross which, he writes, has 'chiefe dignity' in comparison to 'Materiall Crosses' (25–6). Such preference appears contradictory in proximity to the carnal image of a cross 'dew'd on mee in the Sacrament,' as does the poem's emphasis on self-scrutinizing moral censure when juxtaposed with the earlier negative allusion to 'Pulpit.' The transition from 'Materiall' to 'spirituall' crosses is effected, in part, by a Paracelsian analogy that helps to explain what Donne is up to:

> These [spiritual crosses] for extracted chimique medicine serve,
> And cure much better, and as well preserve;
> Then are you your own physicke, or need none,
> When Still'd, or purg'd by tribulation.
> For when that Crosse ungrudg'd, unto you stickes,
> Then are you to your selfe, a Crucifixe.   (27–32)

Material crosses are rejected not so much for their materiality as because they are not as effective as that which 'ungrudg'd, unto you stickes.' The implicit alignment of 'spiritual crosses' and 'extracted chemique medicine' is a clever conceit, but the medical analogy also plays on the semantic complexity of 'spirit' in Renaissance thought. Physiologically indicative of the subtler of bodily fluids (which in turn are vectors of the operations of the soul or psyche), the term also allows the disembodied entity to which modern definitions are restricted. Like a sacrament, therefore, a spiritual cross somehow literally penetrates the body of the recipient, sacrament and cross each a kind of purge in the Paracelsian sense of natural antipathy. While the preferred Cross is representative of an inward spiritual process, it is nevertheless invested with a wider symbolic currency, drawing its devotional power from an analogy that renders the Atonement, with its insistence on the torture and death of a historical body, visceral and personal.

In his anti-royalist reading of the poem, P.M. Oliver aligns subversion of the Jacobean Oath of Allegiance with a move away from ritual, public gesture toward more private and 'metaphorical crosses.' At the same time, however, he erroneously characterizes Calvinism as reinforcing the king's authority, the doctrine of predestination as theoretically denying the self-determination involved in making these metaphorical crosses. 'The Crosse,' writes Oliver, 'enforces a concentration on the steps individuals can take toward their own salvation' and is thus, presumably, an anti-Calvinist poem.[33] Calvinism is more complex than this allows, particularly the second-generation variety with its implicit voluntarism that encourages precisely the kind of speculation and self-determination predestinarian doctrine theoretically denies. Oliver himself seems to recognize this when, in another context, he writes that the 'Calvinist doctrine of the limited Atonement directly challenged the individual to believe that he or she was among those for whom Christ died.' There is, moreover, a 'difficulty inherent in Calvinist doctrine with regard to the desirability of receiving tangible confirmation of elect status.'[34] One can only speculate as to why, given such qualifying remarks, Oliver argues that Calvinist orthodoxy, and especially the doctrine of predestination, supports royal power. While undoubtedly Calvinism was of ubiquitous influence in Elizabethan and early Stuart religious thought, identification of its central tenets with the interests of the throne is an oversimplification. Benjamin Carier's 1615 warning to James that the doctrine of predestination undermines episcopacy and thus, according to James's famous formula (no bishop, no king), the crown itself, proves that at least one contemporary thought Calvinism a threat to rather than reinforcement of royal authority.[35] Because Reform doctrine paradoxically encourages both an intense awareness of one's lack of agency and a determination to be among the chosen, the relative material/spiritual status of sacraments is all the more urgent. For while material objectification or 'real presence' promotes universal grace, it is 'thy heart' (51) in its 'dejections, when it downeward tends, / And when it to forbidden heights pretends' (53–4) that finds the more subtle 'spirituall' cross devotionally compelling. Grace is never more one's own than when 'are you to your selfe, a Crucifixe' (32).

The intersection of external ritual and internal deliberation, of sacrament and word, is perhaps more properly understood as a conflict between claims to spiritual authority. 'The Annuntiation and Passion,' framed by reference to the Eucharist, begins as a meditation on the paradoxes suggested by the coinciding in 1609 of Good Friday and the feast of the Annunciation, goes on to credit the church as the proper sphere in which to appreciate such wonders, and concludes with a conflation of messianic blood, church body, and individual soul. The motion from bodily ritual toward inward deliberation is again traceable, though here the transition is obvious and sudden:

> Tamely, fraile body,'abstaine to day; to day
> My soule eates twice, Christ hither and away.   (1–2)

The speaker's body is to be fasting and silent witness to the soul's meditation, the latter then repeatedly referred to in the third person as 'she': 'she sees him man, so like God made in this' (3); 'shee sees him nothing twice at once, who'is all / Shee sees a Cedar plant it selfe, and fall' (7–8); 'shee sees at once ...' (11–12). By the end of the poem, however, 'she' has become the church itself while the entity addressed directly in the second person has become 'my Soule' (45). The mother church has gradually displaced the speaker's soul as meditator on and mediator of Christian paradox (including, of course, the eucharistic paradoxes of both the Incarnation and Atonement), while the 'fraile body,' once silent witness, now appears to be absent altogether. What remains is the interplay of church and soul, the former both an encouragement of and refuge from the perplexities of faith, not unlike the great wheel of the English church envisioned by Sir Thomas Browne: 'so God by his Church,' writes Donne, 'neerest to him wee know / And stand firme, if wee by her motion goe' (29–30). This institutional ecstasy is religious counterpart to that of the lovers in 'The Extasie' whose 'two soules' give way to an 'abler soul, which thence doth flow' and 'Defects of loneliness controules' (42–4). It is a communion which recalls 'Vale-diction to his booke,' whose lovers 'for loves clergie only'are instru-ments' (22), they themselves sacramental beings, the intensity of their erotic experience a mythical communion in which they dissolve into the 'Booke' that is 'as long-liv'd as the elements' (19).

The soul, having relinquished its direct apprehension of faith's para-doxes, is now to 'uplay' (45) these as given by the church. The institu-tion's exhaustive authority culminates in the final lines where Christ's 'imitating Spouse' (39) is the conduit through which the blood of Atone-ment flows:

> as though one blood drop, which thence did fall,
> Accepted, would have serv'd, he yet shed all;
> So though the least of his paines, deeds, or words,
> Would busie a life, she all this day affords;
> This treasure then, in grosse, my Soule uplay
> And in my life retaile it every day.   (41–6)[36]

The speaker's body is the effigy or site of convergence between the inner and outer, private and public aspects of religious experience. But it is an impediment in as much as it calls attention to a gap between the fleshly reality of which the speaker is aware (yet apparently embarrassed about) and the corporate body of Christ, the church. This tension is exacer-bated in these final lines where the symbolic or sacramental efficacy of 'one blood drop' is contrasted with the brutal reality of actual crucifix-ion, where 'least' is simultaneously contrasted with and reflective of *all* 'his paines, deeds, or words.' The body silenced at the outset and eventu-ally dismissed, or at least left in the shadows, is reasserted in the flesh and blood of messianic sacrifice. Like the central symbol of 'The Crosse,' the Atonement represented by the sacrament on this day when the speaker's 'soule eates twice' is inextricable from a discourse simultaneously de-pendent on and threatened by the reality of a historical body. What Donne writes of Christ's coming and of man's brief life might also describe the human experience of an elusive presence in the Eucharist: 'He shall come, he is gone' (40).

In moving toward a psychological as opposed to a symbolic, ceremoni-ally oriented religious experience, the affective dimension of devotional poetry nevertheless allows the carnal imagery of sacrament to penetrate and help to realize the inner recesses of religious desire. Barbara K.

Lewalski cites a letter to Goodyere in which Donne defends 'The Litanie' as avoiding both Roman and Reformed criticism and confirms a notable feature of the poem, namely, its appropriation of ceremonial form for inward, spiritual examination. Donne refers to two ancient 'Letanies in Latin verse' which provide him with 'a defence, if any man; to a Lay man and a private, impute it as a fault, to take such divine and publique names, to his own little thoughts.'[37] In the poem the penitent longs for tribulation, to be purged of all 'vicious tinctures' (8), and to do so through vivid identification with the Crucifixion:

> O be thou nail'd unto my heart,
>   And crucified again,
> Part not from it, though it from thee would part,
> But let it be by applying so thy paine,
> Drown'd in thy blood, and in thy passion slaine.   (14–18)

The emphasis on messianic identification, bordering on the blasphemous in 'The Relique' and 'The Funerall,' is here, as in 'The Crosse,' an important feature of the devotional experience; for it is in such identification, encouraged by both the Gospels and St Paul, that the Christian finds refuge from the sin that condemns. Also similar to 'The Crosse' is a reluctance to allow such identification to go unqualified. Whereas in the former poem both idolater and idol are indicted – it is the eye that 'most ... needs crossing' (49) – in 'The Litanie' it is the sacramental referent itself that appears to encourage misguided affection. The prayer includes a petition to be delivered 'From trusting so much to thy blood, / That in that hope, wee wound our soule away' (138–9). The danger here, however, may not be overreliance on the blood given in the Eucharist so much as on the theological abstraction declaimed from puritan pulpits at least as often as it found concrete expression in the Communion wine. The same stanza cautions against 'thinking us all soule, neglecting thus / Our mutuall duties' (143–4), so that together these lines condemn the antinomian tendencies of a Calvinism that leaves little room for human responsibility. 'Blood,' then, manifests the arch-liminality of sacramental discourse, the symbolic hinge on which depend both sacramental efficacy and the doctrinal abstractions that support it. But if the letter to Goodyere advocates a balance of public and private pieties, here, in this most Roman Catholic of poems, Donne directs his criticism primarily at pious enthusiasts, even when a more general target is apparent:

> When plenty, Gods image, and seale
> Makes us Idolatrous,
> And love it, not him, whom it should reveale.   (185–7)

'Seale' suggests a sacramental reference in so far as its proximity to 'image' and 'Idolatrous' evokes puritan criticism of the Roman Mass. These terms, however, are presented in such a way as to be subversive of that anti-Roman discourse. They now indicate the gifts of wealth and affluence and thus a warning against finding in social or economic status signs of God's special favour; the alliance of wealth and spiritual security is an idol no less insidious than any universally accessible 'breadengod.' (While my observations here might support the disappointed courtier theory of religious zeal, it should be noted that the letter to Goodyere is dated 1610, some five years prior to Donne's Ordination.) Donne's ironic association of sacramental topoi such as 'blood' and 'seale' with 'plenty,' the nonsacramental sign of divine favour, thus may be a deliberate taunt directed at anticeremonial precisians. But given the poem's intended audience identified in the letter to Goodyere – Donne's 'own little thoughts' – such passages are as much theological reflection and deliberation as they are polemic. A collective prayer whose liturgical tone and formality are complemented by the repeated first person plural 'us,' 'The Litanie' allows the line separating idolatry and authentic worship to run through the speaker's own heart. This is perhaps most apparent in the supplication, 'When wee are mov'd to seeme religious / Only to vent wit, Lord deliver us' (188–9), Donne earlier having assured God, 'I ... excuse not my excesse / In seeking secrets, or Poëtiquenesse' (71–2).

This fear that his art might constitute a form of idolatry is rare in Donne, more a feature of George Herbert's verse than his own. Yet it does surface occasionally, as in 'To the Countess of Bedford, On New-yeares day' where the speaker's poem, like an idolatrous Roman Catholic sacrifice, 'made of miracle, now faith is scant,/ Will vanish soone, and so possesse no place ... and it, too much grace might disgrace' (23–5). A surprising fusion of artistic prowess with a specifically Calvinist rather than Roman Catholic self-pride is suggested by the final image and context of 'The Crosse.' Here, Donne's identity as poet emerges as an integral part of his religious orientation:

> Crosse those dejections, when it downward tends,
> And when it to forbidden heights pretends.

And as the braine through bony walls doth vent
By sutures, which a Crosses forme present,
So when thy braine workes, ere thou utter it,
Crosse and correct concupiscence of witt.   (53–8)

This indictment of wit is startling given the brilliance of the conceit, while the manic-depressive extremes of downward dejections and 'forbidden heights' – the latter not unlike the preacher Donne's warning 'not to get above [God] in his unrevealed Decrees' (*Sermons*, 7.228–9) – suggest the alternating despair and bold presumption of a predestinarian sensibility, which, it appears, is complicit with the wit in need of venting. This head of steam, moreover, finds relief through none other than 'a Crosses forme,' the latter's ceremonial status and power inherent in its liminal spanning of inner and outer aspects of religious experience, a 'materiall' cross inscribed on the speaker's skull/psyche.

Is it possible Donne recognizes for poetic wit a decorum analogous to that of sacrament? The Eucharist, after all, brings together widely disparate things (bread and body, wine and blood), even if their otherwise remote similarities are more readily apparent than those comprising even the least jarring of Donne's conceits. Similar to the linguistic alchemist of the secular verse, the poet here performs a task not unlike that of the God who becomes present in the Eucharist. For the poet's is the power of the magus, an occult craftsman who prises words from their commonplace referents to recombine and imbue them with new meaning and significance in a manner analogous to the startling kerygmatic assertions, *hoc meum corpus est, hoc meum sanguis est.* In 'The Crosse' it is the intersecting axes symbolic of the fleshing of the word – the 'Crosses forme' through which devotional 'witt' finds appropriate and sober expression – that provide Donne with a model for the creative process. DiPasquale also observes the paradox that Donne's poem exemplifies the wit against which it so vehemently cautions. Her answer to this conundrum, however, is that Donne intends simply to demonstrate the very danger of which he writes, the 'idolatry that he sees inherent in all sacramental actions.'[38] This, it seems to me, unnecessarily tames a poem whose vitality consists precisely in the poet's willingness *not* to resolve the difficulties he raises, to display openly not only his inability to reconcile the ideological poles traced by 'The Crosse,' but also his failure to contain the potential idolatry he recognizes in his art. Fully aware of the dangers, Donne directs the carnal language of sacrament to an internal application even as the denigration of wit is a half-hearted attempt to subordinate art to the devotional stirrings of the Spirit. But perhaps that distinction collapses, finally, under the weight of a sacramental application that is the convergence of internal and external, of spirit and artifice, on the very body of the recipient – the 'Crosses form' that is 'dew'd on me in the sacrament.' The point at which material and spiritual crosses overlap is a dew that congeals as earthly bread without ceasing to be manna from heaven – that which in Andrew Marvell's version of the same paradox quivers on a liminal 'point below,' mirroring the 'greater heaven in an heaven less' before 'dissolving ... Into the glories of th'almighty sun' ('On a Drop of Dew,' 35–40).

The relationship between devotion and the external means of grace – whether these latter be sacraments proper or the poetic utterances that incarnate and ceremonialize devotional experience – is a central feature of Donne's sacred verse. If the material aspects of ceremony advance the radical claims of the Incarnation, they do not obviate the need to internalize spiritually the grace they embody. An exclusively word-centred, psychological piety, on the other hand, in celebrating a spiritual experience which transcends the constraints of confessional and doctrinal identity or ceremonial obligation, tends to attenuate if not to obliterate the historical, corporate, and somatic exigencies of Christian worship. A Calvinist view of sacrament locates presence primarily within, so that the presence or absence of grace, in practice if not in theory, depends on the subjective disposition of the communicant. Donne's carnal modification of this view externalizes the divine and locates the drama of personal salvation in a broader mythical context, one reinforced by the ceremonies and rituals of a tangible and inclusive institutional reality. The divine lyrics are thus public, performative manifestations of religious interiority, their function analogous to that of sacraments. Just as the eucharistic elements are invested with a presence that transcends their materiality, so these poems are ritual enactments of rarefied spiritual processes, the 'visible sign[s] of invisible grace,' to borrow the English reformer Nicholas Ridley's phrasing of a theological commonplace.[39] Their 'experimental' dimension in Donne more often than not yields to an external means of grace. The personal, introspective quality of his devotional lyrics does not, as Anne Ferry argues, preclude their being a 'public voice [by which] to utter what is in all hearts.'[40] As sacraments communicate a grace not finally constrained by subjective anxieties, so Donne's devotional poems externalize the interiority they articulate, rendering their speakers' isolation a communal space to be shared by other similarly afflicted souls.

CHAPTER THREE

Eating the Word: Donne's 1626 Christmas Sermon

In 'A Hymn to Christ, at the Author's last going into Germany,' Donne's dismissal of his talents, along with the 'Fame, Wit, Hopes (false mistresses)' (28) they afford, is solemnized in a sacramental commitment to his new vocation, a poetic self-Ordination. The occasion is Donne's chaplaincy on the earl of Doncaster's diplomatic embassy, 1619–20, and anticipates his promotion to Dean in 1621. The denial here of artistic autonomy, a requisite part of his devotional strategy, is, as in 'The Cross,' both eloquent and disingenuous. Recalling 'The Calme' and its sailors who 'on the hatches as on Altars lye / Each one his owne Priest, and owne Sacrifice' (25–6), 'A Hymn' begins with the promise that

> In what torne ship soever I embarke,
> That ship shall be my embleme of thy Arke;
> What sea soever swallow mee, that flood
> Shall be to mee an embleme of thy bloode.   (1–4)

That same sea is to be put 'betwixt my sinnes and thee' (13), and in the final stanza Donne speaks of his forsaken past in terms of a 'seale' of divorce (25), thus reinforcing his vocational commitment through a sacramental consecration appropriately invoking both Marriage and Ordination. The exchange of past exploits for 'An Everlasting night' (32), however, is despairing. While equally a legal term and thus appropriate when speaking of a bill of divorce, 'seale' is also applicable to sacraments, including, in a Roman Catholic context, the sacrament of Marriage. Thus, in marrying 'those loves, which in youth scattered bee,' God, in keeping with biblical tradition, is assigned the groom's role, but in another sense becomes surrogate for those 'false mistresses' (27–8). '[S]eale,' then, in signifying both divorce and remarriage, marks Donne's transition from courtier, lover, and poet to devout and priest. He never-theless retains a predilection for courtship, the poetic concern to estab-lish union with the object of devotion, whether mistress, king, or deity – the propensity to exercise what Northrop Frye has described as the Renaissance artist's 'centripetal gaze.'[1] The doubly sacramental seal in 'Hymn to Christ' thus functions as the temporal indicator of conversion, a transformation wherein the essential characteristics of one life are reconstituted and redirected in another.

Initially resisted, Donne's final succumbing to Ordination in 1615 no doubt was a significant moment for one whose secular aspirations and disappointments had consumed a considerable portion of his career. However we characterize his decision – whether that of authentic con-vert or frustrated courtier – it is clear that Donne the English divine never relinquished his earlier identity as a poet of remarkable intelli-gence and daring. The same ability to establish sometimes astonishing connections among the elements of his experience we find in the secu-lar poems is evident also in the sacred verse and in the sermons of the dean of St Paul's. It is in the relatively greater public dimension of the sermons especially that Donne's rhetorical skills are brought to bear on pressing ecclesiastical and political concerns.

Donne's 1626 Christmas sermon contains both his most explicit treat-ment of sacramental doctrine and a sustained attempt to reconcile the potentially conflicting ceremonial and predestinarian imperatives of English Protestant divinity. Eleanor McNees has written extensively on this sermon and its importance for our understanding of Donne's sacra-mental theology,[2] but her 'Anglican' reading assumes that Donne's is a confidently worked out *via media* rather than, as I will argue, a reflec-tion of ideological conflict within the religious establishment. Recent historiography cautions against accepting at face value Jacobean and Caroline divines' claims that their church successfully negotiates an Aristotelian mean between doctrinal and ecclesiastical extremes vying for control of its confessional identity. Notions of an English *via media*, like the religious 'polarizations of opinion' identified by Anthony Milton, were 'a *function* of polemical debate, rather than its trigger.' As we shall see, the 'polemical categories through which modes of controversial discourse operated during this period'[3] fail adequately to describe Donne's unique contribution to the ever-elusive middle way.

Elizabethan and early Stuart churchmen whose religion was predomi-nantly sacramental, ceremonial, and sacerdotal were at odds with those who placed greater emphasis on doctrine, preaching, and a puritan devotional piety. Though most mainstream bishops and ministers sought to combine the ceremonial and doctrinal elements of English Christianity, conflict over the church's confessional identity intensified and threatened seriously to erode relations among the establishment clergy. With its strained fusion of Reform doctrine and Roman Catholic ecclesiology, the English middle road tended to veer off course when fondness for sacrament and ceremony on the one hand conflicted on the other with a religious practice more devotional, scriptural, and homiletic in orientation. While sacrament and sermon had always been, ideally, complementary components of English Protestant divinity, from as early as the 1590s prominent churchmen such as Richard Hooker, Thomas Buckeridge, and Lancelot Andrewes feared that undue emphasis on preaching threatened to diminish the sacramental dimension of the ministry. This opposition became more apparent in the 1620s when the ideological progeny of these avant-garde conformists began increasingly to assert the role of sacrament and ceremony in providing the means of salvation and thus to foster divisions among an otherwise unified religious establishment. This division is particularly evident whenever sacramental ministry, the chief instrument of visible religious conformity, is contemplated in light of the Calvinist doctrine of predestination. For in so far as sacraments advanced Richard Hooker's vision of a broad-based church membership, they conflicted theoretically with Calvinism's implicitly exclusionary view of an elect minority. Because predestination threatened the inclusivist policies and unity of a state institution, conforming Calvinist divines were often careful to downplay or even positively to dismiss the more distasteful elements of predestinarian doctrine in favour of an edifying emphasis on sacraments and the grace they were believed to confer.[4]

The combination of inward and outward dimensions of religious experience suggested by my phrase 'sacramental puritanism' was thus far from stable. The Elizabethan Settlement was less the emergence of a distinctively English Christianity than an attempt to establish as broadly inclusive a state institution as was possible in a country to be torn apart by religious strife. Donne's gestures toward the middle road that the church sought to pave and maintain, however, represent a significant attempt to reconcile the ceremonial and sacramental impulses of the 'old religion' with the predominantly introspective, word-centred, and predestinarian pieties of English Calvinism.

The 1626 Christmas sermon is a telling example of Donne's effort to negotiate contrary visions of the church and thereby to advance his own unique version of that most elusive of religious ideals, the English *via media*. The sermon addresses both sacramental and predestinarian controversy at a time when such issues had become once again problematic for Donne's contemporaries. As might be expected of any seasoned proponent of middle-road policies, Donne deftly traces a way between the perceived idolatrous excesses of Roman and Lutheran sacramentalism on the one hand and pious disregard for ceremony on the other. As we shall see, however, Donne's formula for 'real presence' in the sermon differs little from that of his supposedly idolatrous foes, even while accompanied by customary dismissals of Roman Catholic doctrine and practice. Similarly, whereas he scathingly dismisses Calvinist extremists for regarding Holy Communion as a lottery, Donne, I argue here, subtly advances a sacramental piety that includes the exhortation that individuals privately reflect on their status with respect to divine election. Inviting them to receive sacramental grace, Donne encourages his auditory to have no regard for the more extreme predestinarian notion of a *decretum horribile*. But just as vehement antipopery in the sermon does not preclude his advancing a subtly carnal sacramental formula, so Donne's apparent dismissal of predestinarian extremism does not prevent him from cultivating in his flock an 'experimental' Calvinist interiority.

It is not clear finally that Donne's sacramental homiletic indicates support for the proto-Laudian sympathies of the Caroline court, at least not in 1626. If by sacramentalizing the word Donne accommodates an innovative, avant-garde fondness for ceremony alongside more puritan proclivities, doing so also allows the otherwise prominent status of ceremonial forms to be subordinated to private enthusiasms. We will see that even in direct violation of a royal decree in June of the same year, Donne had not refrained from expressing distaste at the then ascendant political fortunes of anti-Calvinism. It is thus in the wake of theological controversy and amid the changing face of establishment divinity in the 1620s that Donne advanced the integration of sacramental and Calvinist devotional experience – the primary symbol and instrument of ecclesiastical unity, and that nether psychological realm wherein the devout negotiate God's hidden decrees. That Donne in one and the same sermon combines a carnal sacramental position with predestinarian sympathies may seem to some a contradiction of the highest order. Thus Peter McCullough describes Donne's ecclesiology as inhabiting a 'muddled space' somewhere between 'anti-Catholic Calvinism' and 'numinous sacramentalism.'[5] While the present chapter does not claim for the sermons as a whole the site of a sustained set of religious conflicts, it does aim to explicate one of the more muddled moments in a theologically evolving and complex religious career.

For the English church the question of sacramental efficacy had never been simply a matter of endorsing or rejecting outright the notion of 'real presence.' Establishment divines, as Christopher Hodgkins has demonstrated, could rely on the fact that both the Articles and Calvin himself asserted the presence of the body and blood of Christ in the sacrament.[6] Difficulty arose only with inordinate speculation as to the precise *modus* of eucharistic presence. Whereas Calvin had emphasized the spiritual mode and corporate act of receiving while nevertheless maintaining a functional importance for the species of bread and wine,[7] sacramental thought among the English church establishment of the 1620s became explicitly more concerned with the connection between presence and the externals of ceremony. To the degree that the question of 'real presence' was concentrated on the species, just so did ceremonies and their priestly overseers come increasingly to be regarded as the proper institutional media of sacramental grace. Conversely, a sacramental theology which identified the psyche or soul of the communicant as the primary site of a largely noncorporeal immanence suggests a diminished role for institutional trappings and the ecclesiastical authority of which they were an extension.[8] This institutional authority, facilitated and reinforced by public ceremonial worship, met in Calvinist doctrine a potential threat. This is apparent, for example, in Benjamin Carier's 1613 letter to James I, where the recusant-to-be is adamant that predestination subverts both sacramental worship and the episcopal discipline it reinforced.[9] While Calvin's doctrine theoretically denied the possibility of knowing one's status with respect to election, predestination inevitably encouraged the elitism (or despair) Calvin himself had cautioned against. The local presence of Christ among the species of the Eucharist, on the other hand, implied a universal view of the Atonement and the availability of grace to all who willingly and worthily received them. Richard Hooker, as Patrick Collinson has shown, had sought to skirt over the problem by allowing that the godly might worship alongside the wicked; the non-elect, for the sake of peace in the realm, were thus obligated to conform to the same rites and ceremonies enjoyed by their more fortunate contemporaries.[10] As Protestants 'distinctive in their enthusiasm and zeal for the cause of true religion in a way in which both they themselves (regarding themselves as a "godly" elite) and their hostile opponents ... could and did recognize,'[11] puritans were suspicious of those whose emphasis on sacrament and ceremony implied a far too inclusive ministry. Even if the Articles provided that the wicked do not share in the benefits conferred at Holy Communion, not everyone in the church was as content as was Hooker to remain wheat among the tares.

To the extent that predestination suggests a limited Atonement, the question of the *modus* of sacramental presence becomes a matter of some urgency, even if both Donne and Calvin were eager to rest secure in the mysteries of eucharistic grace. 'Although my mind can think beyond what my tongue can utter,' writes Calvin, 'yet even my mind is conquered and overwhelmed by the greatness of the thing. Therefore, nothing remains but to break forth in wonder at this mystery, which plainly neither the mind is able to conceive nor the tongue to express.'[12] Echoing St Paul, Donne hoped that one day 'I shall see all problematicall things come to be dogmaticall, I shall see all these rocks in Divinity, come to be smoothe alleys' (*Sermons*, 3.111). In the Christmas sermon he has little patience for those disinclined to stand and wait:

> They that will assign a particular manner, how that body [of Christ] is there, have no footing, no ground at all, no scripture to Anchor upon: And so, diving in a bottomless sea, they poppe sometimes above water to take breath, to appeare to say something, and then snatch at a loose preposition, that swims upon the face of the waters; and so the Roman Church hath catched a *Trans*, and others a *Con*, and a *Sub*, and an *In* ... and rymed themselves beyond reason, into absurdities, and heresies. (7.296)

'Face of the waters' here suggests criticism less of a too superficial or literal reading of Christ's words of institution than of an erroneous insistence on deciding one way or the other. 'We offer to go no farther, then according to his Word,' says Donne following his dismissal of the drowning heretics, 'and in that light wee depart in peace, without scruple in our owne, without offence to other mens consciences,' that is, men other than those who would snatch at a 'Trans' or 'Con' or 'Sub' or 'In' (7.296). Reference to scripture as the final authority is always soundly orthodox; but it may also be a convenient evasion. Those refusing to exercise Simeon's, St Paul's, and Donne's patience could also point to scripture, presumably, to authorize their snatching. Indeed, just as Calvin himself eventually went so far as to endorse a theory of 'real presence' that goes considerably beyond mere assertion toward rational explanation, so Donne's lawyerly mind was far from immune to theological curiosity.

Defining a position via dismissal of that which it is not is typical of those churchmen who, like Sir Thomas Browne, would 'keep the road, the great wheele of the Church' while avoiding a too explicit confession of the theological particulars of their commitment.[13] Donne also shares with the author of *Religio Medici* a strategic fondness for litotes, the negative construction of an essentially positive statement. In the Christmas sermon, following a lengthy anti-Roman attack and just prior to the 'face of the waters' passage, Donne provides a list of patristic authorities on the Eucharist, beginning 'we refuse not the words of the Fathers ... Not *Irenaeus* ... Not *Tertullians* ... Not *Cyprians* ... Not *Damascens*,' for all of whom the bread undergoes some sort of change, 'not only changed so in use ... but changed supernaturally.' Having gone explicitly beyond an innocuous emphasis on corporate 'use,' the ritual *act* of receiving, Donne now must grapple with a positive formulation of the presence he would assert, his commitment to doing so highly appropriate given the calendrical context – the Christmas celebration of the Incarnation:

> for this transforming, cannot be intended of the outward form and fashion, for that is not changed; but be it of that internall form, which is the very essence and nature of the bread, so it is transformed, so the bread hath received a new form, a new essence, a new nature, because whereas the nature of bread is but to nourish the body, the nature of this bread now, is to nourish the soule. (7.295)

Momentary focus away from the communal act and toward the bread itself gives way finally to the end for which the bread is intended: soul nourishment. But the terms Donne uses to characterize the transformation here give pause, for they suggest the scholastic categories of substance and accident and thus the very doctrine Donne has been at pains to denounce. The second Tridentine canon on the Eucharist, in its final form, includes the following:

> Should anyone ... deny this wonderful and unique changing of the whole substance of bread into the body and of the whole substance of wine into the blood, while the species of bread and wine nonetheless remain, which change the Catholic Church very suitably calls transubstantiation, let him be excommunicated.[14]

Donne's 'outward' and 'internall' forms are compatible with Reform theological discourse in so far as they may correspond merely to the outward trappings of ceremony and the inward realm of the individual soul. Eleanor McNees and, more recently, Theresa M. DiPasquale, advance just such a reading.[15] Indeed, Donne's evocation of the Aristotelian categories is followed soon after with the assertion that the bread is 'of another nature in the use, though not in the substance' (7.296). Not long after the Christmas sermon, moreover, he speaks of a 'true Transubstantiation, that when I have received it worthily, it becomes my very soule; that is, My soule growes up into a better state, and habitude by it, and I have the more soule for it, the more sanctified, the more deified soule by that Sacrament' (7.321). Earlier in this same passage Donne asserts that Christ is the 'forme, the Essence, the substance, the soule of the Sacrament' (7.320), thus lending support to R.V. Young's Roman Catholic emphasis. This indeed is 'theologically loaded language,' as Young writes,[16] but even here Donne adds the caveat that 'To take the body, and not the soule, the bread, and not Christ, is death' (7.320). If the bread were truly transubstantiated in the scholastic sense, it would be impossible to take it and not the 'forme, the Essence, the substance.' Donne deliberately plays with scholastic language in anticipation of the even more surprising phrase, 'the true Transubstantiation.' His emphasis there is on reception and the transformation of the communicant's soul. It is the soul that is 'transubstantiated,' not the bread and wine. Indeed, Donne has just insisted that 'What the bread and wine is, or what becomes of it' is 'impertinent to be inquired' (7.321). The 'true Transubstantiation,' then, is a deliberate parody of Roman Catholic doctrine, a subversive appropriation of scholastic discourse in the service of Reformation theology. Nevertheless, there is more than a little ambiguity in the Christmas sermon as to what, exactly, Donne's categories – 'outward form,' 'internall form,' and 'essence' – apply. Even if the 'soule' is the ultimate beneficiary, the focus on 'bread' discloses what may be a more carnal preoccupation. The final word of the previous paragraph, the object of Donne's apparent ire, 'Transubstantiation,' together with the opening of the present paragraph, 'But yet, though this bread be not so transubstantiated, we refuse not the words of the Fathers,' seems to deny the possibility such a doctrine might be entertained. And no, substance and accident are not the terms Donne uses; in fact, in the previous paragraph he insists that the bread is not 'Transubstantiated to another substance.' He goes on, moreover, to denounce the 'absurdity' of the 'Trent Canon' (7.296). And yet that glaring target of a moderate's criticism, 'Transubstantiation,' is followed immediately with the equivocating 'But yet' introducing Donne's positive formulation – a formulation which quite explicitly allows that one aspect of the bread changes while another remains – precisely the Roman Catholic position at Trent.

Donne's formula does not include mention of the body or blood; the bread undergoes a change, but to what is not clear. The metaphysical division of the bread into conceptual categories, however, whether substance and accident or outward form and essence, is remarkably similar to the Tridentine formula. Indeed, the substitution of 'species' for 'accident' while nevertheless maintaining 'substance' – a feature of the Council's desire to shed Thomist and Aristotelian associations while retaining an essentially scholastic metaphysical framework – is not unlike Donne's own combining of 'outward form,' 'internall form,' and Aristotelian 'essence.' The vehemence with which Donne in the sermon attacks transubstantiation is qualified by a formula remarkably similar to the one it would displace. He thus goes momentarily and considerably beyond what C.W. Dugmore has called the *mysterium tremendum* approach to the Eucharist, a view of real presence that stops short of identifying its *modus*, opting instead for an agnostic awe.[17]

The sermons are filled with attacks on the Roman Mass: papists 'mold [Christ] up in a wafer cake' (5.135), a 'sacramentall box' (7.139); they 'make millions of these bodies in the *Sacrament*,' dishonouring 'this body, whose honour is to sit in the same dimensions, and circumscriptions, at the right hand of God' (8.288–9); and in the Christmas sermon, theirs is 'a Pharisaicall Superstition' (7.289), an 'Atheisme' that 'impute[s] contradictions to God' (7.294). In a slightly earlier sermon Donne refers to Aristotle as the 'Pope' of 'Philosophical Divinity in the Schoole' (7.131). Elsewhere, however, he criticizes the Roman church precisely for their condemnation of '*Aristotles Metaphysicks*' as 'Heresie' (10.149). The ambivalence over Aristotle, moreover, extends to the Counter-Reformation church itself:

They know the people doe commit Idolatry, in their manner of adoring the bread in the Sacrament, and they never preach against this error of the people, nor tell them wherein that Idolatry lies; It is true, that in their Bookes of Controversies, which the people could not understand, if they might read them, in those bookes they proceed upon safer grounds; There they say, that when a man adores the Sacrament, he must be sure, that he carry not his thoughts upon any thing that he sees, not only not upon Bread and Wine, (for, that they must not beleeve to be there, whatsoever they see or taste) but not upon those species and apparences of Bread and Wine, which they seem to see, but he must carry all his thoughts upon the person of Christ, who is there, though he see him not; for otherwise, say, they, if he should adore that which he sees, he should commit Idolatry. (7.333)

Eucharistic idolatry is more the province of the people than official Roman doctrine, even if the church leaders are in part responsible for popular ignorance. Donne may have been aware that Aristotelian substance, according to Aquinas, is a pure potentiality which achieves actualization only through its corresponding accident: 'It offers no footing to any organ of sense or to the imagination, but only to the intelligence, whose object is the essence of things, as Aristotle says.'[18] In any event, Donne's equivocating around a distinction between official Tridentine doctrine and popular or vulgar misconception is a significant concession for one otherwise inclined to call the Roman church an '*Italian Babylon*' (10.153). When Donne in the Christmas sermon challenges the papists to go all the way and procure 'a trans-accidentation, that since the substance is changed, the accidents might have been changed too' (7.295), he may thus have in mind some but not all Roman Catholics, berating the former only for an insufficient understanding of Aristotelian metaphysics. Donne's disdain for the philosopher as scholastic pope might thus best be understood as a reaction against the Roman church's failure to discourage the perverting of otherwise sound doctrine. In the Christmas sermon Donne may have wanted to wrest Aristotle back from the papists, replacing the terms 'substance' and 'accident' with 'outward' and 'internall' forms in order to avoid the controversy which the former might arouse. Donne does not deny, however, the possibility of a separation of inner from outer; rather, he mirrors very closely the Roman doctrine's categorical division. The stable, unchanging 'outward form' and the efficacious 'internall form' or 'essence and nature of the bread' thus avoid the dangerous notion of transubstantiation in name only.

How do we account for the accommodation, in a single sermon, of both vehement anti-Roman sentiment and a sacramental formula strikingly similar to that of the notorious enemy of English Protestants? Donne's strategy is decidedly not an example of what Anthony Milton has identified as 'negative popery,' the tendency among some late Jacobean and Caroline divines to introduce innovative or potentially controversial ideas minus the usual caveats affirming the Church of England's distinct confessional identity vis-à-vis the Roman church.[19] Donne apparently wanted to dissociate himself from such churchmen even if the view of 'real presence' he advocates in the sermon would have complemented their increasing reluctance to perpetuate the anti-Roman polemical tradition. It may be that the average lay person would not have recognized the subtleties of Donne's appropriation of scholastic language. But the fact that such a formula is immediately preceded by a standard antipapist litany suggests Donne's sensitivity to his auditory's theological sophistication. Even couched in acceptable anti-Catholic guise, however, recourse to a specific formula, however uncharacteristic of the eirenical preacher, suggests Donne's recognition of the Church of England's failure to develop a sacramental theory distinct from that of Rome yet adequately suited to the church's traditionally sacramental orientation. Despite its denial of a purely signifying function for the elements and insistence on the presence of the whole Christ, Calvinist sacramentalism for Donne simply may not have gone far enough in recognizing the incarnational dimension of Holy Communion.

A potentially controversial eucharistic formula in the 1626 Christmas sermon is accompanied by anti-Roman diatribe and thus differs from Donne's more avant-garde contemporaries' negative popery, the deliberate failure to buffer popish innovation with antipapal remarks. Similarly, his contempt for extreme predestinarian views in the same sermon precludes what might be called negative puritanism – but it does not of Donne an anti-Calvinist make. Indeed, he advances in the Christmas sermon a convergence of ceremonial and devotional aspects of religious experience in which the sacrament of Holy Communion is wedded to an experimental predestinarian interiority – this despite apparently anti-Calvinist remarks and thus not unlike his offering a quasi-Tridentine view of sacramental presence amid conventional dismissals of Roman transubstantiation.

'Man,' Donne assures his Christmas auditory, 'comes not to the Sacrament, as to a Lottery, where perchance he may draw Salvation, but it is ten to one he misses' (7.283). It is crucial when evaluating Donne's attitudes toward Calvinism and predestination to distinguish between infralapsarian (sometimes called sublapsarian) and supralapsarian approaches to the doctrine. The infralapsarian position, not unlike the Roman Catholic, held that the elect are those who willingly and actively respond to God's grace freely offered to all members of fallen humanity; they are foreseen by God as having responded positively to his saving grace. Regarded as such, the decree, in Anthony Milton's formulation, 'proceeded from prescience of original and actual sin, and was *not* an absolute act of God's will and purpose.'[20] However, because such a view encroaches on divine sovereignty by allowing human effort a role in the soteriological process, supralapsarians held that God did not simply foresee but rather foreordained just who would 'willingly' respond (the elect) and who would not (the reprobate). Jeffrey Johnson emphasizes Donne's rejection of supralapsarian Calvinism and the importance of that rejection for his understanding of the sacrament. Holy Communion would be little more than a lottery if communicants' willingness to receive sacramental grace were to have no bearing at all on whether or not it is in fact conferred. Nevertheless, while justifiably critical of those who overstate Donne's obsession with divine power, Johnson too hastily separates Donne from Calvin's 'theologically foundational' view of sovereignty.[21] Calvin was more equivocal and less absolutist than Johnson implies, writing, for example:

> If anyone approaches us with such expressions as: 'Why from the beginning did God predestine some to death who, since they did not yet exist, could not yet have deserved the judgment of death?' let us, in lieu of reply, ask them in turn, what they think God owes to man if He would judge him according to His own nature. As all of us are vitiated by sin, we can only be odious to God, and that not from tyrannical cruelty but by the fairest reckoning of justice. But if all whom the Lord predestines to death are by condition of nature subject to the judgment of death, of what injustice toward themselves may they complain?[22]

It is the phrase 'condition of nature' that is crucial here for it suggests an infralapsarian as opposed to supralapsarian decree. All are reprobate by virtue of original sin unless redeemed by God. Calvin does go on to add, however, that the reprobate, presumably in keeping with divine justice, are 'justly charged against the malice and depravity of their hearts,' but in order to maintain God's radical sovereignty, Calvin cannot refrain from providing that 'it be added at the same time that they have been given over to this depravity because they have been raised up by the just but inscrutable judgment of God to show forth his glory in their condemnation.'[23]

Passages in Donne which seem to critical proponents of Anglican moderation evidence of anti-Calvinism are better seen as reflecting a doctrinal heterogeneity both among his Calvinist contemporaries and, as above, in Calvin himself. Just as the latter claims Augustinian authority for his formulation of predestination, so Donne cites Augustine in order to downplay a strict determinist position: 'There is no predestination in God, but to good' (5.53; see also 7.74). This clearly promotes an infralapsarian position, which locates election after the Fall and holds that all therefore are justly doomed save those whom God redeems. Elsewhere, however, Donne finds it difficult to avoid the conflict between human autonomy and Calvin's notion of an all-consuming, irresistible will:

> God hath elected certaine men, whom he intends to create, that he may elect them; that is, that he may declare his Election upon them. God had thee, before he made thee; He loved thee first, and then created thee, that thou loving him, he might continue his love to thee ... God hath not left out my selfe; He hath been my Helpe, but he hath left some thing for me to doe with him, and by his helpe. (7.63)

As if aware of entertaining Pelagian notions Donne buffers his personalized claim for human agency with not one but two qualifying reminders of God's help. Indeed, the preposition 'with' quickly becomes 'by' – 'with him, and by his helpe' – the passage thus ending on a note that reiterates divine sovereignty. Moreover, Donne barely maintains an infralapsarian predestination, 'before he made thee' suggesting at the very least that God's declaration of 'Election' hovers precariously between his consideration of original and actual sin. Indeed, the passage might easily be construed to refer to the Creation per se, in keeping not only with the Pauline notion that the elect are chosen in Christ before the world existed (Eph. 1.4) but also with Beza's supralapsarian position that God's double decree precedes both Creation and Fall and depends not at all on foresight of sin. Donne's doctrinal elusiveness here may be part of an eirenic strategy or it may suggest what Joshua Scodel has identified as the persistence in the *Sermons* of the devout sceptic of 'Satyre III,' a Donne who 'continually sought to distinguish the true Christian from the easy-going conformist and to require from the sincere conformist some of the sceptical seeker's commitment to "inquiring right."'[24]

Whatever the intricacies of his views on predestination elsewhere, in December 1626 Donne emphasized human responsibility as an important component in the redemptive scheme. 'Man comes not into the world, nor he comes not to the Sacrament, as to a Lottery, where perchance he may draw Salvation, but it is ten to one he misses, but upon these few and easie conditions, Beleeve, and Love' (7.283). That same month the Arminian John Cosin criticized those who

> preach us all Gospel and put no law among it, bishops and priests that will tell the people all is well if they can but say their catechism and here

sermons [and] make them believe that there is nothing to be done more but to believe and so be saved.[25]

Cosin would have approved of Donne's remarks about a predestinarian 'Lottery' and both would have concurred with Carier that the sacramental grace offered by a state church to all who would (and ideally should) receive it is simply incompatible with luck-of-the-draw notions of Holy Communion. Donne's 'Beleeve, and Love,' moreover, unlike the 'believe and so be saved' to which Cosin objects – and in an order opposite to that urged by Una on Spenser's Redcrosse – adds works to faith, evident also in the sermon's earlier rendering of the phrase: 'Beleeve, and live well: More he asks not, lesse he takes not for any man, upon any pretence of any unconditioned decree' (7.282).

Might we not count Donne among the Arminian insurgents of revisionist historiography? Or might his 'Beleeve, and Love' be a moderate's nuancing of his own anti-puritan provocation, his 'few and easie conditions' perhaps construed by such as Cosin as *too* few and *too* easy?

Cosin's sermon, delivered '*Prima Adventus, Decembris 3, 1626*' at the consecration of Bishop Francis White, is a vehement defence of episcopal Ordination, quoting 1 Tim. 5.22, 'lay hands suddenly on no man.' Insisting that only the bishop and not the priest 'hath authority to put into the priesthood, or to give any orders at all,' Cosin adds that this is by express authority of 'the God both of Law and Gospel.' He concludes by sealing White's commission with an invitation to receive Holy Communion; the new bishop of Carlisle will 'kneel here alone till that [his consecration] be past.'[26] Donne, in contrast, does not hesitate in the Christmas sermon to refer to his entire auditory as a '*Royall Priesthood,*' one, albeit, that is neither 'knighted, nor ennobled,' but whose 'good soule[s]' nevertheless are 'crowned' with a '*Regale Sacerdotium.*' Their reception of the sacrament, moreover, is also characterized as a sacerdotal occasion: 'to come to the Communion Table, is to take Orders; Every man should come to that Altar, as holy as the Priest, for there he is a Priest' (7.286–7). The thrust of the passage is perhaps merely figurative – those to whom it is addressed, after all, are neither 'knighted, nor ennobled' – but it does confer on Donne's lay audience a dignity Cosin would reserve for an apostolic élite and, directly contrary to Cosin's admonition, grants Priest John Donne the bishop's otherwise exclusive authority to ordain.

The young Cosin was friend to Bishop Richard Neile and an associate of the latter's Durham House Circle, a group whose Arminian views, as

Nicholas Tyacke has shown, well may have facilitated their increasing influence at court. The new bishop was a notorious anti-Calvinist whose public criticism of Reform doctrine, like Cosin's, was aimed not only at the second-generation Calvinism of Beza but also at Calvin himself and the Genevan church in general.[27] These divines surely would have approved of Donne's disparaging remarks about a predestinarian lottery and its threat to the institutional cohesiveness promoted by sacrament and ceremony. But eagerness to avoid contentious doctrine does not make Donne an anti-Calvinist. That the Arminian potential of his remarks may derive more from pastoral concern than doctrinal conviction becomes evident in light of a sermon and events of six months earlier. In early June, notes Tyacke, a proclamation urging 'the peace and quiet of the Church of England' was issued by Charles I in response to the intention of the Cambridge Commencement to maintain the thesis, 'No one disputes, save in error, against predestination.'[28] The decree, which included affirmation of the Elizabethan Articles as sole doctrinal authority, prompted a largely Calvinist parliament to respond with a bill appropriating Charles's appeal for peace, but for an altogether different purpose. For 'the better continuing of peace and unity in the commonwealth' the 14 June parliamentary bill sought, to no avail, to expand the moderately predestinarian 1563 Articles to include the Irish Articles of 1613, notorious for containing the unmistakably (and rejected) Calvinist Lambeth Articles of 1595.[29] The Commencement affair, royal proclamation, and subsequent parliamentary unrest were in part occasioned by controversy over Richard Montagu's *Appello Caesarem* (1625) and its explicit endorsement of Arminian doctrine. In February the York House Conference under Bishop Neile had convened with a view to resolving the debate provoked by Montagu. That Charles a year earlier had intervened in parliament on Montagu's behalf provided support for Cosin's remarks at the close of the conference proceedings that the king 'swears his perpetual patronage of our cause.'[30]

Joshua Scodel cites the June 1626 proclamation as a factor in the apparent anti-Arminianism of a sermon Donne addressed to the king in April 1627.[31] Donne's response to the royal decree, however, was much swifter and more direct. Disappointment at the Durham House divines' potential for influencing policy is evident in a sermon Donne preached on 21 June, just one week after the parliamentary bill had been introduced. There he offers comments which, because potentially inflammatory, might be construed as an affront to the king's order. Countering the Roman Catholic polemicist Bellarmine's appropriation of patristic authority in support of Baptism for the dead, Donne conveniently allows that the early fathers were sometimes mistaken. Included among patristic error is the affirmation that 'the cause of God's election was the foresight of the faith and obedience of the Elect' (7.202). Though not an explicit endorsement of supralapsarian predestination, the remark denies a tenet central to the Arminian position on election. Donne does not offer a positive alternative to the 'error,' but his silence only partially attenuates a critical position fully compatible with the more blatantly Calvinist designs of the Cambridge Commencement. Bellarmine is thus but the decoy of a polemic aimed closer to home. Qualifying his remarks about patristic error, Donne goes on to say that 'in the heat of disputation, and argument, and to make things straight' the fathers sometimes erred by countering one heresy with an equally heretical opposite. Even Augustine, in seeking to maintain human free will without encroaching on divine prerogative, was 'transported sometimes with vehemency against his present adversary, whether Pelagian, or Manichean' (7.203). Donne then adds that this same tendency

> is a disease that even some great Councels in the Church, and Church-affaires have felt, that for collaterall and occasionall, and personal respects, which were risen after they were met, *the maine doctrinall points, and such as have principally concerned the glory of God, and the salvation of soules,* and were indeed the principall and onely cause of their then meeting there, *have been neglected.* (7.203, my emphasis)

Just a few lines earlier Donne refers to the 'Councel of Trent' as having taken place 'the other day' (7.202). But for the 1620s English Church the most recent of 'great Councels,' one concerned precisely with the doctrinal mare's nest of divine sovereignty and the Atonement – 'the glory of God and the salvation of soules' – was the 1618 Synod of Dort. Indeed, the heading for the second chapter of the Synod's proceedings is 'Christs death and the redemption of men by it.'[32] Donne's charge that such 'main doctrinall points ... have been neglected' is significant in light not of the Tridentine proceedings of some seventy years previous but rather of both Dort – which, comparatively, *was* just 'the other day' – and more recent events. The doctrinally Calvinist outcome of Dort, notes Tyacke, was denied authority by Richard Montagu in *Appello Caesarem* on the basis that it had never been officially endorsed by the English Church, even if the anti-Arminian delegation to the 1618 synod was supported by James and by the Abbots, both Archbishop George and Bishop Robert.[33] Montagu's supporters at York House in February 1626, holding that Dort in effect denied the universal efficacy of the Atonement, opposed a Calvinist presence which called for an enshrining of the Dort findings as authoritative.[34] Charles's proclamation in June, favouring Neile and his associates, effectively sealed the fate of Dort's authority, the baldly predestinarian bias of the Cambridge Commencement having played a card too provocative to ignore. That Donne thought overzealousness a chief cause in the failure of those wanting for Dort a more explicit political and ecclesiastical authority is evident in his disappointment at the 'neglect' of 'some great Councels in the Church':

> Men that came thither with a fervent zeale to the glory of God, have taken
> in a new fire of displeasure against particular Heretiques, or Schismatiques,
> and discontinued their holy zeale towards God, till their occasionall dis-
> pleasure towards those persons might be satisfied, and so those Heresies,
> and Heretiques against whom they met, have got advantage by that passion,
> which hath overtaken and overswayed them, after they were met. (7.203–4)

Donne echoes here the moderate Calvinist Bishop George Carleton, whose *Examination* of Montagu's Arminian claims for English orthodoxy, notes Anthony Milton, was published in two editions of 1626. Carleton wrote of those who, 'in zeale to correct [Arminian] errour have gone somewhat too farre on the right hand.'[35] Such fears are also similar to those of John Davenant who, in a letter to Samuel Ward of 22 June – a week following the parliamentary bill and the day after Donne's sermon at St Paul's – expressed concern that Charles's proclamation would be used by the Durham House divines to vilify the Cambridge Calvinists as doctrinally novel and therefore divisive.[36]

I have been suggesting Dort as the principal 'Councel' Donne has in mind. But given the failed Calvinist efforts at York House and the sermon's immediate proximity vis-à-vis the events of June, the more recent conference is as likely a target as any. Indeed, the plural 'Councels' allows both possibilities, just as it allows a generic and politically innocuous reading of the passage as referring to no council in particular. This latter reading Donne is at some pains to encourage when, after further admonishing the zealous not to let God's 'Lieutenant and Vicegerent [be] wearied, and hardened towards us,' he recognizes for his earlier comments a too specific political currency:

> God forbid that my praying that things may not be so, should be interpreted
> for a suspicion in me, that things are so; God forbid, that invocation upon

> God, should imply a crimination upon men; The Spirit of God, in sense of
> whom, and in whose presence I speake, knowes that my prayer is but a
> prayer, and not an Increpation, not an Insimulation. (7.204)

If, as Walton claimed, Donne was careful to 'cast his sermons into form'
and to 'commit his meditations to his memory' in preparation for mount-
ing the pulpit, here he appears to have left intact the window on a mind
at work – to pervert Morris Croll's well-known formulation, an actual
polemic in progress.[37] If he was later to become more explicitly supportive of what may be called Arminian ideas, here Donne cautiously voices
both resistance to a central tenet of such beliefs and regret that very
recent events suggest favour for those who hold them. The 21 June
sermon was thus part of a concerted Calvinist effort to rebuff the proto-
Laudian divines of Durham House, one which culminated in Archbishop James Usher's more vehement attack on the Arminian faction in
a court sermon just four days later.[38]

If Donne is critical of overzealous Calvinists it is more because such
eagerness is advantageous to their opponents than because their theology is erroneous.

Donne recognized among some of his conformist contemporaries a
tendency to favour a priestly, ceremonial, and sacramental style of divinity over one more pastoral, word-centred, and even predestinarian in
emphasis, all the while cautioning Calvinist divines against too vehemently voicing their angst at doctrinal innovation and the political developments that supported it. Indeed, in the Christmas sermon Donne
offers what could be construed as outright contempt for those too vocal
about their predestinarian convictions. Perhaps it is no coincidence that
in early October 1626, between the June controversy and Christmas, the
man who one day would replace Ussher at Canterbury had just been
informed of his imminent appointment as dean of the Chapel Royal.
How does the dean of St Paul's negotiate the contrary imperatives of
sacrament and English Calvinism at a time when anti-Calvinist divines
were advancing their doctrinal and ecclesiastical biases at the Caroline
court and thus precipitating the Laudian archbishopric?

Donne's usual quietism with respect to controversial doctrine suggests
that he was what Kendall would call a 'credal' predestinarian. In the
Christmas sermon, however, Donne offers a reconciliation of sacramental and devotional imperatives that recalls the 'experimental' Calvinism
of *Holy Sonnets*. This should not be surprising, for Kendall's categories

suggest not so much doctrinal as pastoral differences, the issue less one of theological preference than of emphasis. Acutely aware of the value of the individual devotional pilgrimage and the theological deliberations it might entail, Donne was also very fond of the extra-verbal, corporeal dimensions of worship and their role in uniting a church body otherwise divided along doctrinal lines. He advances in the Christmas sermon a convergence of predestination and ceremony through a combination of temporal condensation, typological layering, and, above all, a figurative identification of word and sacrament, thereby directing his auditory toward their own epiphany, an encounter with the divine in which past and future, along with individual identity, are subsumed by a universal and sacramental present. The encounter may be understood conceptually as two interdependent axes: the horizontal flow of history comprising and comprised of the lives of Donne's auditory, and the vertical or transcendent moment of communion with God in the sacrament. Directed toward that ritual moment is an examination of Simeon's qualifications and the effects of his encounter – the Epiphany of the Christ child, and the *Nunc dimittus* or Song of Simeon (Luke 2.29–32) that is Donne's text: 'Lord now lettest thou thy servant depart in peace, according to thy word: for mine eyes have seen thy salvation.' These qualifications serve in turn as a measure against which each communicant is to examine his or her own spiritual status. Described as an act of writing, a re-inscribing of scripturally valorized 'characters' on the collective church body, this examination follows the rhetorical procedure outlined in the *divisio*, explicitly said to resemble the breaking, ingesting, and assimilating of the sacramental gifts:

> The end of all digestions, and concoctions is assimilation, that that meate may become our body. The end of all consideration of all the actions of such leading and exemplar men, as *Simeon* was, is assimilation too; That we may be like that man. Therefore we shall make it a first part ... (7.280–1)

By drawing an analogy between sermon and Eucharist, both of which are to be received and applied by his auditory, Donne sacramentalizes the word and renders the sacrament a repository of homiletic exhortation. Receiving the material elements,[39] it remains only that communicants ingest and assimilate the moral actions and 'characters' of the exemplar Simeon, the preacher's strategy here perhaps influenced by Richard Hooker's remarks advocating frequent singing of the *Nunc dimittus* and the other New Testament hymns as a participation in the experience that first inspired them, 'because the mysticall communion of all faithfull men is such as maketh everie one to be interested in those precious blessinges which anie one of them receiveth at God's handes.'[40]

Having delineated in detail Simeon's godly qualities and characteristics, Donne turns to his spiritual beneficiaries:

> We cannot pursue this Anatomy of good old Simeon, this Just, and Devout Priest, so farre, as to shew you all his parts, and the use of them all, in particular. His example, and the characters that are upon him, are our Alphabet. I shall only have time to name the rest of those characters; you must spell them, and put them into their syllables; you must forme them, and put them into their syntaxis, and sentences; that is, you must pursue the imitation, that when I have told you what he was, you may present your selves to God, such as he was. (7.289)

Donne's pun on 'character' extends beyond the double meaning of moral quality and grapheme to include a sacramental sense in as much as it is Simeon's characters that are 'that meate' to be digested, concocted, and assimilated by his auditory.[41] This 'spelling' of Simeon as a personal imitation, moreover, is to be accompanied by a manifestation of the Holy Ghost as a strikingly predestinarian 'spirit of Prophesie': 'Thou art a Prophet upon thy selfe,' writes Donne, 'when thou commest to the Communion; Thou art able to foretell, and to pronounce upon thy selfe, what thou shalt be forever.' Here, however, Donne advocates precisely the position he had eschewed as Patristic error in the June sermon – namely, that 'the cause of God's election was the foresight of the faith and obedience of the Elect' (7.202):

> Vpon thy disposition then, thou maiest conclude thine eternall state; then thou knowest which part of St. Pauls distribution falls upon thee; whether that tribulation and anguish upon every soule of man, that doth evill; Or that, But glory, and honour, and peace to every man, that worketh good. Thou art this Prophet; silence not this Prophet; doe not chide thy conscience for chiding thee; stone not this Prophet; doe not petrifie, and harden thy conscience against these holy suggestions. (7.289–90)

Holy Communion is a fulcrum upon which turn the past and future events of each individual life, which, from this vantage point, is viewed as a narrative that variously either conforms to or departs from the ideal embodied by our friend Simeon. It is here that one decides 'what thou shalt be for ever.' Donne thus combines an exhortation implying the possibility to change with an urgent call to look within for evidence of election. The introspective communicant who does the examining, the 'conscience' that 'chides,' is itself to be comprised of the 'example' of Simeon, the 'characters that are upon him' – 'our Alphabet.' Though moderate endorsements of predestination typically discouraged speculation as to one's elect or reprobate status, even Calvin himself, as we have seen, knew that refraining from doing so was very difficult. Indeed, it is his auditory's concern for their eternal destiny that Donne deliberately exacerbates. Sacramental participation is intimately associated with the question of whether one's life as a whole, as a complete story made up of characters, syllables, words, and sentences, does in fact bear the status of election. Donne, we saw, explicitly opposes a supralapsarian doctrine of predestination to reprobation, the strictly arbitrary and terrible decree that would make of the sacrament a mere lottery. But his exhortation here appears to exploit the anxiety attendant upon consideration of God's foreknowledge and 'St. Pauls distribution,' the outcome of an obscure but, from God's perspective, already written text. Good works are less the effort to obtain divine favour than they are the evidence that favour has indeed been granted, the signs by which one can know that his or her election is sure. Receiving the sacrament, then, is an opportunity to reflect 'vpon thy disposition' and 'conclude thine eternall state.' Donne may identify with those who advocate the Atonement as the very source of good works – who hold, as Donne says elsewhere, that Christ has 'given us money to pay [our debt] our selves' (7.227). But in the Christmas sermon, the question of to whom in the end the Atonement will apply is concomitant with the call to scrutinize one's 'disposition' at the Lord's table. The prophet conjured at Communion to 'chide' is called upon to rewrite Simeon's characters on the parchment of a contrite, penitent soul. But it would appear that he or she is less co-author than copyist of a completed work – one that, according to the logic of predestinarian doctrine, is to remain unpublished even if accessible to the more extreme optimists and pessimists alike.

As Donne and his auditory are identified with this early recipient of salvation, so is Simeon but one of several related biblical types:

> Simeon had informed himself, out of Daniel, and the other Prophets, that
> the time of Messias coming was neare: As Daniel had informed himselfe out
> of Ieremy, and the other Prophets, that the time of the Deliverance from
> Babylon, was neare: Both waited patiently, and yet both prayed for the

accelerating of that, which they waited for; Daniel for the Deliverance, Simeon for the Epiphany. (7.290)

By placing the communicant in proximity to a scriptural character who in turn is prefigured by others, Donne exploits a popular method of biblical interpretation. Barbara Lewalski points out that typology for Donne, as for others, is not confined to scripture as its fit object; rather, it expands from exemplary biblical models to include the seventeenth-century Christian within whom 'God's vast typological patterns' operate.[42] The alphabet which constitutes Simeon's exemplary status, drawn from both scripture and the church fathers, is to be spelled out again in the life of each communicant. Simeon's age, priesthood, righteousness, devotion, and patience have their own scriptural correspondents, their own series of types; and all are brought to bear on the present repository of these reconstructed 'characters': each celebrant present this day at St Paul's.

There is also a sacrificial aspect to this conflation of types. Jesus' parents offered him at the Temple as 'the little body of a sucking childe,' which 'in the Sacrament' is 'not sucking, but bleeding.' So Simeon made a customary offering, a pair each of turtledoves and pigeons, and so is a similar sacrifice required of Donne's auditory. Turtle and pigeon represent, respectively, 'solitary and contemplative' and 'active, and sociable' lives, both affirmed as 'indifferent' – that is, good and acceptable in so far as offered to God (7.282–3). Donne's is a humanist Simeon for whom private devotion and public obligation are intimately related, thus comprising for Donne's auditory an ideal model of behaviour and attitude. The motion from Temple Presentation of the Christ child, to Simeon's sacrificial offering, to the supreme sacrifice of the Atonement, 'not sucking, but bleeding,' is extended finally to the sacrifice of the corporate body at the sacrament of Holy Communion:

> And so having thus far made this profit of these circumstances in the action it selfe, appliable to us as receivers of the Sacrament, that as the childe Jesus was first presented to God in the Temple, so for your children, (the children of your bodies, and the children of your mindes, and the children of your hands, all your actions, and intentions) that you direct them first upon God ... (7.283)

These temporal offspring are analogous both to the sucking child of Simeon's epiphany and to the bleeding sacrifice of the Atonement; and all are gathered together 'in the action it selfe' at the sacrament, an observation made poignant by Donne's reference to Simeon's characters as 'Elements in the making up of this man' (7.290). These 'Elements' include not only the present disposition of the participant and the 'characters' derived from exemplary models in the past, but also future attitude and actions. As members of a '*Regale Sacerdotium ... a Royall Priesthood*' (7.286), Donne's auditory are cautioned to be mindful of their priestly status. To come to Communion 'is to take Orders' and 'no man that hath taken Orders, can deprive himselfe, or devest his Orders, when he will. Thou art bound to continue in the same holinesse after, in which thou presentest thy selfe at that Table' (7.287). Present spiritual disposition thus both dictates and depends on that of the past and future: 'the life that thou leadest all the yeare, will shew mee, with what minde thou camest to the Sacrament, to day.' The communicant's assimilation of Simeon's 'characters' includes a commitment to the responsibilities of priesthood. And just as the official priest is to live in a 'continuall Epiphany,' so is the individual believer bound through the Communion ceremony to imbue all of his or her remaining earthly moments with the same holy intentions exercised during that pivotal occasion. The vertical relationship of the communicant with the divine at the Eucharist is to inform all the lived plane of temporal existence, for the Priest/believer 'should never looke off from God' (7.286). As Donne advises elsewhere, 'Wish every day a Sunday, and every meale a Sacrament, and every discourse a Homily' (5.373), so that both sacrament and word inform the religious quotidian. The Eucharist thus takes on an apocalyptic dimension, its temporal, ritual status gesturing beyond the present moment toward the whole life of each participant and his or her place in God's scheme – in short, one's 'eternall state' or 'what thou shalt be forever.'

Donne's use of temporal condensation and typology complements a figurative identification of homily and sacrament. His auditory are encouraged to contextualize their religious duty and obligations as part of a vast design, just as local participation in the Eucharist places each communicant within immediate proximity of a dramatic, spiritual reality for which the trappings and gestures of ritual are a continual reinforcement. Spiritual reflection aided by homiletic exhortation is the psychological counterpart of an external ceremony, this relationship brought into relief through the suggestion that Simeon's 'characters' are 'meate' and 'Elements' to be consumed by the auditor-communicant.

Not unlike the poet of 'The Crosse' and 'The Litanie,' Donne recognizes here his predilection for witty verbal constructions and thus cautions his auditory to hear the 'Sermon of the Sermon' rather than merely the 'Retorique, or the Ethique, or the poetry of the Sermon' (7.293). If a *via media* equilibrium is envisioned in Donne's careful approach both to sacramental and to predestinarian doctrine, so does his attitude toward the *ars prædicandi* include a warning that the preacher's artistry might impede rather than mediate the communication of God's grace. This would support Dennis Quinn's observation that Donne, while an enthusiastic proponent of rhetorical eloquence, also was aware of the danger of indulging *elecutio,* the expression of truth, at the expense of *inventio,* the discovery of truth in its transcendent, pre-verbal state.[43] Doubt as to the extent rhetoric can be extricated from the truths it conveys is not unlike Donne's varying opinion as to the extent and manner of the Eucharistic species' participation in the gifts they represent, or, again, of the role of the saved in their salvation. In all three cases, it is a question of the degree to which spiritual realities are dependent upon external mediation, whether bread, works, or word. Sacrament and homily have in common the problem of communicating divine truths even while constituting, in their very mediatory status, a reminder of just how distant or ineffable those truths ultimately are. Debora Shuger identifies a tension in Renaissance thought, stemming from Aristotle, between *magnitudo* and *præsentia,* terms roughly corresponding to Donne's 'Sermon of the Sermon' and 'poetry of the Sermon.' The sermon's doctrinal core, the sermon of the sermon, is humanly inaccessible, of course, apart from the logic and rhetoric which render it intelligible. But this does not preclude its pre-verbal ontological status. According to Aristotle, writes Shuger, there is a gap between that which is intrinsically knowable and that which is knowable by the finite human intellect. In other words, what humans know is only a partial apprehension of what is – reality in its fullest sense – access to which, presumably, is enjoyed only by the mind of God. Renaissance continental rhetorics advocate the role of affectivity in addressing the gap between *magnitudo* and *præsentia* and thus moving the emotions to the love of God. They promote an Augustinian psychology in which affectivity, far from being considered irrational, is seen as a central element of the properly religious mind. At the same time, however, Renaissance psychological theory maintained a hierarchy which, while affirming the ontological priority of images in cognition, nevertheless cast suspicion on their power. Ideally, reason processes and censors the image before granting access to other psychological faculties, but occasionally fails to intercept it, thus allowing for the danger of an unmediated image-idea reaching the appetitive faculty and moving the will to irrational action. But 'whether or not they believed in certain innate principles or moral axioms, those who wrote about the soul in the Renaissance accepted the Aristotelian postulates that all substantive knowledge derives from sense experience and that the mind cannot think without images of sensation.'[44] Whereas in the Christmas sermon Donne is careful to distinguish between the 'poetry of the Sermon' and the 'Sermon of the Sermon,' elsewhere he acknowledges the art of preaching, along with sacraments, as effective means of marrying *magnitudo* and *præsentia*. Rhetoric for Donne, notes Shuger, is that which makes 'absent and remote things present to your understanding,' while sacraments bring Christ 'nearer ... in visible and sensible things' (5.144).[45] The parallel suggests that the rhetorical dress of homily, with its images, figures, and conceits, corresponds to the material aspects of sacrament. Though both Simeon and Christ are otherwise absent, the former is in effect reconstituted by the faithful as they inscribe within themselves his 'characters' as 'syntax and sentences,' while the latter is present via the sacrament accompanying the word. Both processes involve a kind of ingestion, 'that that meate,' both Christ's body and Simeon's exemplary characters, 'may become our body.' That which is absent and remote is brought near, rendered audible, visible, and sensible by sacrament and word.

Donne might have hesitated to identify his auditory's assimilation of homiletic instruction and exempla explicitly as a sacramental process. Indeed, the importance of a reverential attitude toward the 'Sermon of the sermon' is differentiated from that which should apply to reception of the sacrament. To come to the sermon with a 'licencious' attitude is one thing; but 'he that brings this disposition to the Sacrament, ends not in the losse of a benefit, but he acquires, and procures his owne damnation.' Both sermon and sacrament offer benefits to those who would come with a righteous and just attitude not unlike Simeon's. They would appear to differ quite markedly, however, when it comes to the ill-disposed, for whereas the sermon is perhaps but an empty husk of human ingenuity for those whose approach is a 'treacherous comming' to church, the sacramental sign, on the other hand, retains a connection with its signified, only now it is a source of damnation, or, as Donne also says in this context, an ill-disposition is 'at the Sacrament, deadly' (7.293). It would appear that the Eucharist is never an empty sign – as the logic or rhetoric of a sermon may be – but rather is always associated with presence, whether as a blessing to the righteous or damnation to the ill-disposed. Nevertheless, the relative literal or figurative extent of the eating metaphor is far from clear when it is considered that the Eucharist itself inspired no little controversy over the extent to which its signs participate in their holy referents. Just as it is more important to accept than fully to comprehend the mystery of sacramental presence, so is Donne's auditory expected to receive and assimilate Simeon's exemplary godliness as if it were 'Elements' to be ingested. While it is perhaps finally impossible for us to know the actual psychological effect of Donne's conceit on his hearers, neither can we assume its purely figurative status. If rhetoric involves a reconciliation of *magnitudo* and *præsentia*, then the rhetoric of the sermon is never *merely* the rhetoric of the sermon; rather, it is instrumental in bringing remote things near, a means of grace not unlike the word's sacramental coadjutor.

Homily and rhetorical procedure are eucharistic. 'The end of all digestions, and concoctions is assimilation, that that meate may become our body. The end of all consideration of all the actions of such leading and exemplar men, as Simeon was, is assimilation too; That we may be like that man' (7.280–1). Donne's *divisio*, the rhetorical organization whereby the relationship of scriptural text to sermon is established and anticipated, is imbued with sacramental significance. Analogous to the breaking of the consecrated bread and, by extension, to the sacrificial breaking of the Christ body, the sermon has become a means of grace, a necessary component in the soteriological scheme. Division, assimilation, and their subsequent effect – the ability, like Simeon, to 'depart in peace' – are aspects of both sermon and sacrament, each of which, in its own way, manifests the Word become flesh. For Donne, it is a thin line that separates ritual and homiletic art; like ritual, art facilitates greater comprehension of the ineffable truths theology can only dryly assert. The danger, however, as Donne well knew, is that the 'Logick' or 'Retorick' or 'poetry of the Sermon' may somehow contaminate, render less pure, the eternal verities that are the 'Sermon of the Sermon.' The same tension informs both Calvinist soteriology, which is reluctant to compromise God's radical transcendence and sovereign will, and Donne's diatribes against Roman Catholic transubstantiation, the local manifestation of Christ's body and blood. By focusing his auditory's lives, past, present, and future, on the sacramental moment; by promoting a typological fluidity whereby communicant, Simeon, and Christ, sacrament, epiphany, and Atonement, are the interpenetrating topoi of metaphysical wit; by drawing attention to the locally historicized, bodily and sacramental dimensions of the word – through all these means Donne excites a vivid apprehension of the truths he imparts. Hearing the word might thereby approximate Simeon's experience of the Word: 'actually, and really, substantially, essentially, bodily, presentially, personally' (7.280).

Donne sought to combine reverence for sacrament and the ceremonial marks of religious authority with an inward-looking Reform piety. His analogy sacramentalizes the word and thus reifies the effects of pulpit oratory. His method would reconcile a potentially divisive Calvinism with the increasingly sacramental orientation of the religious establishment – the inward spirituality of a scripture- and preaching-centred puritanism with the ceremonial enthusiasm of Donne's avant-garde contemporaries. Donne advances as complementary the potentially contrary imperatives of word and sacrament by conferring eucharistic status on both the 'elements' of his sermon and their desired or intended effect on his auditory. Hearing the word in a ceremonial, sacramental, and public context involves a spiritual ingestion whereby an exemplary moral figure, Simeon at the Temple Presentation, is analysed according to his various attributes or 'characters,' which are then consumed and assimilated by each communicant. Donne's strategy thus exemplifies what Ramie Targoff describes as 'the direct correspondence between outward behaviour and inward thought' in early modern religious subjectivity. But this is far from being, as Targoff implies, just another Foucauldian *régime* penetrating the frontiers of private consciousness.[46] For by capitalizing on the Eucharist's role in self-reflection, by encouraging speculation as to 'what thou shalt be forever,' by bringing that nebulous devotional interiority within such close proximity of the institutional signs that are its surface, Donne promotes the introspective curiosity whose excesses he is also eager to discourage. Public ceremony and ritual may extend, through word and pulpit, beyond the altar to define and regulate religious subjectivity; but there is little to prevent a bridge thus established from personalizing public ritual and thus rendering Donne's auditory priestly agents in their religious edification. Unlike Benjamin Carier in 1613 and the proto-Laudian divines of the early Caroline era, Donne at Christmas 1626 was determined to maintain a moderate predestinarian Calvinism even while advancing sacrament and ceremony as essential elements of Christian worship. The result is an idiosyncratic contribution to the elusive English *via media*, one that promoted ceremonial law and order while careful to maintain that election is finally a private matter.

CHAPTER FOUR

Heart's Altar: Herbert and Presence

If Donne managed to advance a Calvinism compatible with his enthusiasm for sacrament and ceremony, he did so by downplaying and even attacking the predestinarian extremism latent within Reform theology. The potentially dichotomous relationship between predestinarian doctrine and the ritual is evident particularly in his assertion about the sacrament not being a lottery. So explicit a caveat as that found in the 1626 Christmas sermon – an otherwise subtle reconciliation of ceremonial and puritan pieties – derives from the need to confront an issue that had troubled the Elizabethan church, and that for Donne and other moderate English Calvinists in the 1620s had again become controversial.

Whereas the Dean of St Paul's allowed an 'experimental' impulse to inform his sacred verse and, occasionally, his preaching, George Herbert's evangelical and pastoral piety is, with very few exceptions, devoid of predestinarian references. There is some evidence in *The Temple*, however, suggesting Herbert's tacit approval of the more contentious aspects of Calvinist doctrine. In 'Love Unknown' he implies that the 'many' who 'drunk bare wine' suffer considerable disadvantage relative to the speaker for whom 'A friend did steal into my cup for good' (42–3).[1] Herbert was far from reluctant to indulge a sensual view of sacramental grace and these lines may indicate only that he had little sympathy for those who regarded the elements merely as commemorative signs. And yet what is most striking about the passage is its predestinarian suggestion: Herbert allowing, as did Hooker, that the godly might worship alongside the wicked.[2] This subtle manoeuvre maintains both a carnal emphasis and the broad-based vision of church membership sacraments support, while at the same time allowing for the possibility that some who drink and eat are not among the spiritually regenerated. It recalls Donne's playful treatment of the sacramental-predestinarian connection in 'Loves diet' where the mistress's tears and favours, her 'drink' and 'meate,' must for some be 'counterfeit,' for 'eyes which rowle towards all, weepe not, but sweat' (17–18). It echoes indeed the sacramental lottery overtly denigrated in Donne's 1626 Christmas sermon but accompanied nevertheless by implicit endorsement of Reform doctrine. It would appear that predestinarian Calvinism for the speaker of 'Love Unknown' is compatible with an avant-garde fondness for ceremony. The passage is thus an exception to Peter Lake's alignment of sacramental enthusiasm with anti-Calvinism.[3] Herbert does not seem to have shared the concern of those who, like Benjamin Carier, worried that predestination compromises the sacramental dimension of Christian ministry and the social cohesion it supports.

In 'The Water-course,' more famously, Herbert allows that God

gives to man, as he sees fit, $\left\{\begin{array}{l}\text{Salvation.}\\\text{Damnation.}\end{array}\right.$ (10)

In this uncharacteristically controversial lyric Herbert is perhaps deliberately playful, never clarifying the pronoun's antecedent – God or man? R.V. Young calls Herbert's position here Thomist, one that sustains *both* free will and predestination.[4] But if this is meant to distance Herbert from Calvin, it does not suffice, for surely Calvin maintained that *his* position retains human free will, at least with respect to sin, insisting, for example, that the reprobate are 'justly charged against the malice and depravity of their hearts.'[5] Whatever the logical contradictions involved in such assertions, Calvin was as concerned as Aquinas and the church fathers both to make sin a strictly human responsibility and grace an unmerited gift. Differences – and they are significant – arise only in working out the technical details involved in reconciling such claims with free will. A more general difference is the extent to which Calvin was willing logically to go in support of these cornerstone truths. By raising the issue of predestination so explicitly in 'The Water-course,' Herbert thus reveals his affinity with Calvin's own willingness to force consideration of the issue even while demurring from stating clearly his own place within the English Calvinist tradition. As David Como has argued, the 'hegemonic force of the predestinarian consensus' among English Calvinists 'was strongest when it was tacit, assumed and unquestioned.'[6] His reluctance to divulge anything like a firm doctrinal position, however, did not prevent Herbert from expressing his confidence in God's mercy, for it is the overwhelming presence of sacramental grace, joined to the communicant's willingness to receive it, that permeates both poem and title:

> turn the pipe and waters course
> To serve thy sinnes, and furnish thee with store
> Of sov'raigne tears, springing from true remorse.   (6–8)

Whatever his predestinarian theology, Herbert does not seem to have been troubled by Calvinist doctrine even though the psychological intensity sustained in *The Temple* evokes an acute spiritual diffidence and awareness of human depravity. Herbert's sacramental puritanism, unlike that of *La Corona* and *Holy Sonnets*, is less an escape into sacrament from a subjectively-mediated grace than a sacramentalization of the devotional sphere itself. Eucharistic topoi for him were not only necessary and effectual means of grace but also the conceptual and psychological framework within which to imagine its application to the human heart.

Historian Anthony Milton has identified Herbert as among the earliest of divines 'to proclaim the new Anglo-centric orthodoxy' of the seventeenth-century church. Whereas for earlier conformists the Church of England was a champion of true religion against supposedly anti-Christian Rome, the later Jacobean and Caroline ecclesiastical establishment sought to extricate itself from the confessional struggles of European Protestantism. This middle road was based not on the ideal moderation it eventually came to signify in later historiography, but rather on a complex mixture of nationalism; the growing inclination to jettison an earlier Protestant identity; and the need to establish a greater sense of contiguity with pre-Reformation ecclesiastical and theological tradition. Distinct from foreign Calvinism, the English middle way in the 1620s and 30s yielded increasingly to an emphasis on sacrament and ceremony to support the inclusivist and erastian policies of a state institution. However, if Herbert could be said implicitly to have been an exponent of Peter Lake's 'avant-garde conformity' – the aggressive promotion of a preeminently sacerdotal and sacramental vision of the church – his poetry nevertheless exemplifies the 'internal religious experience' Milton identifies as a distinctive feature of both moderate and more radical puritan divinity.[7]

R.V. Young is the most recent and a very formidable critic of the Protestant poetics that has dominated Herbert studies during the last several decades. His observation that such work 'fails to do justice to either Catholic or Protestant, forcing both parties into narrow ideological categories' is long overdue. Particularly relevant to the present study is Young's recognition of the relevance of sacrament for meditational practices. 'The most intimate and withdrawn of *private* devotions,' he writes, 'involves the urge to escape the self' so that 'solitude is only the means to a profounder communion.'[8] Young does not consider, however, the extent to which the relationship between sacrament and devotional solitude could be one of conflict rather than cooperation, a conflict rooted in the confessional struggles of the English church. Critical of the 'new-historicist inclination [to] try to explain devotional and doctrinal motifs in *The Temple* in terms of the socio-political imperatives of Jacobean and Caroline culture,' he is concerned that 'unless the poetry is, at some point, considered in its own right as poetry, then there is, finally, no point in studying it at all.' The detailed close readings provided here should allay such concern. But Young's insistence that Herbert 'was not bound to any of the particular party platforms current in his day' too hastily dismisses the considerable body of Church of England historiography produced in recent years and its relevance for our understanding of the period's literature. Herbert's doctrinal elusiveness, I suggest, is itself a political strategy – eirenic in intent and pastoral in motivation – but deeply aware of the controversies it navigates. His eventual removal to Bemerton no more placed him beyond the polemical fray than his devotional inwardness can be separated from its ceremonial contexts. Reading *The Temple* in light of church politics is neither 'reductive' nor does it 'threaten' the author's 'poetic vitality.'[9] On the contrary, that very vitality is evident in his subtle and often dazzling engagement with the socio-religious turbulence of the period. Herbert's heavenly verse in this respect is firmly on the ground, whatever our definition of poetry 'as poetry.'

Young likely would endorse C.A. Patrides' observation that in the Eucharist lies 'the marrow of Herbert's sensibility,'[10] but this attractive phrase does not account for the tensions informing the English *via media*. Herbert's middle road is far from straight. The path he forged is best thought of not as one nor even as a harmony of disparate theologies but rather as a dissonant blend of the potentially contrary imperatives of public ceremony and private devotion. There is in his oeuvre a marked ambivalence toward the relationship between these modes of piety, particularly as they converge on his treatment of the Eucharist. The two are brought together successfully in *The Temple*, but this suc-

cess consists precisely in the drama resulting from the ideological conflict the poems trace.

Herbert was among those English divines whose reluctance to articulate
explicitly the *modus* of divine presence did not prevent them from rever-
ing the material aspects of sacramental ritual. These churchmen, like
Hooker, made some effort to distinguish between simply corporeal and
more mystical understandings of sacramental presence. But if they were
wary of the scholastic accretions attached to the Tridentine doctrine of
transubstantiation, particularly the Aristotelian categories of substance
and accident, English divines in the 1620s began to entertain the possibility of alternative interpretations. As Dugmore observes, the Roman
doctrine actually denied presence *in loco*, allowing the body and blood a
reality only *per modum substantiae*. While it is not surprising that many saw
in the Tridentine formula a too carnal and therefore idolatrous rendering, schooled divines would have recognized that the subtleties of the
doctrine did not make such an interpretation necessary.[11] As Milton has
suggested, this may help to explain why such clergy as Andrewes, Montagu,
Neile, Cosin, and Laud advanced a sacramental vision of the ministry
bordering on popery, while maintaining, if sometimes disingenuously, a
hostile stance toward the Roman church per se.[12] It is safe to speculate
that one of the causes why avant-garde and Laudian divines were accused
of popery by their opponents is the spectre of transubstantiation raised
by this emphasis on ceremony and the sacramental dimension of the
ministry. Such fears, notes Milton, were not entirely unwarranted. John
Cosin, for example, endorsed the Jesuit Maldonatus's moderate views
on the eucharistic sacrifice and went so far as to advocate a doctrinal
rapprochement with Rome. Cosin's contemporary, William Forbes, denied
the heretical status of transubstantiation and consubstantiation. Perhaps
most disturbing about such popish flirtations was the implicit suggestion
that the Tridentine canons on the Eucharist or even the Roman Missal
itself could be interpreted in a manner harmonious with English doctrine and that Roman divines such as Maldonatus or Sancta Clara were
willing to offer such interpretations. Cosin, Forbes, and others may have
identified transubstantiation with simplified, vulgar interpretations of
Roman doctrine common among both moderate and nonconforming
puritans. Or they simply may have recognized the futility of encouraging
tolerance for a formula whose complexity precluded popular access, in
which case their occasional anti-Roman outbursts were less doctrinal in

motivation than politically expedient. In any event, it is clear these divines sought not only to promote sacraments as essential means of grace, but on occasion appeared to advance sacramental formulae indistinguishable from that of their supposed Roman foes, and thus inadvertently exacerbated fears of crypto-popery.[13]

Like other establishment divines, Herbert more often than not sought to avoid controversy while maintaining both a sacerdotal and sacramental vision of the church. Richard Hooker provided Herbert and others with a model of behaviour suitable for approaching Holy Communion:

> What moveth us to argue of the maner how life should come by bread, our dutie beinge here but to take what is offered, and most assuredly to rest perswaded of this, that can wee but eate wee are safe? ... Let it therefore be sufficient for me presentinge my selfe at the Lordes table to knowe what there I receive from him, without searchinge or inquiringe of the maner how Christ performeth his promise.[14]

Herbert essentially agrees, even if his approach to such mystery is far from Hooker's measured rationality. The Country Parson,

> being to administer the Sacraments, is at a stand with himself, how or what behaviour to assume for so holy things. Especially at Communion times he is in a great confusion, as being not only to receive God, but to break, and administer him. Neither finds he any issue in this, but to throw himself down at the throne of grace, saying, Lord, thou knowest what thou didst, when thou apointedst it to be done thus; therefore doe thou fulfill what thou didst appoint; for thou art not only the feast, but the way to it. (*Works*, 259)

Poetic endorsement of this *mysterium tremendum* approach is apparent in 'Divinitie,' where theological curiosity is as presumptuous as the new philosophy's obsession with astronomical inquiry. Among the objects cut and carved 'with the edge of wit' (7) is the Eucharist, which Herbert implies should be regarded as a simple matter and exempt from controversy:

> But he doth bid us take his bloud for wine.
>   Bid what he please; yet I am sure,
> To take and taste what he doth there designe,
>   Is all that saves, and not obscure.   (21–4)

It may be that the sacrament is not the least of 'Gordian knots' (20) after all. The first line of this stanza certainly *does* obscure, grammatically allowing both the innocuous analogy 'blood *as* wine' and the literal substitution 'blood *in place of* wine,' the equivocation exacerbated in the third line by 'what,' which invites the gloss 'whatever.'[15] The obscurity does not so much evade doctrinal commitment as deliberately avoid controversy and what can only amount to an absurd probing of that which finally is mysterious. 'Yet,' however, suggests no little reluctance to rest content with the mysterious words of institution. It is as if Herbert either understands the scripture to be saying one thing and proceeds to assert another, or, more likely, is frustrated by an obscurity inherent in the institution itself and, though allowing the ambiguity in his own assessment, has in mind a certain preference nonetheless. It may be recalled that whereas Christ says 'take and eat,' Herbert writes 'take and taste,' which, while not alone conclusive proof, does suggest the need for as physical an apprehension of God's 'designe' as is possible.

Sensual vividness is evident in an earlier stanza, where the mutual proximity of 'broacht' species and pierced side nevertheless is accompanied by a warning against excessive curiosity:

> Could not that Wisdome, which first broacht the wine,
>   Have thicken'd it with definitions?
> And jagg'd his seamlesse coat, had that been fine,
>   With curious questions and divisions?   (9–12)

'Wisdome' indeed eventually did thicken the wine offered his disciples – but with blood, not definitions – which only advances further the notion that the cup received in remembrance is somehow that which it signifies. It would appear on this account that the overly curious 'edge of wit' does not pertain to any particular doctrinal formula. Rather, the poem condemns scholastic rationalism for applying precise formulae to what must remain a mystery, and thus for mocking inadvertantly that for which Herbert would retain the utmost dignity and reverence. In the final stanza we find that 'Faith needs no staffe of flesh, but stoutly can / To heav'n alone both go, and leade' (27–8). Only faith, which, like 'Divinities transcendent skie' is beyond material limitation, can provide the impetus truly to 'take and taste,' to believe that in so doing one receives that which is 'all that saves' (24). Rather than advance theological formulae which render sacramental efficacy rationally palatable, Herbert advocates believing in the means of grace regardless. By instructing the 'foolish man' to burn his 'Epicycles' and 'Break all thy spheres' (25–6) he attacks Ptolemaic apologists desperate to defend their waning cosmology with sophisticated and ultimately misguided models. Trans- and consubstantiation, Calvinist virtualism – these are as inadequate as their scholastic predecessors in addressing the mystery behind Jesus' words of institution. To persist in such scrutiny is tantamount to crucifying him anew, this time with 'curious questions and divisions.'

But perhaps simply to 'take and taste' grace without trying to understand how grace is imparted in the sacrament is as difficult, finally, as retaining for the universe an Aristotelian hierarchy while dismissing the models which render it intelligible. Ignoring his own advice, Herbert left a record of 'curious questions' about the Eucharist by way of two very different versions of 'The H. Communion.' In B and the *editio princeps*, Herbert avoids explicit mention of the various doctrinal formulae evident in the earlier Williams MS.[16] He begins by rejecting the notion that God might be conveyed 'in' such ceremonial trappings as 'rich furniture ... fine aray' and 'wedge of gold' (1–4). It is important to note, however, that even if many of his contemporaries would have recognized these as the trappings of the Roman Mass, Herbert does not dismiss the use of such external finery per se. One reason for this may be the ambiguities built into the Elizabethan Settlement. Whereas the Prayer Book and Act of Uniformity both had called for 'common bread,' the Queen's Injunction stipulated wafers (Herbert's 'wedge of gold'?). In effect, observes Conrad Russell, 'everyone who took communion had to disobey one of these requirements.'[17] Herbert's objection, then, pertains less to ceremonial preference than to the idea that externals of any sort might themselves effectually conjure or somehow contain their divine referents. For if they did, the sacrament's primarily internal and noncorporeal application would be compromised: 'thou should'st without me still have been, / Leaving within me sinne' (5–6). But if the first stanza leads one to expect a moderate regard for the elements of bread and wine, the second describes a sacramental efficacy every bit as carnal as the Roman Catholic doctrine of transubstantiation:

> But by the way of nourishment and strength
>   Thou creep'st into my breast;
>   Making thy way my rest,
>   And thy small quantities my length;
> Which spread their forces into every part,
>   Meeting sinnes force and art.   (7–12)

This essentially physiological description, while seeking to avoid the problem of determining how or at which point in the process the species become involved in conveying the sacrificial body and blood, nevertheless suggests their instrumental and not merely representational status. Sacramental controversy resides in the silence between the first and second stanzas, between awkwardness over the precise role of ceremonial trappings and scrutiny of a mysterious and spiritual process. Herbert deftly avoids such controversy by focusing on the elements' internal operation, maintaining their carnal status while accommodating a Reform emphasis on individuals' souls as the collective and primary site of divine presence.

The separation of 'souls and fleshy hearts' (15) in the following stanzas nevertheless continues to suggest the need for a physical explanation of sacramental grace. God's 'small quantities' cannot overcome the wall which restrains mere 'rebel-flesh' (17). Indeed, the 'souls most subtile rooms' are penetrable only by 'grace,' which, however, 'with these elements comes,' and which, having entered the soul, sends 'Dispatches' to the sentinels or 'spirits refin'd' (19–24) guarding the way. They in turn distribute medicinal sacramental benefits throughout the body. The process, figuratively, is a military coup: external finery accompanies but does not directly communicate divine presence, which, nevertheless, is somehow connected with the elements, but only after they are ingested. The masticated and divinely invigorated species then 'spread their forces into every part'; but it is grace, the commander-in-chief, that breaches the stronghold and secures both the soul's terrain and a hitherto 'rebel-flesh.'

It may be that what I have described as bordering on a Roman Catholic sacramental position is but the poetic description of what is not a physical process after all. This would be in keeping with Calvin's point that God uses material means to communicate a more rarefied grace. The idea that presence is conveyed 'with' or alongside, rather than 'in' the elements is thoroughly in keeping with Reform theology. The sacrament, rather than an accident veiling an inward substance or, as for Luther, a consubstantial manifestation of the hypostatic union, is instead an Augustinian seal ratifying a sacramental reality solely in the heart or soul of the communicant. It is, writes Calvin, 'an outward sign by which the Lord seals on our consciences the promises of his good will toward us.'[18] R.V. Young insists that 'with these elements comes' excludes a Calvinist reading. But the poem does *not* say that either God or grace is, as in Young's gloss, 'present *in* the eucharistic species.'[19] Young quotes

Calvin's view that sacraments 'do not of themselves bestow any grace, but they announce and tell us' that grace has been conferred.[20] The key phrase here is 'not of themselves' – not, that is, *ex opere operato*. 'With' in Herbert's poem upholds rather than excludes Calvin's 'announce and tell us.' 'Nourishment and strength,' on the other hand, would appear to invite Calvin's condemnation of the idea that heaven's king might go a progress through the guts of a beggarly sinner, suggesting that the elements are in fact changed at the moment of ingestion. Just as the idea of the individual soul as site of a cosmic struggle would not have seemed odd to the early modern Christian, so did Herbert regard the personal drama of redemption as a very real rather than merely figurative battle – the arena corporeal, the struggle immanent. Whatever the extent of that war's reality, the forensic and equivocal 'Not,' 'But,' 'Yet,' and 'Onely' introducing each stanza are symptomatic less of a clear and stable *via media* than the eirenic disposition of the Country Parson, who would that he were content to know that God is 'not only the feast, but the way to it.'[21]

The B version of 'H. Communion' is sensitive to ecclesiastical controversy over the relative importance of ceremony and discipline vis-à-vis preaching and doctrine.[22] This becomes even more evident when it is compared with the earlier version of the Williams MS, where Herbert's theological sympathies are more clearly discernible.[23] The first stanza suggests two competing theories which recall early Reformation controversy. Roman trans- and Lutheran consubstantiation offer a choice between the notion that the bread's substance is wholly transformed and a doctrine of ubiquity wherein God's substantial presence does not exclude that of the bread. The choice, in hindsight, suggests a parody of Luther's notorious struggle with Rome, for in the following stanza Herbert dismisses the issue of the bread's status. What really matters is that his 'gratious Lord' (1) and 'all thy traine' (10) are present in the rite: how this comes about, suggests Herbert, is not nearly as important as simply recognizing that it does. In the third stanza, however, this adiaphoric stance yields to a more specifically Calvinist position: presence is asserted, but is confined to the communicant's soul; it is indicated, but not embodied, by the species of bread and wine. Explicit here, it is this doctrine that might be said silently to connect the first and second stanzas of the later version of the poem; and yet there 'nourishment and strength' suggest a physiological grace.

The first stanza's suggestion that Luther was as mistaken as his Roman foes when it comes to sacramental theology is reiterated at the centre of the poem where 'Impanation' (25), the Lutheran view of sacramental presence based on the hypostatic union of the Incarnation, is explicitly rejected. Rather than bread becoming God, according to Luther, the divine substance becomes united with that of bread, just as the Word becomes flesh at its human birth.[24] That God's nature takes on man's is, for this poem, doctrinally sound; but the notion that that nature is united with mere bread is simply intolerable. Herbert here is willing to allow a significant role for the species, but he is wary, as was Calvin, of compromising the divine nature. Rather, it is 'My flesh, & fleshly villany' that 'made thee dead' (29–30). If there is a sacrificial element in Holy Communion it is in God's gracious identification with the communicant's 'rebel-flesh,' the later poem's version of 'fleshly villany.' And yet this new focus on the Incarnation abandons entirely the poem's earlier ecumenism by doubting whether the elements are at all involved in the flesh they supposedly declare: 'That fflesh is there, mine eyes deny: / And what should flesh but flesh discry, / The noblest sence of five?' (31–3). The species point to rather than embody a process that occurs on a strictly spiritual level. As with the later poem, the W 'H. Communion' registers a gap between flesh and soul, though here the absence of any physiological explanation only exacerbates the absence of Calvin's radically transcendent God:

> Into my soule this cannot pass;
> fflesh (though exalted) keeps his grass
>   And cannot turn to soule.
> Bodyes & Minds are different Spheres,
> Nor can they change their bounds & meres,
>   But keep a constant Pole.   (37–42)

Yet in the final stanza the 'gift of all gifts,' unlike flesh, can indeed 'pass.' This gift, of course, is none other than grace, explicitly identified in the later poem where, by dispatching sacramental and physiological 'spirits refin'd,' it overcomes 'the wall that parts / Our souls and fleshy hearts.'

In the earlier 'H. Communion,' then, Herbert allows little if any interpenetration of flesh and soul, maintaining instead a vision of sacramental grace as predominantly noncorporeal. The later B poem, conversely, is eirenic in tone, accommodating a more integrated, amorphous relationship among body, soul, grace, and the material means of grace. Michael Schoenfeldt, in his examination of the eating trope in the poem, gets it right when he remarks that the 'entry of God into his mortal subject through the medium of food at once delineates the border between matter and spirit and proceeds benevolently to transgress it.'[25] These poems thus frame a linear development in Herbert's sacramental thought. The time between their respective compositions parallels a period in Stuart church history, from the 1618 Synod of Dort to the advent of the Laudian archbishopric, in which sacrament and ceremony became increasingly central to mainstream English divinity. Herbert's accommodation of the ecclesiastical establishment's fondness for ceremony may indicate a growing impatience with what some perceived to be immoderate emphasis on preaching, doctrine, and more private pieties. Whether the change is a reflection of spiritual growth or a response to political realities is difficult to determine; such things, of course, are impossible to separate. Whatever his theological itinerary, the two versions of 'H. Communion' document the array of sacramental theories available to Herbert's contemporaries. While there is no doubt that he shared with other establishment divines a concern that the Eucharist somehow communicate divine presence, the *modus* of communication as variously expressed in the poetry suggests he would have been far from embracing wholeheartedly the Laudian ceremonial program first implemented in 1633, the year of his death. Herbert's beloved English *via media* was less a harmonization of competing ecclesiastical and doctrinal ideologies than a way lacking both clarity and certainty.[26]

Similar though less obvious revision is evident in 'The Altar' where Herbert pleads, 'O let thy blessed sacrifice be mine, / And sanctifie this Altar to be thine' (15–16). In the edition of 1633 the printer Thomas Buck rendered 'heart,' 'sacrifice' and both occurrences of 'Altar' in small upper case type, with spaces between each letter, thereby visually evoking the association of Jesus' broken body with the bread of the Eucharist. Whatever the authority of these effects, we do know that in the Williams MS 'blessed' was originally 'onely' before the author corrected it.[27] *Via media* analyses of the poem, though accurate, fail to allow that the balance it strikes is somewhat more precarious than it would appear. 'The sacrificial altar or communion table,' according to McLaughlin and Thomas, for example, 'is in the heart.'[28] Elizabeth Clarke's apparently Anglican view sees a settled balance, 'a thorough mixture' of inner spirituality and outer poetic form.[29] For M. Thomas Hester, similarly, 'the final shape of "The Altar" is *both* an *altar* and an *I* – an image of the speaker's self and his Christ.'[30] Herbert's revision, however, suggests conflicting tendencies not altogether erased from the poem's final state.

It is doubtful that 'onely' was simply an error on the part of an aman-
uensis;[31] more likely, Herbert boldly removed what was a conservative
qualification – namely, the denial that atoning sacrifice is somehow
replicated in the sacrament.

More ambiguous is 'The Invitation.' Whereas Jesus said simply 'drink'
and 'this is my blood,' Herbert adds a rather specific qualification:
'drink this, / Which *before* ye drink is bloud' (11–12, my emphasis). It
certainly is possible that Herbert means only to distinguish between what
is taken in the sacrament and what flowed at Golgotha; but it is at least as
likely that he addresses the issue so carefully avoided in the 1633 'H.
Communion,' namely, the question of the spatial and temporal occurrence of body and blood – of when and where, exactly, the 'friend' of
'Love Unknown' steals into the speaker's cup. Whereas the blank space
between the first and second stanzas of the later 'H. Communion' allows
him to avoid dealing too specifically with the manner of sacramental
presence, here Herbert appears to advocate a change in the species *prior*
to ingestion, thus going considerably beyond the moderate or Calvinist
position which allows only a spiritual presence among the souls of the
elect. Herbert is thus deeply concerned to maintain for the communication of sacramental grace a considerable materiality, however inward
and 'spiritual' its application. 'The Agonie' likewise renders the Atonement personal, intimate, and visceral, Christ's sacrifice and the benefits
it affords communicated via the sacrament:

> Sinne is that presse and vice, which forceth pain
> To hunt his cruell food through ev'ry vein
>
> ...
>
> Love is that liquor sweet and most divine,
> Which my God feels as bloud; but I, as wine.   (11–12, 17–18)

The juxtaposition of these two couplets is startling. The Christ who in
Pauline terms becomes sin (1 Pet. 2.24; 2 Cor. 5.21) is filled here with sin's
poison, which displaces the divine blood that in turn becomes that of the
communicant, who, presumably, was filled hitherto with the sin now
coursing through his saviour's veins. The final line may suggest a moderate sacramental position; indeed, Hutchinson called it 'an inversion of the
doctrine of transubstantiation.'[32] But 'feels' is at best ambiguous, allowing
that the speaker's phenomenal experience of wine may intimate what in
fact is a bloody affair, the two levels, appearance and veiled reality, evoking
the Aristotelian categories of substance and accident evoked in the

Tridentine canons on the Eucharist. Herbert, however, stops short of identifying explicitly the *modus* whereby divine presence is actualized. Young's assertion that in 'The Agonie' Christ 'is truly present under the form of' the elements is unwarranted, for nowhere in the poem is Herbert this specific. The poet indeed may 'not have been happy' with the 1552 Book of Common Prayer and its presence-denying Black Rubric, but the removal of the rubric and an intensification of sacramental language in the 1559 and subsequent versions more provided Herbert with a rationale for specifying the modus of sacramental presence than the poem allows Young's reading.[33] And yet the communicant's *experience* of wine rather than blood may be seen as compatible with transubstantiation after all, his senses apprehending as wine (accident) what is actually blood (substance). By this 'liquor sweet' the benefits obtained by Christ's surrogate sufferings under the winepress of just wrath are transferred – or transfused – minus the sufferings themselves. Recourse 'Unto Mount Olivet' for the speaker is purely imaginative, even if excruciating: 'A man so wrung with pains, that all his hair, / His skinne, his garments bloudie be' suggests a meditative sharing in Christ's sufferings, but poetic artifice renders sweet that which for another was truly agonizing, just as the accidental species of a Roman sacrament veil even as they embody their substantial counterpart.

Herbert's simultaneous appreciation and distrust of the senses are evident in several lines from 'The Pearl':

> I know the projects of unbridled store:
> My stuffe is flesh, not brasse; my senses live,
> And grumble oft, that they have more in me
> Then he that curbs them being but one to five.   (26–9)[34]

In 'The Odour. 2 Cor. 2.15,' on the other hand, '*My Master*' is not only a sweet sound; such words are 'a rich sent / Unto the taster' (2–3) who would

>   thrust into them both:
>   That I might finde
>   What cordials make this curious broth,
> This broth of smells, that feeds and fats my minde.   (7–10)

The poem thus boldly renders reflection on the word a carnal meditation. A gesture returning the favour shows the poet eager to allow even

God the physical indulgences enjoyed by his creatures. Herbert would make of himself a pleasing and, indeed, pleasant offering – to 'creep & grow / To some degree of spicinesse to thee!' (14–15). Though there is scriptural precedence elsewhere for the idea that the devout life is as a sweet-smelling sacrifice to God (Phil. 4.18), the scripture cited in the poem's title hardly seems appropriate, for there St Paul writes of the smell of Christ in his followers as life to the saved or the stench of death to the reprobate. There is no mention there of *God's* olfactory delight.

For Herbert, then, the material, physiological possibilities of eucharistic presence are not only a doctrinal matter; they go to the very heart of his sacramental poetic. An indulgence in the 'beauty of holiness,' the poet's reflection on a stained-glass depiction of the Eucharist in 'Love-joy' is also a pithy reflection on the sacramental sign. While the emphasis is on simply recognizing and accepting the presence of Christ, the speaker cannot resist offering an explanation, to wit, the letters J and C are 'the bodie and the letters both / Of *Joy* and *Charitie*' (6–7). His interlocutor corroborates and adds 'It figures *JESUS CHRIST*' (8). The simultaneous presence of both body and sign is common to most sacramental formulae; here, however, the letters are 'Anneal'd on every bunch' (3), thus suggesting an inscription which goes beyond the surface to share in a portion of the grapes' substance. The fruit is neither merely a vehicle for J and C, nor is it displaced by them. And because they do not simply reside on the surface, the letters are more than disembodied signs; rather, J and C do not cease to be signs even as they are inextricable from the matter to which they are joined. If the poem merely allegorizes presence, it does so by exploiting the incarnational paradox, based on analogy, that a thing can be another thing while not ceasing to be itself, that the Word does not cease being the Word in being united with flesh. The specific theological context here is Lutheran ubiquity and con- rather than Roman transubstantiation, suggested by the fact that both speaker and interlocutor, rather than witness in 'Love-joy' a transformation, discover instead what has always been there. Not that it matters for one who is 'never loth / To spend my judgement' (4–5) on such concerns. What does matter is the end result of meditation, speculative or otherwise, in this case a profound realization in hindsight of the potentially sacramental dimension of ordinary reality.

This need to perceive in creation's signs evidence of divinity is the essence of sacramental desire, for such evidence corroborates the otherwise subjective and fleeting ephemera of faith. And yet, as Herbert insists in the B 'H. Communion,' divine presence and the grace it brings must be experienced internally to be effective. For the early Stuart English devout the inability to do so suggested perhaps not so much atheism as something much worse – exclusion from God's plan and the register or book of life. This is why it was so important for the pastorally inclined Herbert to realize in the sacramental sign an effectual, objective communication of grace and not merely the outward symbol of a process with which it has no material connection. This pastoral concern is effectively combined with Herbert's wonder at the incarnational paradox in 'Sepulchre,' where persistent grace etches out a place in the stoniest of hearts, here a slab on which the crucified body is laid. Notable here is the idea of the body of the word, of the crucified lord as an engraved character:

> And as of old the Law by heav'nly art
> Was writ in stone; so thou, which also art
> The letter of the word, find'st no fit heart
> To hold thee.   (16–19)

It is in Christ's death that the Word become flesh, the Logos as body, is most significant. For it is in death, a death here brought about by the hardness and resistance of stony hearts – figuratively, of the body of the text against its preverbal logos – that the infinite Word 'also [is] / The letter of the word.' This is the Eucharist's true incarnational significance. For by virtue of becoming flesh, the Word undergoes death, sacrifices itself in order to be in the fullest ontological sense. Herbert in no way attenuates the scandal of divine sacrifice; he does not succumb to the temptation to extricate the spirit of the word from the letter, the Logos from its inscribed/inscribing body. Rather, the poem closes with no sign of either love or stony resistance, word or flesh, giving in:

> Yet do we still persist as we began,
> And so should perish, but that nothing can,
> Though it be cold, hard, foul, from loving man
>   Withhold thee.   (20–3)

This acute sensitivity to the scandalous implications of the Incarnation explains why Herbert, like other avant-garde divines, was reluctant to abandon a carnal sacramental orientation; for it is through the insistent fleshly status of the eucharistic species that the paradox of the Word become flesh is stubbornly proclaimed.

Like the Elizabethan Articles, Calvin in the *Institutes,* and Donne in the 1626 Christmas sermon, Herbert recognized the crucial relevance of sacrament for the psychological dimension of Reform soteriology. His emphasis on the carnal features of the Eucharist, however, goes considerably beyond that of Calvin, the Articles, and even Donne, thus evincing a truly avant-garde attitude toward ceremony and advancing the ecclesiastical unity for which sacraments provided the cement. And yet Herbert's lyrics at the same time are among the most personal and introspective of his era. If anyone created a devotional space susceptible to predestinarian anxiety and doubt, it was him. As we shall see, however, it is precisely his stubborn fondness for sacrament and ceremony that allowed Herbert to avoid the potentially paralysing syndromes of an otherwise puritan psyche.

CHAPTER FIVE

Sacramental Puritanism:
Herbert's English *via media*

Undoubtedly a keen proponent of the church's sacramental policies and practices, Herbert nonetheless cautioned against an overly enthusiastic regard for the material trappings of ritual and ceremony. At issue is conflict between, on the one hand, the vision of a church whose collective good consists in public, ceremonial conformity under episcopal discipline and, on the other, a puritan enthusiasm which locates true religious piety in the private and rarefied communion of God and individual. Controversy over the material extent and *modus* of divine presence in the Eucharist, then, is of no little consequence for the perceived role of institutional media in the administration of God's gifts. *The Temple*, however, is powerful evidence that these ideological poles were, in actual devotional as opposed to polemical contexts, far from mutually exclusive: Herbert's celebration of ceremonial forms not only complements but indeed is an integral feature of the devotional subjectivity he cultivates.

Sacramentum sacerdotalis

In 'The Priesthood' Herbert is in awe of the priestly office, especially the administering of sacraments. His profound respect for ritual is anticipated by subtle comparison of the Eucharist with the potter's art, which fits earth by 'fire and trade ... for the boards of those / Who make the bravest shows' (16–18). In the next stanza we find that the inferior art is but earth delighting in earth, 'both feeder, dish, and meat' having 'one beginning and one finall summe' (21–2), and in the following stanza the sacramental pun on 'board' as Communion table[1] is confirmed:

But th' holy men of God such vessels are,
As serve him up, who all the world commands:
When God vouchsafeth to become our fare,
Their hands convey him, who conveys their hands.
O what pure things, most pure must those things be,
Who bring my God to me!   (25–30)

Perplexity results finally in a hyperbolic display of submission, the poet and aspiring priest recognizing his status as 'lowly matter,' the master potter's clay thrown 'at his [God's] feet' (35–6). Such prostration, however, represents more than admiration of and fear for the sacramental office. The Ark of the Covenant he hesitates to grasp, no doubt mindful of Uzzah's fate (2 Sam. 6.6), is typologically the sacrament, the vessel of the new covenant (Heb. 9.4), which here seems to 'shake / Through th' old sinnes and new doctrines of our land' (32–3). It is difficult to determine precisely what is meant by 'new doctrines.' The poem's title and reverent tone suggest Herbert's target is puritan disregard for holy things. Indeed, for R.V. Young 'new doctrines ... can only be an attack upon Puritanism.'[2] Given the probable date of composition it is likely Herbert was responding to excessive fear of the church's increasingly sacramental orientation.[3] On the other hand, Uzzah's presumptuous approach to the presence housed in the Ark suggests Herbert here may just as likely condemn a too familiar, curious, and thus potentially idolatrous regard for sacraments, a charge often laid against the scholastic dissection of the Eucharist associated with the Roman Catholic tradition. The latitude allowed by 'new doctrines' is perhaps deliberately ambiguous, referring to any and all attitudes which threaten an ideal balance of pious restraint and due reverence.

The mutual reinforcement of sacerdotal and sacramental imperatives is evident toward the poem's close, where, following the penultimate stanza's 'I throw me at his feet' (36), Herbert imagines himself an empty vessel not unlike the eucharistic species, presented and now humbly awaiting divine invigoration:

There will I lie, untill my Maker seek
For some mean stuffe whereon to show his skill:
Then is my time.   (37–9)

Quiet anticipation of miraculous transformation, whether of bread and wine or ministerial office, allows Herbert to indulge a celebration of his vocation, tempered by humility and short of endorsing the *iure divino* episcopacy advocated by some of his more zealous peers.[4] Though considerably enamoured of the special privileges such office affords, and relishing the idea of his own hands being such 'pure things' as 'bring my God to me!' (29–30), Herbert is self-effacing sufficiently as to recognize the importance of sober and due submission, 'Lest good come short of ill / In praising might' (40–1). The priest's predicament is not unlike that of the encomiast in Donne's Countess of Bedford poem, 'On New-yeares day,' where it is implied that the art of praise is analogous to the doctrine of transubstantiation, both of which are in danger of exalting the means above their object.

Ceremonial caution and priestly reverence yield to a more relaxed wonder and awe in 'The Invitation,' where poetic structure mirrors the paradox of the Word become flesh, made explicit, as we have seen, by the poem's claim that the sacramental wine is blood 'before ye drink' (12). Here Herbert's dual vocation as priest and poet is most apparent, for 'The Invitation' is not only *about* Holy Communion: the poem's subtle conflation of profane and sacred experiences reflects the incarnational scandal even as it exemplifies Herbert's metaphysical wit. The humble Parson extends generous welcome and mild admonition to those approaching the Lord's table, compared to which all previous meals have failed to satisfy vain appetites: 'taste' is 'waste' (1–2), wine is 'drunk amisse' (10) if not of 'the feast, / God, in whom all dainties are' (5–6). And yet the most exquisite of human experiences is surpassed only by a joy which nevertheless resembles that which it putatively transcends:

> Come ye hither All, whose love
> > Is your dove,
> And exalts you to the skie:
> Here is love, which having breath
> > Ev'n in death,
> After death can never die.   (25–30)

The balanced antithesis of Herbert's stanza lends formal support to the comparison. Secular love is neither dull nor sublunary. Nor does the love embodied in the Eucharist escape the death implicitly associated with sexual fulfilment, the familiar *petite mort* (more typical of Donne or Crashaw, unusual in Herbert) boldly suggesting eucharistic sacrifice. Indeed, the paradox that lovers' orgasm signals the obsolescence of their efforts is analogous to the theological commonplace of the final line. This mirroring in the stanza's second half of qualities associated with the love celebrated by the first is reciprocated, 'dove' evoking the Holy Spirit which descended both on Jesus to inaugurate his ministry, and on the Virgin Mary at his miraculous conception.[5] This in turn suggests for 'breath' an association with the risen Christ's gift of the third member of the Trinity breathed on the apostles just prior to the Ascension (Jn. 20.22). In hindsight, then, the 'All' of this penultimate stanza anticipates the identification of 'All' and 'All' in the final line, extends the invitation, 'Come ye hither,' to God, and thus advances the interpenetration of love and Love.

The hierarchical order evoked by a vertical structural arrangement (the fifth stanza's 'All,' 'dove,' and 'skie' followed by 'breath' and 'death') is dissolved from within when we discover that both the exalting terms and those concerned with more earthly matters are performing double duty. Similarly complementary or imbricate pairs inform other stanzas: profane 'fare' (3) and heavenly 'feast' (5) in the first, 'pain' (13) and 'cheer' (17) in the third, and, above all, 'wine' (7) and 'bloud' (12) in the second. The poem thus is truly incarnational in its treatment of sacramental ritual, both thematically and formally, the careful arrangement of antitheses and their instability reflecting the incarnational paradox that the Eucharist embodies. Finally, as if to render explicit the poem's thematic design, Herbert offers the theological assertion already discussed – 'drink this, / Which before ye drink is bloud' – which appeals to while going beyond messianic authority, thus abandoning eirenic caution for a decidedly corporeal vision of sacramental presence. Poetic ingenuity is a prominent feature of 'The Invitation.' But Herbert is sure to include amid the dazzle a plain, and not obscure, statement of that which is the source of all the fuss. Perhaps in no other *Temple* poem is the Renaissance notion of poet as quasi-divine maker more evident: priestly and poetic authorities combine to assert the Word become flesh offered to all who would receive it.

The priest's sacerdotal authority and preaching responsibilities are potentially at odds in 'The Windows.' Identified with stained glass, he is valued as much for the office he holds as for the word he is charged with administering:

Doctrine and life, colours and light, in one
        When they combine and mingle, bring
A strong regard and aw: but speech alone
        Doth vanish like a flaring thing,
        And in the eare, not conscience ring.   (11–15)

Though focused ostensibly on the relevance of personal conduct and reputation for the pulpit, the metaphor draws on long-standing controversy over the relative value and importance of preaching versus the ceremonial 'beauty of holiness' championed by Laudian divines. R.V. Young writes that the poem is about 'the mutually enhancing effects of "Doctrine and life, colours and light in one."'[6] I would add to that *via media* reading a balance of image and word. Novel in this respect is the antithetical proximity of 'eare' to 'conscience,' these usually being allies in support of a word-centred as opposed to ceremonially based ministry. The preacher here is a living *exemplum*, most valuable as a visible symbol of godliness, part of the very fabric of the church, its buildings, and ceremonies – in short, a window through which the light of divinity might shine. While certainly not denigrating the word, Herbert does seem to suggest that it needs palpable support by way of living example in order to prevent its echoing in his auditory's ear as mere theological abstraction. The preacher's example, then, his doctrine *and* life, his symbolic status in the community, accompany the word in going beyond the 'eare' or mere intellectual comprehension effectively and affectively to penetrate his auditory's conscience. Worth noting here is the confusion of visual and auditory metaphors: 'speech alone ... vanish[es]' while 'colours and light,' like the word, 'ring.' A similar synaesthesia is evident in 'Christmas,' where divine/human union consists in the interpenetration of the speaker's music and God's light: 'His beams shall cheer my breast, and both so twine, / Till ev'n his beams sing, and my musick shine' (33–4). In 'The Windows,' this internal assimilation of the word is augmented by its association with the preacher's sacerdotal role, God's representative contiguous with the beauty of holiness over which he is steward. Herbert's Country Parson, similarly, 'is not witty, or learned, or eloquent, but Holy,' and preaching is sacramentally augmented 'by dipping and seasoning all our words and sentences in our hearts, before they come into our mouths, truly affecting, and cordially expressing all that we say; so that the auditors may plainly perceive that every word is hart-deep.' The blood and Baptism echoes are not merely metaphorical; indeed, the preacher's purpose is 'an often urging of the *presence*, and majesty of God, by these, or such like speeches' (*Works*, 233–4). While ultimately concerned with the internal effect of the word, then, Herbert knows that the priest's moral integrity and sacerdotal authority complement his teaching, just as apprehension of God's presence in the sacrament is unthinkable apart from its material aspect.

Right attitude and conduct are not confined to the ministerial role.

After outlining the various moral and social responsibilities of the candidate poised for entry, the speaker/priest attending the Church-porch turns to the attitudes and behaviour appropriate for temple worship:

> Twice on the day his due is understood;
> For all the week thy food so oft he gave thee.
> Thy cheer is mended; bate not of the food,
> Because 'tis better, and perhaps may save thee.
> Thwart not the Mighty God: O be not crosse.
> Fast when thou wilt but then, 'tis gain not losse.   (391–6)

Hutchinson notes that Communion in Herbert's day was celebrated once per month, 'Twice on the day' therefore suggesting morning and evening prayers rather than the sacrament.[7] It may also be observed that the cautionary 'bate not,' which warns against unnecessary controversy, may apply both to sacraments and to liturgical prayers while, similarly, the qualifying 'perhaps may save thee' is a caution against presumption applicable to both forms of ministry. It is likely that Herbert deliberately associates prayer, which after all is a form of communion, with the spiritual 'food' of the Eucharist.[8] Following a warning in 'The Church-porch' to 'Jest not' at preaching (439), he alludes to the possibility of receiving sacraments in a manner not only ineffectual, but positively damning:

> None shall in hell such bitter pangs endure,
> As those, who mock at Gods way of salvation.
> Whom oil and balsames kill, what salve can cure?
> They drink with greedinesse a full damnation.   (445–8)

As in Donne's Christmas sermon, hearing the preached word is analogous to the bodily ingestion of sacramental benefits, as equally susceptible to abuse and as capable of causing harm. Resonant here, of course, is St Paul's warning that those who receive the Eucharist unworthily bring damnation on themselves (1 Cor. 11.27–30). The final admonition that a contrite attitude and right understanding of doctrine are prerequisite to receiving sacramental grace is underscored in 'Superliminare,' where the 'precepts' (1) documented in 'The Church-porch' are to be assimilated in order to 'taste / The churches mysticall repast' (3–4).

Just as the priest's attitudes and conduct are a model for the laity, so Herbert's respect for ceremony and ritual is not confined to the institutional context they support and perpetuate. Sacramental attitudes, rather, are comprehensive of a faith whose quotidian realities persist beyond religious ritual and observance. The opening stanzas of 'Providence,' for example, render poetic observation of the created world an act of worship. The speaker is God's instrument, Herbert's divine muse, 'through whom my fingers bend / To hold my quill' and who makes man 'secretarie of thy praise' (3–8). All creation, while eager to sing their creator's renown, are 'lame and mute' (12) if not for 'Man,' for whom 'the penne alone into his hand' (7) is given:

> Man is the world's high Priest: he doth present
> The sacrifice for all; while they below
> Unto the service mutter an assent,
> Such as springs use that fall, and windes that blow.   (13–16)

It is man's discursive engagement with creation that both manifests its glories and, in so doing, formally ritualizes the gratitude and praise latent in its myriad being. In addition, then, to its sense of 'place before the altar,' the verbal 'present' also suggests the sacramental intensity of 'make present,' thus intimating man's dignified status as officiating priest over great creating nature. In fulfilling his duty as one made in the image of an infinitely creative being, this quasi-magus brings forth the world in all its splendour. All is possible in the first place only through the ubiquitous presence of God in the world:

> Thou art in small things great, not small in any:
> Thy even praise can neither rise, nor fall.
> Thou art in all things one, in each thing many:
> For thou art infinite in one and all.   (41–4)

Wherever one cares to look, God is already there, present in Nicolas of Cusa's notion of a circle whose centre is everywhere and circumference nowhere. Poetic celebration of the world's beauty is a form of worship, Herbert's reasonable service. A sacerdotal and carnal view of sacramental ministry is here based on a Lutheran doctrine of ubiquity that in turn allows the poet to be a priestly representation of the Word that creates by speaking the world into being.

Religious celebration thus extends beyond the official walls of cathedral and parish church to inform everyday experience. Herbert's spiritual ideal is perhaps most succinctly realized in 'Sunday,' a poem that promotes an integral relationship between the Sabbath and other less celebrated days of the week. Sacraments are a key feature of Sunday's worship, here a divine signature or seal conferring on the day a promissory status:

> O Day most calm, most bright,
> The fruit of this, the next worlds bud,
> Th'indorsement of supreme delight,
> Writ by a friend, and with his bloud.   (1–4)

The fruit of the vine is the seed of graces yet to come, a taste of the marriage supper of the Lamb to be celebrated at the end of history. Such fruit is the harvest rest crowning man's toil, Sundays the 'face' and 'brow' which knock 'at heaven' while 'The worky-daies are the back-part' (9–11). Human labour finds purpose here in relation to the ceremonial rest that is the Sabbath which parts the 'ranks and orders' of the 'fruitfull beds and borders / In Gods rich garden' (26–8). The wine consumed in the Eucharist, while anticipating what Donne in *The Second Anniversary* calls 'essentiall joy' (443), also addresses the effects of Adam's curse, man's share in the sufferings which the second Adam experiences in full. St Augustine's assertion that the church is united with the sacrificial mystery on the altar in the Eucharist[9] is relevant for a garden whose fruit is both delineated by human labour and a source of ease 'for those / Who want herbs for their wound' (41–2). The cyclical aspect of such ritual certainly is no Blakean same dull round: seen as part of a succession 'Thredded together on times string' (30), each Sunday performs an eschatological function, is

> a day of mirth:
> And where the week-dayes trail on ground,
> Thy flight is higher, as thy birth.
> O let me take thee at the bound,
> Leaping with thee from sev'n to sev'n,
> Till that we both, being toss'd from earth,
>   Flie hand in hand to heav'n!   (57–63)

As the eucharistic species combine the fruit of human and divine labours in a healing balm and rest for the weary pilgrim, so is the back-breaking toil of 'worky-daies' joined with the Sabbath to form a devotional pilgrimage almost giddy with its own momentum.

It is this combination of reverence for things divine and homely sympathy for the human condition in Herbert's poetry that allows official observances to reverberate beyond the church's sacred walls. A careful balance of respect and light-hearted familiarity or 'domestic simplicity' integrates stylized ritual with the rhythms of Christian existence.[10] Herbert's awareness of the incarnational paradox proclaimed in the Eucharist, its insistence on the Word become flesh, is the institutional basis for recognizing sacramental significance in daily human life and labour.

Devotio sacramentalis

Contiguity between ritual and quotidian in 'Sunday' is symptomatic of the intimacy among public and private, external and internal spheres of religious experience throughout *The Temple*. Like the speakers of Donne's divine poems, Herbert's devout finds in the institutional media of sacrament and ceremony relief from the oppressive guilt and sense of personal depravity that haunt the isolated devotional psyche. Herbert's crushing realizations of spiritual inadequacy, however, are often accompanied by a measured confidence rarely seen in *Holy Sonnets*. Alluding in 'Repentance' to the wormwood and gall of Jeremiah 9.15, Herbert suggests a eucharistic parody and the possibility of its reversal, the latter turning on a subtle messianic identification:

> Sweeten at length this bitter bowl,
>   Which thou hast pour'd into my soul;
> Thy wormwood turn to health, windes to fair weather:
> > > For if thou stay,
> > > I and this day,
> As we did rise, we die together.   (19–24)

The preceding Confession appropriately anticipates Herbert's hope for sacramental absolution, while his implied identification with the sun and, inevitably, Christ and his Passion, augments this figurative transubstantiation of 'wormwood' to 'health.' The 'bitter bowl' thus recalls Gethsemane even as the confessional context suggests its sacramental function. The dual nature of the eucharistic symbol, signifying both suffering and joy, wrath and mercy, is appropriate for the poem's *felix culpa* theme. But before 'Fractures well cur'd make us more strong' (36), there is a moment of doubt in 'if thou stay,' a doubt which may also mask the rhetorical ploy of one anxious to secure his own interests by implying incompetence for God's failure to act on his behalf. This daring devotional strategy recalls Donne's manoeuvre in the *La Corona* sonnet, 'Resurrection,' where the penitent's 'If' implicitly challenges God to act: 'If in thy little booke my name thou enroule' (8). Insofar as this 'bitter bowl' may not in fact be sweetened there looms the threat of a demonic reversal of the Resurrection scheme; the rising Herbert, sun ('day'), and son thus converge at the zenith of a decision whose outcome is obscured by the silence between Confession and Communion at the structural centre of the poem.[11]

A similar strategy is a feature of 'Grace,' where the elusive gift is typologically associated with sacraments in the third stanza:

> The dew doth ev'ry morning fall;
> And shall the dew out-strip thy Dove?
> The dew, for which grasse cannot call,
>   Drop from above.   (9–12)

As elsewhere, God is challenged to act as much for the sake of his own reputation as in the interest of the plaintiff. Herbert is the incapacitated grass, the depraved sinner in no way able to help himself, while the dew he desires is the manna from heaven which no earthly dew could hope to embody. The dilemma of having to plead for that which no human plea can ever effect is thus alleviated through sacramental allusion, which inadvertently challenges God's apparent reluctance by fleshing out his hidden decrees – to the extent that is possible – as finally favourable to the speaker. This boldness is even more evident in a struck stanza of W:

> What if I say thou seek'st delayes;
> Wilt thou not then my fault reproue?
> Prevent my Sinn to thine own praise,
>   Drop from above.   (43r)

In 'Sighs and Grones,' eucharistic mediation is again the merciful alternative to divine justice:

>   O do not fill me
> With the turn'd viall of thy bitter wrath!
> For thou hast other vessels full of bloud,
> A part whereof my Saviour empti'd hath,
> Ev'n unto death: since he di'd for my good,
>   O do not kill me!   (19–24)

But just as sacraments are not received without due reflection on one's unworthiness, so is mercy rarely without just chastisement, God having command over both 'life and death,' being both '*Judge* and *Saviour, feast* and *rod, / Cordiall* and *Corrosive* ' (26–8). Herbert's final cry, 'My God, relieve me!' (30), is as much exasperation in the face of a paradoxical theodicy as it is a plea for redemption.

Though such exasperation is not surprising given limited human understanding, Herbert's speaker could also face the sinner's predicament with calm acceptance. 'Affliction (V)' begins with reference to God's 'floting ark,' typologically indicative of Baptism, 'whose stay / And anchor thou art onely, to confirm / And strengthen it in ev'ry age, / When waves do rise, and tempests rage' (3–6), initial deliverance from original sin having lasting effects on the baptized. But the many ills of subsequent life require a supplemental grace. The second stanza's final couplet alludes to this intervening sacrament as the point at which the sinner's griefs, drawing him to God, are shared by God, even as God in the Eucharist offers himself:

> At first we liv'd in pleasure;
> Thine own delights thou didst to us impart:
> When we grew wanton, thou didst use displeasure
> To make us thine: yet that we might not part,
>   As we at first did board with thee,
>   Now thou wouldst taste our miserie.   (7–12)

There is an echo here of the struck board of the Lord's Supper in 'The Collar,' though here the recognition of divine empathy precludes frustration and momentary apostasy. The effect of the lines is that God in Holy Communion abandons any claim to the head of the table, rather joining his guests in a repast of shared joys and sufferings. It is this domestic familiarity at an otherwise solemn occasion which allows the fishing trope of the following stanza, where a distant pun on angels (angle? angler?) contributes to the idea that both joys and griefs are baits whereby God with his 'double line' (15–16) furnishes his table with guests. But just as harvest revelry in Robert Herrick's 'Hock-Cart' yields to the 'pain' that inevitably must 'spring again' (54–5), so here is the happy meal tempered by echoes of the pain it salves. The final stanza's trees are both afflicted sinners 'whom shaking fastens more, / While blustring windes destroy the wanton bowres,' and reminiscent of the cross of the Atonement, wherein mercy and justice are reconciled, God's 'bright beams' taming his 'bow' (20–4).

In 'Miserie,' a *contemptus humanitatis* indicting man's blatant disregard for the free gift of grace becomes in hindsight a more private *mea culpa*. God's mercy and grace are so extensive that even in his unbridled appetites man has been provided for, God 'Not suff'ring those / Who would, to be thy foes' (29–30). Ultimate sovereignty and prevenient grace, structurally evident in the poem's framing words – 'Lord' (1) and 'My God' (78) – are also suggested by a sacramental echo: '*Man is but grasse, / He knows it, fill the glasse*' (5–6). Sacramental prevenience becomes apparent in the following stanza where the speaker is astonished at God's patience, regretting that man, unlike God, will 'not lose a cup of drink for thee' (8), and is confirmed later where the same exasperation becomes a potentially heretical denial of the efficacy of the Atonement, the speaker asserting that man's 'humours reign' and 'make his life a constant blot, / And all the bloud of God to run in vain' (62–4). This parodic association of recreational drink and the Eucharist recalls 'The Church-porch,' where intemperance threatens to invalidate God's image and seal:

> Stay at the third cup, or forgo the place.
> Wine above all things doth Gods stamp deface.   (47–8)

Sacramental grace in 'Miserie' subverts its parodic echo, the vain/vein pun complementing the suggestion that even in man's ribald excesses – perhaps especially there – Christ's atoning work has been operative, the sacrament preveniently retroactive even in the debauching of one of its central symbols. Recognizing his own depraved status in the final line – 'My God, I mean my self' (78) – Herbert is now more reluctant to dismiss as 'vain' man's only hope, for he now must know that his own attempt to flatter God has been, like all human praise, but 'infection / Presum[ing] on thy perfection' (35–6). He has allowed that the 'glasse' of sin could only be a drink of condemnation; God, apparently, has always had other plans.

The relationship between devotional and sacramental pieties and its significance for penitential despair is particularly evident among the alternating voices of confident judge and guilty supplicant in 'Conscience,' where the violence of the Crucifixion is directed against the sorrow-dogging 'pratler' (1) and his 'chatting fears' (5). The speaker's only recourse is

> My Saviours bloud: when ever at his board
> I do but taste it, straight it cleanseth me,
>   And leaves thee not a word;

No, not a tooth or nail to scratch,
And at my actions carp or catch.   (14–18)

Notable here is the association of 'word' with the accusing Conscience while the silencing of this 'pratler' is explicitly a matter of eucharistic grace. This sacrament versus word/Conscience opposition is clarified and the tables turned when in the final stanza the cleansing 'bloudie crosse' becomes the speaker's 'sword,' a weapon of 'Some wood and nails to make a staff or bill / For those that trouble me' (21–4). Internal reflection and sacramental relief conflict violently within the devotional psyche itself. The speaker would escape Conscience's psychological tortures, finding in sacramental blood and the cross it stains the instruments of his liberation into an external and mythical ritual. Personal struggle is thus absorbed by its archetypal Christian context which allows the penitent some respite from his incessant self-condemnation. Herbert's poem appropriates the symbols of Christian ritual paradoxically to eradicate the accuser Conscience from whatever might then remain of the speaker's divided self. This sacramentalization of the religious psyche culminates in a devotional version of man-as-microcosm, where inward agony melts into the surrounding heavens: 'My thoughts must work, but like a noiseless sphere' (8). It is perhaps strange that the target of eucharistic grace also happens to be a vital component of the Christian psyche, the censor who convicts of sin. Certain sweet dishes presumably *are* sour, certain fair looks foul. Yet Herbert apparently is concerned more with combating Conscience than those fleshly desires which threaten devotional integrity. It is as though music howls at all only because Conscience chides and clouds the ear, which otherwise might hear the 'Harmonious peace' (9) of 'noiselesse' thoughts and the Pythagorean song they whisper.

The violence that surfaces in 'Conscience' is understandable given the contradiction the poem addresses.[12] That Conscience can be both false accuser and the law which justly convicts is a reflection of God's own paradoxical duality, the same doubleness that allows the ultimate accuser to wreak havoc on poor Job only to restore him in the end (only, of course, after having quelled any hope of a rational explanation). That the Eucharist and that which it represents address this duality by placing God himself (in Christ) in the unenviable position of which Job's suffering is a type is captured by a succinct juxtaposition in 'The Bunch of Grapes': 'the Laws sowre juice sweet wine' (27). Herbert's typological meditation applies scriptural and sacramental topoi to his own spiritual condition, especially the plaint echoing the forsaken Christ in Gethsemane. Of interest here is the sacramental character of certain types or 'adumbrations' of the New Testament in the Old.[13] The 'Red sea, the sea of shame' (7) anticipates and is clarified by 'the Laws sowre juice' in the penultimate line. In fact, the 'vein' (4) of several lines previous is in hindsight suggestive of what follows. 'Noah's vine' not only 'bring[s] forth grapes good store' (24–5) but is also implicitly representative of the law which convicts of sin. We are reminded that the Eucharist for Herbert involves not only the gift of grace and final rest or peace for the weary soul, but also some of the agony – which Christ experienced in full – necessary for the purging of sin. Herbert, like St Paul, would share in Christ's sufferings for the sake of the church. A further typological connection is intimated in the final lines of the second stanza, 'Gods works are wide, and let in future times; / His ancient justice overflows our crimes' (13–14), where 'overflows' recalls 'Red sea' and suggests the blood of the Atonement, thus once again focusing on justice and sin as opposed to mercy and grace-imputed righteousness. It is not until the third stanza that the speaker's questions address this absence. 'But where's the cluster? where's the taste / Of mine inheritance?' (19–20) introduces the object of the poem's title, this explicit eucharistic type complemented in the same stanza by 'scripture-dew' (16) which combines the Israelites' manna with the Word of life that is both scripture and Christ, the bread of life. The speaker's expectation to 'as well take up their joy, as sorrow' (21) is revealed in the final stanza as having already been fulfilled:

> But can he want the grape, who hath the wine?
>   I have their fruit and more.
> Blessed be God, who prosper'd *Noahs* vine,
>   And made it bring forth grapes good store.
>   But much more him I must adore,
> Who of the Laws sowre juice sweet wine did make,
> Ev'n God himself being pressed for my sake.   (22–8)

Nevertheless, while 'sea of shame,' 'justice,' 'crimes,' and the finally sacramental remedy suggest that release from sin's guilt is the primary object of the speaker's desire, 'Canaan,' 'inheritance,' and 'grapes good store' all intimate a more than merely spiritual thirst. Indeed, it is quite possible 'sev'n yeares ago' is an uncharacteristically biographical detail suggesting some sort of worldly disappointment. This is not to imply, as has been fashionable to say of Donne, that Herbert is merely frustrated courtier become godly vassal. It does suggest that his frail humanity is inclined to disguise fears, anxieties, and disappointments in an effort to protect whatever dignity and sense of purpose remain. If in addition to his share of guilt and shame Herbert projects on the Eucharist his worldly frustrations, he only reveals what omniscience must already know.

Vocational anxiety, regret, and disappointment are nowhere more pronounced than in 'The Collar,' the first lines' frustration concentrated on a central symbol of Herbert's ministerial office. 'I Struck the board, and cry'd, No more. / I will abroad' (1–2) is a resolve augmented by a dichotomy opposing the narrow and sober confines of the Communion 'board' to the open vista suggested by 'abroad,' the rhyme anticipating their eventual reconciliation. Like 'The Altar' and 'The Church' as a whole, 'The Collar' is framed by the Word that is all, here the struck board of the Eucharist and the final lines' gently admonishing Father. What happens in between is a rehearsal of Adam's rebellion, the poet's impatience with 'lines and life' which, though potentially 'free as the rode,' are yet 'still in suit' (4–6) – still aspiring, that is, to divine service.[14] Eucharistic topoi continue to inform the rebellion: 'Harvest' expands to embrace a Pauline reference (2 Cor. 12.7) to 'thorn' (7), which in turn evokes the crown of the crucified Christ – an ironic anticipation of the 'bayes' Herbert lacks – and allows transition to the more explicit allusions in 'wine' and 'corn' (10–11). The same grace which stoops in 'The Altar' to identify with that poem's broken heart shares the bitter harvest of the speaker here. The loss of worldly honour – 'cordiall fruit' (9), 'bayes,' 'flowers,' and 'garlands gay' (14–15) – and the 'wine' and 'corn' that were in abundance before his 'sighs did drie' and 'tears did drown' them (11–12) are together the speaker's unwitting oblation, the fruit of a prevenient and incomprehensible grace. He is unaware of his participation in messianic suffering and sacrifice, or that trepidation with respect to religious vocation is not solely his; that Jesus, both in Gethsemane and at the moment of his greatest suffering, expressed considerable reluctance to follow through with his calling. Far from trivial, the doubt, loss, and pain of the speaker are imbued with a divinity that acknowledges their significance, so that in the end the child is not merely obedient, but rather a highly valued creature whose 'fierce and wilde' (33) raving is an honest despair toward which his Lord is more sympathetic than he had imagined. 'Christ's drama,' writes one perceptive critic, 'runs silently and invisibly behind the poem.'[15] Far from dismissing the child's anxieties and frustrations, the final lines acknowledge and validate even as they silence them.

If we see the poem in its entirety as the deliberations of a Herbert about to receive (and administer?) the Eucharist, we are witness to a protracted moment wherein the devout follows the Pauline instruction to examine himself. But rather than indulge a maudlin rehearsal of his undeserving sinfulness, Herbert simply reveals his frustration, chides his piety for depriving him of other pleasures, and thereby allows himself fully to recognize the frustration of which God, no doubt, is already cognizant. Genuine transparency and self-knowledge finally allow the speaker to realize an intimacy with God – 'Child ... My Lord' (35–6). This final resolution is itself anticipated by the second and now considerably subdued 'I will abroad' (28), which occurs in the midst of the child's despair as a significant pause, a final desperate assertion which nonetheless echoes the symbol ('board') of that which has all along been 'cordiall fruit.' Now finally restored, or rather rediscovered, wine and corn re-emerge unsullied – fortified even by hard-won sighs and tears. Having struck the board, Herbert is now able to embrace it with an expanded understanding of its significance. Whereas in 'Conscience' the imperatives of sacrament and word fight an unresolved psychological battle, here the still small voice of the Word facilitates return to the sacramental board and body which celebrate it.

The (in)adequacy of devotional prayer and its relevance for the material dimension of sacramental grace are explored in 'The Search,' where, paraphrasing Psalm 42.3, Herbert is both distressed at God's apparent absence and sustained by his own efforts to rectify the loss: 'My searches are my daily bread; / Yet never prove' (3–4). Seeking God is the Christian's food, the devotional quotidian supplementing occasional sacraments. The devout's posture is one appropriate for prayer but also identical to that which the Country Parson prescribes for receiving the Eucharist: 'the Feast indeed requires sitting, because it is a Feast; but man's unpreparednesse askes kneeling' (*Works*, 259). 'My knees,' writes Herbert,

> pierce th'earth, mine eies the skie;
>   And yet the sphere
> And centre both to me denie
>   That thou art there.   (5–8)

The juxtaposition of rooted knees and sky-piercing eyes suggest that the space separating the speaker and his God traverses his own body, from prostrate flesh to the limits of corporeal vision. Just as bread in the Eucharist is consumed and assimilated by the communicant, so this 'daily bread' combines a hunger for God with an appropriately receptive body, the latter straining its corporeal limitations to accommodate an ostensibly spiritual food. Just as various and often conflicting theologies attest to the *mysterium tremendum* that is sacramental presence, and to the futility of identifying its *modus*, so is the devotional psyche subject to the anxiety of absence. Reluctant to entertain a radically transcendent deity, Herbert reasons that God may be busy attending to a parallel universe: 'Lord, dost thou some new fabrick mould[?]' (25). He discovers, however, that the cause of absence may be the divine will itself, a rather disconcerting notion; he would much prefer the material barriers of 'brasse, / Or steel, or mountains' (34–5) to that for which 'all strength, all subtilties / Are things of nought' (39–40).

To the extent they are thought to embody divine immanence sacraments attenuate the psychological anxiety of a Calvinism sensitive to the vagaries of an inscrutable and alien Will. Yet, as John Donne wrote, agreeing with Richard Hooker and the Elizabethan Articles, on the wicked sacraments confer no benefit at all (*Sermons*, 5.163). And while the elements offered at board are perhaps no guarantee of divine favour, still less is *this* daily bread, kneaded in the close, private realm of the devotional psyche, an altogether adequate sustenance. Indeed, it is considerably less tangible, more elusive. But the marriage of Christ and his body, the church, toward which the Eucharist is a public, ceremonial gesture, can also be a private courtship or pas de deux; just as the ritual ideally is inseparable from the presence it celebrates, so devout searches, while for the most part 'never prove,' are psychologically inextricable from the occasional, fleeting realization of their objective: 'For as thy absence doth excell / All distance known: / So doth thy nearenesse bear the bell, / Making two one' (57–60). Intimate nearness is just around the corner from infinite distance. 'Herbert's God,' writes Helen Wilcox, 'is tasted as much by his absence as by his presence.'[16] Hope, according to Richard Crashaw in a poem of that title jointly composed with Abraham Cowley, is 'our absent presence, and our future now' (70). For Herbert – whose searches are his daily bread – seeking and finding, presence and absence are but sistole and diastole of the same beating heart.

The joy that accompanies fleeting spiritual fulfilment is vividly reified in 'The Glance':

> I felt a sugred strange delight,
> Passing all cordials made by any art,
> Bedew, embalme, and overrune my heart,
>   And take it in.   (5–8)

Wonder and the excitement elicited by analysis rush headlong until overcome by the experience itself, 'bedew' initiating a string of gentle pauses and assonances which together evoke the typologically eucharistic manna. This otherwise ineffable moment is drawn out until it fully assimilates the heart it woos, sating both consumer and consumed. Sacramental consummation is also suggested by the glance's association with 'seal' in the final stanza, 'A mirth but open'd and seal'd up again' (18). Here, however, it is Baptism that is suggested, for in the second stanza we find that this 'first glance' is associated with a 'sweet original joy' continuously working 'within my soul' (13–14). This combination of original salvific experience and its continued effects suggests both sacraments, Baptism providing deliverance from the soul's enslavement by original sin, Holy Communion a perpetual guard against and remedy for 'the malicious and ill-meaning harm' (11) and 'surging griefs' (15) of daily (fallen) life. Both look toward an eventual 'full-ey'd love' (20) and thus anticipate the water of life and wedding supper of the Lamb of which they are types. Structurally, the poem's three stanzas are a progression from initial conversion, through subsequent spiritual struggle and the glance's sustaining power ('surging griefs' antithetically complementing the earlier 'sugred' experience), to final rest 'In heav'n above' (24). Again, it is sacrament which salves the sinner's despair, the fleeting glance of a distant, albeit 'sweet and gracious' (1), eye transubstantiated to penetrate and envelop Herbert's heart, much as a Renaissance sunbeam might congeal upon and bedew the earth it warms.

Herbert's rest in God's presence is usually more hard-won than this. In 'Love Unknown' he sustains simultaneous recognition of both the penitent's spiritual depravity and the depth of God's love. His is a devotional psyche reluctantly assuaged by the assurances of sacramental grace. At the first attempt to appease his Lord the speaker's heart is 'seis'd' and placed in a font

> wherein did fall
> A stream of bloud, which issu'd from the side
> Of a great rock: I well remember all,
> And have good cause: there it was dipt and dy'd,

And washt, and wrung: the very wringing yet
Enforceth tears.   (13–18)

Herbert expands the traditional typology connecting the rock which fed
the Israelites with Christ, Baptism, and a spiritual food and drink (Ex.
17.6; 1 Cor. 10.1–4) to include more explicitly the blood of Atonement.
The qualification 'yet,' moreover, implies the heart's need of continual
sacramental renewal and thus anticipates the eucharistic heart of the
poem. At each painful discovery of the insufficiency of his sacrifices, the
speaker acknowledges his friend's disappointments – '*Your heart was foul
... hard ... dull*' (18, 37, 56) – and follows each with a brief Confession.
The second of these celebrates a remedy that also exemplifies the
caution characteristic of Jacobean and Caroline divines' approach to
sacramental doctrine:

            I found a callous matter
Began to spread and to expatiate there:
But with a richer drug then scalding water
I bath'd it often, ev'n with holy bloud,
Which at a board, while many drunk bare wine,
A friend did steal into my cup for good,
Ev'n taken inwardly, and most divine
To supple hardnesses.   (38–45)

As we have seen, Herbert clearly regards as disadvantaged those whose
views lean toward a merely commemorative ritual, 'bare wine' evoking a
disenchanted, ineffective means of grace. He is careful, however, to
attenuate this assertion of presence with 'Ev'n taken inwardly,' thus
connecting any substantial transformation of the elements with the act
of ingestion. This combination of presence, effectual species, and a
Calvinist emphasis on reception rather than the externals of ritual marks
the threshold between the worlds of matter and spirit Herbert would
fuse. He knows that sin is primarily a spiritual ailment and requires a
penetrating, spiritual cure. But his is an undeniably material and somatic
characterization of sin : 'hardnesses' in need of 'suppl[ing],' or, in 'The
Agonie,' a 'presse and vice, which forceth pain / To hunt his cruell food
through ev'ry vein' (11–12), both suggesting an overwhelmingly physiological need. Whereas for Calvin the material means are but God's
concession to the fleshly limitations of his creatures, Herbert is much
more reluctant to divest spiritual experience of its sublunary component.

The first and third Confessions of 'Love Unknown,' in which the speaker comprehends his failure to merit salvation, are compensated by divine reassurance. Preoccupied with his many faults, the penitent 'still askt pardon, and was not deni'd' (21), for his sins, as it turns out, are 'by another paid, / Who took the debt upon him' (60–1). It is in between, following the second Confession (38–9), that the sacramental grace cited above intervenes to assuage his anxieties. Just as Herbert's poetic and prayerful offerings are a sacrifice acceptable only when fully recognized as divinely initiated and sustained, so Christ's presence among the 'rich furniture and fine array' of ceremonial ritual imbues what is otherwise meaningless custom with true sacramental significance. Carnal and potentially sacerdotal indulgence is softened both by the homely image of Christ as a mischievous friend stealing his way into the cup, and by an emphasis on communal use – 'Ev'n taken inwardly.' This latter allows the potentially controversial problem of *modus* to be avoided, even if the evocative imagery and diction – 'bath'd,' 'bloud,' 'drunk,' 'supple' – complicate such doctrinal evasion. On the one hand, Herbert is reluctant to allow his transcendent Lord to be subjected to the material limitations of carnal being; yet he also maintains the scandal of the Word become flesh, the need for a Christ actually present among both the means and 'suppling' effects of God's supreme gift. If some divines worried that overly carnal notions of real presence compromise divine autonomy and transcendence, Herbert insists that such presence is but the divinely instituted and necessary expression of the Incarnation, a Will paradoxically stripped of power and subjected to history, a body and death.

But does Herbert finally rest secure in a primarily sacramental grace? 'Love Unknown' is a psychological dramatization, gesturing only momentarily toward the soteriological efficacy of sacraments and the escape they provide from inner turmoil and doubt. The poem in this respect exemplifies a devotional tendency in Herbert that Achsah Guibbory has described as focusing 'on the individual believer rather than the corporate religious community.'[17] The external remedy may provide a means of grace independent of psychological disposition, but as significant as it may be, the Eucharist nevertheless is overwhelmed, 'Ev'n taken inwardly' – swallowed, as it were, by the speaker's ever vigilant Conscience. Even the communion with his crucified saviour which the ritual allows is compromised by an anxiety apparently impervious to sacramental persuasion, for immediately following the eucharistic encounter, the still unconvinced penitent hesitates:

But when I thought to sleep out all these faults
    (I sigh to speak)
I found that some had stuff'd the bed with thoughts,
I would say *thorns*.   (49–52)

More than a *meditatio Christi*, the metaphor transfers the crown of thorns
to the speaker's psyche and allows his ephemeral tortures the dignified
status of messianic sacrifice. Though the focus here is inward, it forms
part of what Elizabeth Clarke calls a process of 'mortification-vivification'
wherein Herbert's self-abnegation is a priestly sharing in the far superior
priesthood of Christ. The inward focus, then, is paradoxically an effort
to eliminate the self so that it might be more fully realized as a member
of a greater body. Just as resurrection follows death so does self-affirma-
tion follow self-denial, a resurrection of self Clarke associates with the
externals of ceremonial worship.[18] If Herbert's sacramental vision suggests Roman sensualism and a fondness for ritual, however, these serve
primarily to ceremonialize otherwise inward deliberations. And yet this
fusion of inside and outside may not have the desired effect, for while
ceremony provides escape from existential isolation, Herbert's distinctive self permeates rather than becomes lost in its institutional context.
There is perhaps no rest for one who knows that even his prayers are
inseparable from ritual, reverberating as they do between ceremonial
and devotional, institutional, and private spheres: 'Though my lips went,
my heart did stay behinde' (59). The crucial question is whether or not
he can accept finally that his friend's suppling 'holy bloud' might indeed
render the heart '*new, tender, quick*' (70).

The liminal frontier between ceremony and devotion, the site of a
psychological drama animated and reified by sacrament, is important for
our understanding of Herbert's verse and its ostensibly inward focus.
Inwardness in Herbert does not result in the desacramentalization of
Christian worship identified long ago by Malcolm Ross as a central (and
regrettable) feature of seventeenth-century religious poetry.[19] Eucharist
and ritual, rather, are inseparable from the *The Temple*'s interiority, the
latter an extension of its public, ceremonial context. The result is nothing less than a sacramental puritanism, the integration of institutional
and private aspects of religious experience, as in 'Sinne (I),' where
God's 'fine nets and strategems to catch us in' include not only 'laws,'
'Pulpits and Sundayes,' but also 'sorrow dogging sinne' and 'anguish of
all sizes' (3–7); together, these are 'Without, our shame; within, our
consciences; / Angels and grace, eternall hopes and fears' (11–12).

Woven into the fabric of a devotional life, sacramental topoi for Herbert alleviate a self-absorbed psychomachia. The external means of grace provide a healing balm for 'sorrow dogging sinne,' sacraments penetrating the private psyche and materializing the otherwise ephemeral processes of Christian salvation.

In addition to addressing the theological controversies of his era, sacrament in *The Temple* advances the Christian paradox of Incarnation as central to Herbert's interrogation of the relationship between spiritual and material aspects of religious experience. The integration of internal and external modes is essential to both sacramental worship and devotional versification, for the Christian *mythos* attending ceremonial forms encompasses also the communicant's private reflections, whether at 'board,' prayer, or quill and 'little book.'[20] Herbert's poetry addresses matters of concern to the members of a faith community even as it portrays one individual working out his salvation in fear and trembling. Central to this integration of communal context and private devotional space, sacramental topoi establish the individual penitent's rôle in a larger scheme, both his or her performative ritual duty, and status with respect to the register or book of life to which all hopeful souls aspire. The measured yet energetic creativity discernible in Herbert's verse is a result of his efforts to find in sacraments the mediation of a grace the apprehension of which the most sincere and constant of devotional psyches is unable otherwise to sustain. It is only through continual return to its institutional and carnal status as sacrament that Herbert can imagine the Word become flesh and the supreme gift it declares.

CHAPTER SIX

Poetry and Self: The Eucharistic Art of Devotion

The invitation to receive sacraments is ultimately an invitation to identify with their source, to commune with the Christ whose death and atoning work they proclaim. Though sometimes sacerdotal in emphasis, Herbert's sacramental images are often presented in surprisingly familiar guise and thereby facilitate an understanding of the Incarnation as rendering immanent and intimate that which is otherwise remote. This colloquializing of the ceremonial is part of Herbert's broader design, namely, to envision human intimacy with God through identification with Christ, the raison d'être of both devotional and sacramental enterprises. As viewed through a ceremonial lens, Herbert's devotional efforts avoid devolving into the despair of which even the most confident of religious psyches is susceptible. Sacraments, like the cross in Donne's poem of that title, are instrumental in avoiding 'those dejections' both 'when it downward tends, / And when it to forbidden heights pretends' (53–4). It is a similar sacramental view of self that allows Herbert to develop his art without succumbing to the maudlin humility an otherwise severe recognition of human depravity demands. If the Herbert persona is not nearly as playful as Donne's or that amazing free artist of himself,[1] Michel de Montaigne, it nevertheless shares with the great French essayist energies which no mere ego could ever contain. That persona is at once both Herbert and not Herbert, a sacred Other the depths of whose mysteries coincide with those of the poet's devotional interiority. That Herbert's poetry is as good as it is, then, derives from a rare and difficult-to-sustain aesthetic poise: that of one whose deeply personal art is, after all, not really about him.

Following St Paul's example of seeking to share in Christ's sufferings, Herbert at once entertains and interrogates an identification of his penitential griefs with Jesus' own sacrifice and sorrows. But accompanying this need to understand his devotional efforts as somehow contiguous with the Passion is Herbert's keen awareness of the ultimately insignificant role they play in his own salvation. Sacramental topoi in this context are central to the crisis of identity, famously illuminated by Stanley Fish, according to which Herbert's spiritual autonomy must confront the Word he knows is All. Fish's observation that external poetic form in *The Temple* is always 'mended or completed or given meaning by God,' however, is offered in the context of a study which pays little attention to sacrament and the role it plays in Herbert's efforts to retain for his devotion and his art a personal agency compatible with that all-consuming Word.[2]

The sacramental-devotional identification of Christ and communicant is particularly evident in Herbert's poetry of tears. Lachrymal images not only allow the identification of penitential grief with Jesus' Passion, the latter inaugurated in the garden of Gethsemane where he is said to have wept or sweated blood (Lk. 22.44). Like sacraments, tears span internal and external dimensions of religious experience, both in their material manifestation of an inward process, and by facilitating devotional reflection through a shared discourse, in this case a common religious and literary topos. Southwell's devotional lyrics anticipate in this respect Herbert's sacramental interiority. In 'Davids Peccavi,' for example, the speaker's 'teares' are 'my drink, my famisht thoughts my bread' (7–8). In 'A Phansie turned to a sinners complaint,' similarly, the speaker's 'hart the Altar is, / And hoast a God to move' (29–30), while later in the same poem, 'teares shall be my wine' (133). Herbert, however, was much more acutely aware than was Southwell that tears potentially are inadequate or even false indicators of an authentic penitential attitude. Elizabeth Clarke believes that the extreme baroque conceits in Herbert's poetry of tears manifest an ironic reluctance to allow external forms to communicate devotional sincerity. 'Concentration on the outward and physical effects of emotion without regard to the inward cause,' writes Clarke, is 'foreign to Herbert.'[3] But the sincerity topos might include an equally ironic self-aggrandizement. Herbert knows that inward sincerity is at least as ephemeral as its outward manifestations, so that his sacramental appropriation of the tears tradition is but another attempt to give voice to his private fears and anxieties, to provide yet another avenue of escape from devotional isolation. The excessively lachrymose penitent of 'The Dawning,' for example, is admonished, 'with his buriall-linen drie thine eyes' for 'Christ left his grave-clothes, that we might, when grief / Draws tears, or

bloud, not want a handkerchief' (14–16). Directed toward a communally
valorized symbol, Herbert's private grief is externalized and subsumed
by the broader tradition and Christian *mythos* to which he belongs. We
are reminded of Donne's frustrated lover in 'Twicknam Garden,' who,
by conflating his own tears with 'loves wine,' would transform his agony
into a sacramentalized asceticism, his passion into the Passion. But
whereas in his messianic posturing Donne's speaker is the victim of a
deliberate Chaucerian irony, Herbert's penitent comes to understand
his devotional isolation and pain as an experience shared by one from
whom grief drew both tears and blood. Donne's speaker indecorously
appropriates the Passion for his own purposes; the devout subject in *The
Temple* is overwhelmed by the messianic drama. If sacramental lachrymae
in 'Twicknam Garden' are but ammunition in the frustrated Petrarchan
lover's arsenal of wit, for Herbert they represent an ideal communion in
which self is subsumed wholly by the divine.

In 'The Sacrifice,' Herbert's speaker assumes the messianic perspective, albeit with little of the blasphemous potential of Donne's 'Spit in my
face you Jews.' Thorns, grapes, and vine combine to recall the vineyard
of Isaiah 5.1–7; but the lines also suggest *bloody* grapes, divine fruit
among oppressive briars:

> Then on my head a crown of thorns I wear:
> For these are all the grapes *Sion* doth bear,
> Though I my vine planted and watred there.   (161–3)

Earlier, blood is 'temper'd with a sinners tears' (25) to form a healing
balm, the Gethsemane context suggesting Jesus' blood-tears, confirmed
later in reference to the Apostles in the garden who failed to keep watch
(Matt. 26.40–1): 'When all my tears were bloud, the while you slept'
(150). Given the mix of atoning blood and penitential tears – and the
previous mention of 'cup' (23) – we are not far from the combined water
and wine in the eucharistic chalice. Indeed, the poem's penultimate
stanza explicitly refers to Christ's pierced side from whence 'sacraments
might flow' (247), an allusion to the water and blood of St John's Gospel
(Jn. 19.34). Though 'the combination of sacred word and Holy Spirit'
are prominent, it is not necessary, as Elizabeth Clarke has argued, that
they attenuate significantly the poem's visual detail.[4] If ever Herbert
indulged an *imitatio Christi*, this is it. The dual significance of 'cup' – both
the Passion, which for Jesus at Gethsemane is imminent, and the reconciliation it procures – together with its combined contents of blood and

'sinners tears' advances the poet's messianic perspective not only as mere role-playing, but as an empathetic communion. For while dramatic verse demands that the poet assume for creative purposes the perspective of the character he or she portrays, Herbert's vivid portrayal of the Passion necessarily derives its emotional and psychological impact from his own experience. The poem fuses a human understanding of grief with that which nevertheless must be thought finally to exceed human grasp. The interrogative refrain, 'Was ever grief like mine,' in addition to being a rhetorical question eliciting the implied and emphatic response 'No!' is thus also a genuine inquiry into the extent and nature of human involvement in the Atonement. So while 'The Sacrifice' is ostensibly a Passion poem, Herbert's representation of the suffering Christ suggests a problem central to the debate surrounding Holy Communion: to what extent is the Atonement replicated in the Eucharist, or, to put the question another way, what is the nature of 'the sacrifice' in the rite – human, divine, or both? If the dramatic voice of Herbert's poem is any indication, the answer is 'both,' for in that voice are registered the plaints not only of the Paschal Lamb but also the penitent whose human experience informs divine suffering. Moreover, because the poet contrives this communion of the human and divine, he is an officiating priest, his poem both a ritual dramatization of the Passion and a sacrament replete with celebrant, communicant, and sacrificial Host.

If 'The Sacrifice' allows Herbert's speaker a formal identification with Christ, the combining of blood with sinner's tears elsewhere suggests for human suffering and Christian penitence a status of which the poet was nevertheless a little wary. In 'The Thanksgiving,' for example, he doubts his own can ever match his saviour's grief: 'Shall I weep bloud? why, thou hast wept such store / That all thy body was one doore' (5–6). The connections among Gethsemane, the Crucifixion, and the Eucharist are certainly not exclusive to Herbert. In 'Christ's Bloody Sweat,' for example, Southwell imagines Jesus' Gethsemane tears as 'grape of bliss' (1), untouch'd of press,' and 'sweet wine at will' (3–4):

> Thus Christ unforc'd prevents in sheeding blood
> The whips, the thorns, the nail, the spear, and rood.   (5–6)

Again, however, the Gethsemane allusion for Herbert demands that he question the notion that tears in any way can approximate the blood of the Atonement: 'Shall I weep bloud?' asks the incredulous speaker in 'The Thanksgiving.' It is one thing for the messianic speaker of 'The

Sacrifice' to assume as much; it would be quite another for the penitent here, who instead halts at the thought of the Passion, recognizing his utter inability to offer anything in return. Similar reluctance to assume penitential agency is a feature of 'H. Baptisme (I),' where the source of baptismal water, like the eucharistic wine, is 'my deare Redeemers pierced side' (6). Indeed, just as early in 'The Church-porch' Herbert warns that lust 'doth pollute and foul / Whom God in Baptisme washt with his own blood' (7–8), here both sacraments are suggested by the following line's plural 'blessed streams' (7), which in turn are associated with the poet's tearful contribution (9). Just as the poem closes by affirming the prevenient exhaustiveness of Baptism in anticipating the speaker's 'future sinnes' (13), earlier lines also find his tears subsumed by an all-encompassing grace:

> O blessed streams! either ye do prevent
> And stop our sinnes from growing thick and wide,
> Or else give tears to drown them, as they grow.   (7–9)

Likewise, comparing human grief to that of his Lord in 'Affliction (II),' Herbert recognizes that the 'broken pay' he offers in dying 'over each houre of Methusalems stay' is no match for 'thy one death' (2–5):

> If all mens tears were let
> Into one common sewer, sea, and brine;
> What were they all, compar'd to thine?
> Wherein if they were set,
> They would discolour thy most bloudy sweat.   (6–10)

Prevenience is the culprit usurping autonomous and pious grief, this time by way of an irrevocable down payment: 'Thy crosse took up in one, / By way of imprest, all my future mone' (14–15), the final pun (mone/money) emphasizing the inadequacy of the speaker's devotional efforts in the divine economy. Indeed, the alternative spelling, antedating *The Temple*, appears in the *OED* under a lemma particularly relevant to the poem: 'designating a sum applied to a particular purpose or in the possession of a particular person.'[5]

To the extent tears are aligned more with sacramental grace than with human devotional effort are they invested with soteriological efficacy. Rather than inadequate sacrifice, they coincide in 'The Church-floore' with the crucial recognition that mere human effort cannot satisfy divine justice. Associated less with the devotional psyche than with a place of communal gathering, tears' sacramental value is indicated by their capacity to purge Adam's curse:

> Hither sometimes Sinne steals, and stains
> The marbles neat and curious veins:
> But all is cleansed when the marble weeps. (13–15)

'Patience' (3), 'Humilitie' (6), 'Confidence' (9), and 'Charitie' (12) are Christian virtues destroyed by sin and restored through penitence. Yet because weeping *follows* the description of an ideal 'floore,' the suggestion is that the attempt to recover these virtues is both necessary and doomed to failure. Recognition of the extent of its collective depravity is a prerequisite for the church's genuine repentance. *Felix culpa* is evident in 'Death,' who, 'while he thinks to spoil the room ... sweeps' (16–18), just as abrogation of the law is turned through grace to salvation. Similarly, as the floor 'weeps' blood through its 'curious veins,' the process allows grace to do its work, the 'Architect' having overseen his design from the beginning.[6]

If penitence alone, however genuine, is insufficient, 'Ephes. 4.30' nevertheless emphasizes the paradoxical necessity of an appropriate devotional posture. The penitent mourns the Holy Spirit's grief and regrets his own inability to conjure adequate tears. The poem reconciles this lack by closing with a typical identification of tears and blood, the inadequacy of Herbert's grief supplemented by his saviour's: 'Lord, pardon, for thy Sonne makes good / My want of tears with store of bloud' (35–6). This final stanza in hindsight suggests sacramental/typological significance for an earlier:

> Then weep mine eyes, the God of love doth grieve:
>> Weep foolish heart,
>> And weeping live:
> For death is drie as dust. Yet if ye part,
>> End as the night, whose sable hue
>> Your sinnes expresse; melt into dew. (7–12)

If dew suggests manna and, typologically, the bread of the Eucharist, then Herbert expands the tears/blood conceit to include the sacramental body. As night dissolves into dew, so sin, distilled through genuine repentance, is transubstantiated into the bread of life, the Christ who was made a body of sin so that man and God might be reconciled (1 Pet. 2.24; 2 Cor. 5.21). Tears, blood, and bread combine to sacramentalize the penitential psyche so that the weeping heart undergoes a kind of reverse alchemy, the alembic of eucharistic topoi dispersing the self among the dust and dew shrouded by night sky. By allowing otherwise private tears to be absorbed in a wider communal and mythical context, sacrament relieves the isolation and guilt inevitably attending an inward devotional piety. Once again the devotional self achieves transcendence only through obliteration, the process in this case a subtle melting of private griefs into sacramental dew. We are reminded of Donne's lovers in 'Valediction to his booke' whose erotic encounter dissolves calmly into the 'Booke' that is 'as long-liv'd as the elements' (19). As is typical of Donne's sacramental poems, however, the Christian *mythos* in 'To his booke' does not so much subsume the lovers' experience as become the vehicle of a hyperbolic comparison. Herbert's devotional tears, in contrast, without exception are subordinated to the messianic. They are never those which in Crashaw's 'The Weeper,' for a more stark comparison, are so bold as to teach 'Waters above the Heavens, what they be' (23) or 'Whose sacred influence / Adds sweetness' (27–8) to the lips of the 'brisk cherub' (26) whose 'breakfasts' they are (30) – though it must be allowed that in a Roman Catholic context the immaculately conceived Virgin sheds tears as significant as her son's.

The relevance of sacrament for Christian identification with an all-consuming Will is not confined to Herbert's lachrymal poems. 'The Banquet,' which, for obvious reasons, follows 'The Invitation,' shares its companion's metrical arrangement and rhyme scheme, though here the priest turns from his auditory and addresses the elements of the Eucharist themselves. Though ceremonial in tone and context, the poem is less public proclamation than personal reflection, and thus more typical of Herbert's inward focus. He begins by drawing tentative parallels between sacramental incarnation and several natural phenomena, including the occult suggestion that in the Eucharist 'Is some starre (fled from the sphere) / Melted there, / As we sugar melt in wine' (10–12). Unlike Donne in his secular poems, Herbert rarely submits sacramental topoi to the play of extended metaphor; and even when he does, as here, the sacrament overwhelmingly carries the tenor of the verbal relationship. Indeed, Herbert ultimately denies his chosen examples any true resemblance:

> Doubtlesse, neither starre nor flower
>   Hath the power
> Such a sweetnesse to impart:
> Onely God, who gives perfumes,
>   Flesh assumes,
>   And with it perfumes my heart.   (19–24)

The phrase 'Onely God' dismisses both star and flower but immediately appropriates yet another figure. The pious assertion approximates the middle of the stanza and thus occupies the nether space between tropes, on one side a familiar occult analogy, on the other a slightly more playful metaphor. This motion from analogy to metaphor is an appropriate rhetorical accompaniment to the concern with identification indicated by 'Flesh assumes': God, flesh, perfume, and the speaker's heart meld in the brevity of the final line. An immanence based on medieval synthesis thus yields to one based on subjective experience. But if the devout gaze turns from the sky inward, olfactory and kinaesthetic figures maintain the emerging persona's stubbornly outward orientation.

Having achieved the poetic equivalent of eucharistic identification and drawn yet another analogy, this time comparing Jesus' broken body with 'Pomanders' (25) that in 'being bruis'd are better sented' (27), Herbert then describes the effects of sacramental union as three distinct stages. Identifying with the very sin that makes the Atonement necessary, 'God took bloud, and needs would be / Spilt with me, / And so found me on the ground' (34–6). From this prostration, evocative of ceremonial kneeling, the speaker looks up toward God who 'In a cup / Sweetly ... doth meet my taste (38–9).' He is thus empowered to 'flie / To the skie' and finally 'see / What I seek, for what I sue' (45–6). The final stanza completes the motion from ceremonial proclamation to private spiritual drama by requesting sacrificial status for the poet's devotional efforts: 'Let the wonder of his pitie / Be my dittie, / And take up my lines and life' (49–51). Echoing 'The Collar,' where Herbert strikes the Communion board, proclaiming his 'lines and life ... free as the rode,' (4) he now submits the same 'under pain of death' (52) to approximate Christ's own sacrifice, to 'Strive in this, and love the strife' (54).

In 'The Crosse,' identification with Herbert's crucified saviour is frustrated by recognition that whatever he offers was never his to give. Total corruption of the sinner's will ensures that any just motions it might entertain are attributed solely to God's saving grace:

things sort not to my will,
Ev'n when my will doth studie thy renown:
Thou turnest th' edge of all things on me still,
Taking me up to throw me down: (19–22)

Not content as was Donne in 'Hymn to God my God in my sicknesse' to
stop here – 'Therefore that he may raise the Lord throws down' (30) –
Herbert's recourse in the end is to plead the Lord's Prayer, which in this
context suggests a messianic identification:

And since these thy contradictions
Are properly a crosse felt by thy sonne,
With but foure words, my words, *Thy will be done.*   (34–6)

The final referential ambiguity for 'my,' however, is presumably intolerable earlier where the sacrificial status of all-too-human efforts are dismissed at the foot of the cross which cancels

My power to serve thee; to unbend
All my abilities, my designes confound,
And lay my threatnings bleeding on the ground.   (10–12)

In Donne's poem of the same title the cross is approached with a sober
confidence critical of the psychological paralysis evident here, the 'selfe-
despising' that in its own way threatens to become a kind of pious
posturing and 'selfe-love' (38). Donne, like Herbert, never fully avoids
the extremes of presumption and despair, ceaselessly crossing both
'dejections' and 'forbidden heights' (53–4). What both poems share is a
determination to find in this central Christian symbol the reconciliation
of otherwise irreconcilable divine and human wills. Herbert, more than
Donne, is alert to the problem that any attempt to imagine such a
reconciliation is inappropriate because its very success would threaten
the radical autonomy of divine grace. He is nevertheless just as tenacious
as Donne, if more subtle, in his reluctance to abandon personal agency.
Having wrestled with the 'contrarieties' (32) and 'contradictions' (34) of
his status as grace-awarded yet undeserving sinner, Herbert finds relief
by projecting psychological paradox back onto the arch-symbol of its
source, closing with a vision of the cross that is as much the embodiment
of, as cure for, his 'smart' (31). And while the poem as a whole documents an essentially psychological drama, in another sense it seeks to

escape those tortuous confines by allowing the paradoxes to be played out on that shared symbol of Christian suffering. Even as he assumes the 'crosse actions' which 'cut my heart' (32-3) and straps himself to the object that is both his relief and bane, this first Adam's voice – 'my words' – melts into that of the second. We are not altogether certain – as neither, perhaps, is Herbert – just who is quoting scripture here, and for whose purposes. In hindsight, then, the bloody status of the poet's 'threatnings,' sacrificed at the altar that is the cross, is perhaps indicative less of a desire to share in Christ's sufferings than for Christ to absorb his.

Poised on the brink of tasting the ultimate repast, the marriage supper of the Lamb of which the Eucharist is but a type, the guest of 'Love (III)' continues to resist a thoroughly undeserved grace until the sacrament intercedes to silence soteriological anxiety. Michael Schoenfeldt, pace Marion Singleton, places the exchange firmly within the conventions of Renaissance courtship and hospitality. Love, he writes, 'stoops to conquer' in order, finally, to become the dominating Host.[7] Helen Vendler, anticipating Schoenfeldt and Singleton, gets it right, I think, in recognizing for the poem's 'contest in courtesy' a 'gentle irony.'[8] Love's invitation and tender encouragement resemble, in Chana Bloch's formulation, the consolation offered an inadequate lover who 'grow[s] slack' (3) at the initial encounter and whose confidence subsequently is restored.[9] Such confidence, however, consists not in a new-found ability to perform. Indeed, he who finally tastes is denied even the most menial of contributions to the impending union, Love sharply responding to the guest's offer to 'serve' with 'You must sit down' (16–17). This final communion, rather, marks the completion of a process wholly attributed to God, beginning with the Atonement and ending with the gift of grace it affords. Because Love 'bore the blame' (15) and has thus anticipated or 'prevented' the guest's 'shame' (13), the latter's sins are drawn back, going where they 'doth deserve' (14) – in effect, back out the door – even as the guest himself moves forward to receive his (un)due reward. As a response to the guest's perceived inability to 'look on' (10) him, Love's 'Who made the eyes but I?' (12) reminds the guest of his creaturely status while at the same time cautioning him against implying for God a faulty workmanship. Crossing the threshold thus inaugurates a radical separation – the husk of sin from its redeemable kernel – the guest's reluctance deriving from the extent to which he so thoroughly identifies with the former and thus sees in its eradication a threat to his very being. As the condemned sings in Bruce Springsteen's contribution to the *Dead Man Walking* soundtrack, 'I can't ask for forgiveness; my sins are all I have.'

To accept the invitation and accede to Love's conditions, however, is to experience not a disintegration of the self but rather a transformation at once desired and truly frightening. Far more than the most intense of human love affairs, the speaker's relationship with God requires the utmost giving of self in order paraodoxically to achieve its fullest realization. That process only begins when Love takes the guest's hand and asks, 'Who made the eyes but I,' the graphic identification – 'I' and 'I' – suggesting a semantic one – 'me' and 'Love.' But if this dual 'I' is an instance of what Heather Asals has called equivocal predication, there is no question of democratic balance among its components. The sacramental context may require the guest to eat, but in the end it is not only the Host of this intimate and private Mass that is consumed. *Contra* Stanley Fish, however, the speaker of 'Love (III)' is not *self*-consuming. He or she, rather, consumes God in the sacrament even while being consumed *by* God, the result a true *consummation*, a marriage of human and divine in a poem that boldly invests spiritual experience with erotic intensity. Profane and sacred loves are not equivocal, one necessarily cancelling the other; they are the same, rather, in the sense that they share in the same animating presence. R.V. Young thus rightly dismisses the self-consciously 'daring candor of postmodern criticism.' Neither erotic nor divine love in the poem is merely collapsed one into the other. Rather, 'sacred and profane love are analogous' and thus 'mutually illuminating.'[10]

Ceremony, the Art of Devotion

Because *The Temple* as artifact constitutes a sacramentalization of private religious experience – or, conversely, an internal application of the grace that sacraments publicly symbolize and confer – Herbert is also concerned with the role of priest/communicant *qua* devotional poet. In 'The Church-porch,' for example, 'A verse may find him, who a sermon flies, / And turn delight into a sacrifice' (5–6), proverbial wisdom anticipating the invitation in 'Superliminare' to receive the sacrament, the 'churches mysticall repast' (4). Rosalie Colie long ago recognized that Herbert's is an 'immanent God' whose involvement in the minutiae of existence is the model for continual poetic recreation.[11] Yet it must be allowed that Herbert's Reform piety and its severe self-abnegation are of considerable consequence for his sense of creative autonomy and the character of his art. C.A. Patrides, for example, sees Herbert's piety in the context of a 'controlled turbulence' and avers that his apparent artlessness is qualified by a forceful and complex self-consciousness.[12]

Herbert's lines, like his life, look to heaven even as they are rooted in earth. His verse is sacramental in that it embodies that which otherwise transcends embodiment, paradoxically gesturing beyond itself even while stubbornly and sometimes dazzlingly declaring its artifice. Herbert's eucharistic verse exemplifies the observation of F.W., a seventeenth-century English Catholic poet who, notes Alison Shell, writes in the preface to a manuscript sonnet sequence, 'It seemethe verie conforme, to reason, that poetrie and divinitie shouldbe matched together, as soule and bodie, bodie and garment, *substance enwrapped withe hir accidents.*'[13]

Divinely inspired human creativity is an integral feature of Herbert's sacramental world view. The waters in 'Man' which, 'Below,' are 'our drink' and 'above, our meat' (40), are also 'our cleanlinesse' (41). These 'inescapable'[14] eucharistic allusions anticipate Herbert's prayer that God 'afford us so much wit; / That, as the world serves us, we may serve thee, / And both thy servants be' (52–4). Wit is contiguous with this 'meat,' part of a unified sacramental world wherein 'symmetrie,' proportion, and correspondence (13–14), describe a web of analogies and likenesses among creation's constituents, all centred around the microcosm, man, whose 'head with foot hath private amitie / And both with moons and tides' (17–18). The curative power of sacraments, this cleansing 'meat' from above, is reflected by a cosmology wherein the medicinal properties of plants derive from their affinity with human bodies: 'Herbs gladly cure our flesh; because that they / Finde their acquaintance there' (23–4). The capacity for devotional and creative wit is thus among a myriad of divine gifts, the meat from above whose sacramental contiguity revolves around man who 'is one world, and hath / Another to attend him' (47–8). Realizing that world in all its splendour is an aspect of the service to which Herbert aspires, not unlike the 'Man' in 'Providence' made 'secretarie of thy praise' (6–8).

Analogous to the Eucharist, writing in 'H. Baptisme (II)' supplements and reinforces the effects of the primary sacrament. The speaker's soul is opposed to flesh, the 'growth of flesh ... a blister' (14), while spiritual innocence is associated with childhood, and poetic effort a subsequent writing of the soul back into innocent flesh:

> O let me still
> Write thee great God, and me a childe:
> Let me be soft and supple to thy will,
> Small to my self, to others milde,
> Behither ill.   (6–10)

And in 'The Quidditie,' though poetry is no 'crown, / ... point of honour,' great courtier or the rest, it is, nevertheless, 'that which while I use / I am with thee, and *Most take all*' (11–12). Not merely self-reflective, verse actually facilitates communion with the presence it celebrates. That presence itself can never be adequately described; indeed, it is known only through a *via negativa* that places it above the more tangible of human experiences. However, the poem's title – which means something like the essence of a thing – together with the final '*most take all*,' insists that the divine presence is the source of all these lesser pleasures and honours. Herbert in effect applies sacramental theology to poetic craft, asserting the latter's status as a manifestation of the essence by which it is sustained, much as sacramental signs convey that which invests their otherwise mediatory, representational status with transcendent value. That the speaker is intimately familiar with the earthly pleasures he subordinates is evident in the possessive '*my* great stable or demain' (8, my emphasis). It is interesting to note that while both B (47r) and W (48r) (where the poem is called 'Poetry') have 'my,' 1633 has 'a' (61). Thomas Buck's Herbert evidently was more pious than the speaker in the manuscripts. In distinguishing between devotional writing and courtly pursuits Herbert maintains for the former a status which, if it surpasses worldly pleasures, can be understood only in proximity to them. Divine poetry, like the sacramental bread and wine, comprehends the ineffable only in respect of the familiar. Herbert's devotional art is based on the same Word/flesh paradox at the heart of the Incarnation: it is only by dwelling among us, as John's Gospel proclaims, that the Word for Herbert is. This keen sensitivity to the liminal nature of devotional verse is also a feature of the acrostic 'Coloss. 3.3' through which runs the motto, '*My Life Is Hid In Him That Is My Treasure*.' The poet's 'words & thoughts do both expresse' a 'double motion,' one 'wrapt *In* flesh' and tending 'to earth,' the other 'wind[ing] towards *Him*,' a duality fleshed out, so to speak, in the motto's oblique presence, just as the second of the sun's motions 'doth obliquely bend' (1–6). The device, like Herbert's shape poems, is clever; but it is also sacramentally appropriate, both in the way it fleshes out the Word (here scripture), and in its homely portrayal of the sun's (son's) role as 'our diurnall friend' (3). Not only is his life hidden in Christ; Christ is also Herbert's '*Treasure*,' even if hidden in a poetic jar of clay.

Herbert was not always at ease about the status of his devotional art relative to that which it celebrates. Crossing the river in 'Jordan (I)' typologically anticipates Baptism and silently allegorizes Herbert's self-

proclaimed overcoming of poetic artifice: whereas others are fond of the
'course-spunne lines' of 'enchanted groves' and 'sudden arbours shadow,'
the speaker 'envie[s] no mans nightingale or spring,' and would rather
'plainly' assert 'My God, My King' (6–15).[15] This simple proclamation
implies the possibility of a poetry paradoxically free of poetic convention, a poetry *sans* poetry. But just as sacraments provide material reinforcement for the spiritual communion they promote, so does 'Jordan
(I)' reify the importance and necessity of art even as it asserts the latter's
earth-boundedness. This all turns out, however, to be rather disingenuous. If Herbert had in fact written only 'My God, My King,' there would
be no poem at all. The second stanza's subtle assonances and alliteration
help to evoke the very world of Spenserian romance and pastoral they
ostensibly dismiss, just as the poem's overall formal and metric consist-
ency attest to a firm control and calculated artlessness. It would seem,
then, that the interrogative dismissal is less absolute than genuinely
perplexing, both suspicious of and indebted to the poetic artifice leading to – and rendering all the more effective – the supposedly 'plain'
proclamation of the final line. This tension is exacerbated by the ambiguous characterization of 'Shepherds' in the final stanza: 'Shepherds
are honest people; let them sing' (11). Following immediately upon
'Must all be vail'd, while he that reads, divines, / Catching the sense at
two removes' (9–10), the shepherd/poet trope both appeals to long-
standing tradition and suggests an affirmative answer to the question,
even if 'honest' suggests the need for a finally *true* bard, a *pastor fido* who
will 'plainly say' what his predecessors obscured with the rich furniture
of poetic finery.

Is Herbert's the voice of the honest shepherd? This is far from 'plainly'
evident. Here is the entire final stanza:

Shepherds are honest people; let them sing;
Riddle who list, for me, and pull for Prime:
I envie no mans nightingale or spring;
Nor let them punish me with losse of rime,
    Who plainly say, *My God, My King.*   (11–15)

Alluding to a game, the speaker challenges the reader to continue
playing – refusing, at this point anyway, to declare his hand. Echoes of
Bacon's 'Of Simulation and Dissimulation,' which cautions that 'if a man
engage himself by a manifest declaration, he must go through or take a
fall,'[16] reverberate not only here but also in another of Herbert's refer-

ences to primero. Addressing the 'sweet youth' of 'The Church-porch' Herbert avers that in discourse one may 'preserve' his own 'stock' by focusing on and drawing out that of his interlocutor. Particularly telling are the stanza's parenthetical lines – both strategic caution and ironic comment on the speaker's own position:

> Entice all neatly to what they know best;
> For so thou dost thy self and him a pleasure:
> (But a proud ignorance will lose his rest,
> Rather than shew his cards.) Steal from his treasure
> What to ask further. Doubts well rais'd do lock
> The speaker to thee, and preserve thy stock.   (295–300)

Even if we allow that 'proud ignorant' corresponds to 'him,' there is an ethical tension here between what Bacon might have called 'openness and frankness of dealing' and the first degree of dissimulation: 'closeness, reservation and secrecy.'[17] Enticing his reader/opponent to 'pull for Prime' (12) in 'Jordan (I),' Herbert is divided between the honest shepherd's plain song and the 'vail'd' sense that is the poet's stock and trade. If, by his own definition, he refrains from divulging his answers to the poem's pressing questions and is thus 'a proud ignorant,' he effectively both raises doubts and preserves his own 'stock,' shifting the burden of speculative interrogation to the imagined interlocutor or reader. An alternative explanation, however, is that the poet himself is among the puzzled members of his own audience. Herbert's vocational conflict, the poet's doubt as to the status of his craft in knowing and communicating the divine, is never resolved. He may conclude with plain and simple assertion, but the effectiveness of that conclusion is fully dependent on the dazzling artistry that on one level it forsakes. It is not that Herbert here fails to say what he means; rather, he fails (fortunately) to practice what he preaches. Artifice in devotion is, apparently, like the river Jordan: an obstacle to overcome. But immersion in its waters is the only way across.[18]

'Love (II),' like its namesake at the close of *The Temple*, is concerned with the interpenetration of identities that Holy Communion affords. And just as the extent to which the eucharistic species participate in conferring grace is potentially controversial, so here Herbert grapples with the value of his fleshly art relative to the spiritual truths he would have it communicate. The lesser flame of human lust inspires wit and invention, which the poet offers on the altar of 'Immortal Heat' (1).

Whereas Donne's *Holy Sonnets* retain obvious traces of profane love, here such love is fully identified as belonging more to that divine flame than to 'usurping lust' (12). The poem suggests less a strict dualism, however, than a hierarchical contiguity wherein the greater flame subsumes the lesser. In laying 'All her invention on thine Altar' (7) the poet's brain recognizes this contiguity, his now mended 'eies' seeing

> thee, which before saw dust;
> Dust blown by wit, till that they both were blinde:
> Thou shalt recover all thy goods in kinde,
> Who wert disseized by usurping lust.   (9–12)

The legal terminology clarifies the fact that human love has always belonged to God, that lust excludes recognition of this fact and is thereby the expense of spirit in a waste of shame. Lust seeks to consume all rather than allow itself to be consumed on Love's altar. In sacrificing his energies to this Heraclitean fire, the poet seeks a greater union than that in which the object of his love is consumed by his own wit. And while it is that wit which fashions this very sacrifice, the poetic act, because an act of recognition, is but the return of a flame to its origin, allowing lesser heat 'in hymnes [to] send back thy fire again' (8).

Love for the divine is appropriately self-consuming. Stanley Fish rightly observes of Herbert that 'the moment of highest artfulness always coincides with the identification of the true source of that art' and that Herbert, 'in losing title to his poem also loses (happily) the presumption of its invention.'[19] Consummation in the Eucharist, the reception of ultimate sacrifice, asks sacrifice in return. The recipient thus reflects on his sin and subsequently relinquishes his corrupt will to God's. The grace allowing him to do so is effected in the sacrament, so that even as he eats he himself is consumed. Human offering at the sacrament, the submission of a corrupt to an incorrupt will, is a sacrifice made possible by the original Atonement. Consuming and consumed, both God and speaker, as in 'Love (III),' participate in a consummation. In 'Love (II)' that process is reflected in a consuming fire, the encompassing perimeter of poetic heat ultimately swallowed by the immortal it cannot finally contain. But in being consumed, Herbert's art is far from erased; rather, the 'brain' which 'All her invention on thine Altar lay' (6–7) is the source of such hymns as fuel 'Immortal Heat' (1), by whom they are refined and, like the Atonement, anticipate Resurrection.

Poetic identification with atoning sacrifice is also the subject of 'Good

Friday,' where Herbert struggles to 'measure out thy bloud' (2). Christ's 'foes' measuring his sufferings; all stars his death like the one that 'show'd thy first breath'; and falling leaves his griefs (6–10) – these are expanded in the fourth and fifth stanzas to include the poet's life through which Christ's 'distresse ... may runne, / And be my sunne' (15–16). Herbert's turning away from conceits based on his experience of the external world toward his own sin and griefs immediately follows the poem's structural and sacramental centre:

> Or cannot leaves, but fruit, be signe
> > Of the true vine?   (11–12)

The inward turn suggests a complete severing of spiritual truth from the material world and the poetic wit by which both are comprehended. This is particularly true of the poem as it appears in W. But in B and 1633 a revised version of W's 'The Passion' follows 'Good Friday,' sans title, suggesting the two actually may be one poem.[20] These latter stanzas once again recall the sacramental status of the sinner's private anguish, this time explicitly conflating the acts of sacrifice and writing. The sinner's heart is both inkwell and store of sin from which (and paradoxically on which) may be drawn the 'whips ... nails ... wounds' and 'woes' (26) of Jesus' bloody Passion:

> Since bloud is fittest, Lord, to write
> Thy sorrows in, and bloudie fight;
> My heart hath store, write there, where in
> One box doth lie both ink and sinne: (21–4)

The idea of righteous blood displacing sinful blood in 'The Agonie' is also apparent here, but the pen through which flows this blood/ink may be more than merely figurative:

> Sinne being gone, oh fill the place,
> And keep possession with thy grace;
> Lest sinne take courage and return,
> And all the writings blot or burn.   (29–32)

That the ambiguous 'writings' bears the trace of a sacramental role for Herbert's verse is evident in the W version of this stanza's final couplet: 'ffor by the writings all may see / Thou hast an ancient claime to mee'

(25v). If the revision shows greater sensitivity to the ephemeral status of verse relative to the grace which makes it possible, there nevertheless remains the poet's conviction that his life *and lines* are somehow integral with the whips, nails, wounds, and woes he would have lodged in his heart. Just who wields the pen is not finally clear.

The poet's heart in 'Obedience,' finally, 'doth bleed / As many lines, as there doth need / To passe it self and all it hath' (6–8) to God. The poetic 'Deed' (10) is compared to Christ's, whose

> death and bloud
> Show'd a strange love to all our good:
> Thy sorrows were in earnest; no faint proffer,
> Or superficiall offer
> Of what we might not take, or be withstood. (26–30)

Herbert then dismisses any legality which might make some portion of the deed a 'gift or donation' (34). Rather, further to 'exclude the wrangler from thy treasure' (15), he adds a clause insisting that any such gift will 'by way of purchase go' (35); that is, the paper only formally grants what has always belonged to God in the first place. In hindsight, then, poetic bloodshed is at best imitative, the poet discovering that the power to write the deed was never his; the blood/ink that falls to the page may merge with Herbert's, but originates in quite another well. This sacramental gesture is finally extended to the reader:

> How happie were my part,
> If some kinde man would thrust his heart
> Into these lines; till in heav'ns Court of Rolls
> They were by winged souls
> Entred for both, farre above their desert! (41–5)

The poem is thus truly evocative of Holy Communion. In its implicit conflation of poet and priest it may even be described as sacerdotal: the one to one negotiations of lone devout and his God are expanded laterally to include a broader social awareness and pastoral responsibility, finally spanning both vertical (devotional) and horizontal (communal) axes of sacramental experience. The first seven stanzas set forth a legal representation of the speaker's obligations to God, but these legalities are exploded and mocked when his 'Deed' is compared with Christ's atoning work: in the seventh stanza he can only shrug and hand over what he knows is not his to give. So that poetic agency is not entirely lost, however, Herbert now extends the gesture to his fellow debtor who 'may set his hand / And heart unto this Deed, when he hath read' (37–8). The same ink/blood which ratifies that deed is now inclusive of the poet/priest's beneficiary, the reader/communicant.[21]

The Temple documents one weary soul's efforts to find in sacrament an expansion of the devotional self beyond mere ego and the conscience that chides, a desire to identify with the Christ whose body is consumed in the ritual. At stake is the identity of a persona divided between its sense of personal autonomy and the Christian *mythos* with which it would merge. Stanley Fish has argued eloquently that Herbert's poems are self-consuming artifacts. Even Fish cannot deny, however, that *The Temple* is the work of a distinctive and innovative artist, that at those moments when it is most self-censuring and deferential, the penitent's voice is most conspicuously the poet's own. It is only in relinquishing his life that Herbert's Christian Everyman truly knows what it is to live, just as the increate Logos, in becoming flesh and dying, redeems a world otherwise left to its own devices. Consuming and consumed, Herbert's devotional verse is fully sacramental, a liminal fleshing of the Word wherein both deity and religious artist together might declare, as in 'The Sacrifice,'

> my hearts deare treasure
> Drops bloud (the onely beads) my words to measure.   (21–2)

Such confidence in his art emerges despite Herbert's knowledge that *The Temple* might at best embody only approximately the grace whose reality surpasses human understanding. As he writes in *Outlandish Proverbs*, 'Weening is not measure' (*Works*, 348).

CONCLUSION

Sacramental Poetics

Commenting on Herbert's eating images, Heather Ross observes that 'it is through indulgence in the senses that one transcends them and finds God, whereas it is through the repression and denial of our senses, our appetites, that we find ourselves.'[1] If hyperbole, the statement nonetheless is a frightening vision of where a devotional piety stripped of sacrament, ceremony, liturgy, and other universalizing features of religious worship might lead. However inward Donne's and Herbert's devotional enthusiasms, both recognized the importance of incorporating ceremonial forms within the framework of prayer, meditation, and homily. Their efforts to establish a *via media* between sacramental and word-based styles of divinity, moreover, were not only spiritual but also political, for they involved issues central to the early Stuart church's struggle over its confessional identity. The spiritual success of *The Temple* and Donne's divine poems and sermons consists not in a happy reconciliation of religious ideologies, but rather in their being driven paradoxically by the failure finally to provide one. Indeed, the aesthetic and, from the historical scholar's point of view, socio-cultural importance of their work derives precisely from that failure. Political success? Well, there is the 1630s, the Laudian archbishopric, and the English Civil War.

These observations, however, are not meant merely to be some smug dismissal of religious or spiritual ideals and objectives. The failures suggested here would not have surprised divines so thoroughly cognizant of human limitations as were Donne and Herbert. 'Caught between the Passion and its final fulfillment,' writes Martin Elsky of Herbert, 'the poet is plagued by a gnawing sense of incompleteness as he tries to accomplish the final fulfillment of his Eucharistic offering.'[2] As the frustrated lovers of Donne's 'Relique' observe, in a very different context, 'Comming and going, wee, / Perchance might kisse, but not between those meales' (27–8), where 'those meales,' we observed, are the Last Supper and the heavenly wedding banquet framing history that sacramental discourse recalls and anticipates. Donne's profane sacramentalities, as much as his own and Herbert's devotional lyrics, attest both to this rupture between human and divine histories and to the redemptive scope of the Incarnation that bridges them. For the application of sacramental topoi to the various worldy concerns of the secular verse is at once a parody highlighting the chasm that separates the divine aspirations of the soul from the body's historical contingencies, and a radical extension of the Incarnation's unique claims.

This study closes with a brief consideration of two later seventeenth-century devotional poets, Richard Crashaw and Henry Vaughan, as representative of opposite edges of the periphery circumscribing the *via media* that Donne and Herbert sought to formulate and expound. Like them, Crashaw and Vaughan explored the devotional dimension of the Eucharist and the relevance of ceremonial forms for the progress of the soul. Their respective approaches to such matters, however, differed considerably both from one another and from those of their predecessors. The following observations, then, review and indicate later developments of the sacramental poetics that has been the subject of this book.

Other than the occasional reference to pagan altars, as in the closing dedicatory lines of the panegyric, 'To the Queen, Upon her numerous Progenie,' there are no sacramental conceits in Richard Crashaw's secular verse, whereas the Eucharist, not surprisingly, is a prominent feature of the sacred. His conversion experience from son of a puritan and rabidly anti-Roman Catholic polemicist to a priest suspected of the very popery William Crashaw had devoted his career to stamping out entailed a neophyte's zeal for those features of his adoptive religion so beloved of its adherents – the worship of the Virgin and the Real Presence of the Eucharist. These are even combined, for example, in 'The Tear,' where Crashaw's Mariolatry bestows on the Virgin's sorrows a sacramental significance: 'This watry Blossome of thy Eyne / Ripe, will make the richer Wine' (4–5). A more daring conceit, replete with puns on 'host' and 'board,' is the celebration of incarnational paradox in 'O Gloriosa Domina':

He that made all things, had not done
Till he had made Himself thy son.
The whole world's host would be thy guest

And board himself at thy rich BREAST.
O boundless Hospitality!
The FEAST of all things feeds on thee.   (5–10)

That eucharistic topoi are entirely absent from Crashaw's secular poems is consistent with his deliberately separate treatment of the sacred and the profane. It also suggests his reluctance to allow a central feature of his new-found faith to be contaminated by more worldly concerns. The young John Donne's intimate familiarity with the trappings and conventions of his inherited rather than acquired Roman Catholicism by contrast would appear to have allowed him to indulge a greater liberality in his treatment of sacramental ideas from within ostensibly profane poetic contexts. It is perhaps because of an increase in religious zeal following his own Protestant conversion that sacramental topoi are comparatively absent from Donne's divine lyrics. For while it continued to play a prominent role in post-Reformation English divinity, sacrament also was the site of some of the most heated polemical battles. But the diminished presence of sacrament in Donne's sacred verse relative to that of Crashaw or even Robert Southwell was not merely an eirenic reluctance to stir the pot of religious controversy. Whereas Crashaw's and Southwell's largely didactic, liturgical, and ceremonial treatment of sacrament indicates a strong sense of Christian community and ecclesiastical tradition, Donne's comparatively inward focus in the sacred poems was a product of English Calvinism and its need to combine sacramental worship with the private deliberations of the predestinarian psyche.

The tension between devotional and sacramental imperatives in English Protestantism is not entirely absent from Crashaw's verse. With a didacticism similar to that of Southwell's sacramental poems, Crashaw's emphasis on human culpability in 'The Hymn for the Blessed Sacrament' suggests that the predestinarian disputes which plagued the Reformation years continued to be at issue when it came to the question of eucharistic efficacy:

    on the same (life-meaning) Bread
  The child of Death eats himself Dead.
  Nor is't love's fault, but sin's dire skill
  That thus from LIFE can DEATH distill.   (Stanza IX)

That assertion, 'Nor is't love's fault,' like Southwell's own observation a half century earlier in 'Of the Blessed Sacrament of the Aulter' that 'The fault is in the men, not in the thinge' (42), is one with which Calvin would have agreed. But that the notion of divine responsibility needs to be addressed at all is surely a legacy of Calvin's predestinarian soteriology, Crashaw's and Southwell's poems in part a polemical response to its implications. The logical difference between strictly Calvinist and Roman Catholic views of the predestinarian dimension of the sacrament is an important one. Whereas for the latter God's election is based on his foresight of the one who freely chooses to 'eat himself Dead,' as it were, for the former – both the experimental and credal varieties (if pressed on the issue) – the distillation of death from life in the Eucharist has finally little if anything to do with human agency and volition, even as so unfortunate an outcome is held to be entirely the communicant's responsibility. The doctrinal thrust of Crashaw's 'Hymn for the Blessed Sacrament' is evident throughout, the poem's liturgical character reinforced by the almost exclusively plural first-person references. At one point only does Crashaw allow the repeated 'we's to yield to the more intimate and personal 'me.' This occurs, significantly, at the mention of faith and belief in Stanza VII:

> Where nature's lawes no leave will give,
> Bold FAITH takes heart, and dares believe.
> In different species, names not things
> Himself to me my SAVIOUR brings,
> As meat in That, as Drink in this;
> But still in Both one CHRIST he is.

The inward turn is clear enough, but the poem continues to be strongly didactic and dogmatic in substance. The inwardness, moreover, is somewhat disingenuous, a quasi-heuristic device, so that the speaker's priestly duty includes a modelling of personal piety woven into the ceremonial, a piety which consists largely in the internalization of doctrine. The Pauline imperative to examine oneself prior to receiving the species is never in Crashaw's sacramental poems an experimental search for the marks of election or a preoccupation with 'what thou shalt be for ever,' nor even a sustained reflection on personal depravity. The Eucharist is neither an escape from predestinarian doubt nor, worse, a predestinarian lottery. It is rather to be received as a simple and universally accessible act of faith, an effectual remedy for the sins of those willing to acknowledge them and be renewed.

That even so limited a personal moment as that of the 'Hymn' is

uncharacteristic of Crashaw's liturgical poems is evident in his modern
editor's remarks about the opening reference to 'my soul' in the 'Dies
Irae Dies Illa': Crashaw, writes G.W. Williams, 'robbed the opening of its
universality and much of its dignity.'[3] But Crashaw the mid-seventeenth-
century English Roman Catholic was gesturing only toward what in
Herbert the English Protestant and Donne before him had been more
fully explored – the ceremonialization of private devotion. If, as Heather
Ross suggests, sensual indulgence leads ultimately to a transcendence of
the senses, perhaps the obverse is that private enthusiasms might lead
back to the universal, the ceremonial, and the sacramental. Indeed, the
personal dimension of Crashaw's 'Dies Irae' does little to attenuate the
poem's public aspect. In a moment that recalls the despair, supplication,
and subsequent relief frequent in Herbert's poetry of tears, the speaker
avers that

> Though both my Prayres and tears combine,
> Both worthless are; For they are mine.
> But thou thy bounteous self still be;
> And show thou art, by saving me.   (Stanza XIV)

This measured opening of the self to the Other is a confident gesture, a
gentle prodding of the divine will fully expectant of a favourable response. We recognize this tone as resembling not that of the anxious
Donne, but rather of George Herbert's devout, a sinner as convinced of
his salvation as he is conscious of his fallen status. Like Donne's, however, Herbert's devotional inwardness is far more extensive than that of
Crashaw, lingering for entire poems and for much of *The Temple* as a
whole on the condition of his world-weary soul. And yet whatever his
position on predestination – whether, that is, his considerable doubts
and fears derived from such doctrine or simply from a keen sense of
guilt – Herbert embraced the sacrament as a means of grace all but
impervious to the transient whim of the devotional subject.

Herbert's sacramental psychology was of considerable influence on
his poetic successor, Henry Vaughan. Whereas for Herbert, however, the
Eucharist provided a devotional apparatus essential to his articulation of
the workings of grace, Vaughan's sacramental devotion was less a central
than a subsidiary element of his own unique religious sensibility. The
motion from despair and penitential effort to sacramental grace is there,
certainly. Recalling the synaesthesia of the well-known 'Regeneration,'
Vaughan's speaker in 'Admission,' for example, realizes the insuffi-

ciency of such effort and desires that God listen to a more effective
plaint: 'O hear! yet not my tears alone, / Hear now a floud, / A floud
that drowns both tears, and grones, / My Saviours bloud' (29–32). But
Vaughan here fails to forge the tears/blood conceit at which his observation only hints and whereby he might have suggested a self-affirming
rather than self-obliterating transcendence. By uniting his tears with his
'Saviours bloud,' Vaughan, like Herbert in, say, 'The Collar,' might have
realized that his suffering has always been already Christ's own and he
thus might have bestowed on it the dignity it is perceived so sorely to
lack. Paradoxically, this Donnean desperation to drown the self altogether in a sacramental Lethean flood has the opposite effect, the plea
growing louder even as it anticipates the rushing waters: Vaughan's
penitent, like Donne's in *Holy Sonnets*, doth protest too much. The
penitent in 'Praise,' very much like the guest of Herbert's 'Love (III),'
would bring 'to thy board ... a flowre' or 'some such poor Off'ring' (46–
50). But whereas Vaughan's poem closes with the speaker stubbornly
imploring his lord to 'Let him (though poor), / Strow at thy door / That
one poor Blossome' (54–6), Herbert's God mercilessly (-fully) gets the
final word in the exchange: 'You must sit down, sayes Love, and taste my
meat.' It is only in calmly accepting these conditions and yielding to the
Host's hospitality that the guest's 'I' is restored in the final line to its
rightful place and dignity: 'So I did sit and eat.'

Vaughan's affirmations of sacramental presence share also with
Herbert's a physiological concern that grace be communicated both to
soul *and* body. In 'Repentance,' for example, both 'are well drest' in
'him, on whom I feast' (79–80). In 'The Feast,' similarly, 'My soul and all,
/ Kneel down and fall' to receive 'this taste of living glory' (57–9). And in
'The Search,' Christ's 'bloudy sweat' (40) is both a '*Balsam* of Soules' and
'the bodyes blisse' (44). In the same poem, however, 'The skinne, and
shell of things / Though faire, / are not / Thy wish' (81–4), while 'To
rack old Elements, / or Dust ... Is not the way, / nor just,' (88–90) for
'who studies this, / Travels in Clouds, seeks *Manna*, where none is' (95–
6). The eucharistic echoes in 'Elements' and '*Manna*' accompany what
ostensibly is the *contemptus mundi carnalis* of Vaughan's mystic pilgrim.
The Neoplatonic paradox that souls attain their final rest only in being
reunited with a purified body explains the dual application of sacramental grace alongside so vehement a rejection of elemental being. That
Vaughan's hermetic suspicion of the senses is extended obliquely to the
eucharistic species is consistent with this paradox. Though formally
maintaining the double emphasis found in the B version of Herbert's

'H. Communion,' Vaughan is reluctant to sustain so fine a balance of competing claims to the nature of eucharistic presence or to explore possible physiological models, preferring in his own 'Holy Communion' a luminous, pneumatic experience – that the sacramental blood 'unto thy self betroth / Our souls, and bodies both / In everlasting light' (29–31). To be fair, however, we must recall that Herbert in both versions of his Communion poem is reluctant to posit anything like a full interpenetration of bodily and spiritual experiences. Even in the more sensual later version, the elements remain sentinels at the door to the soul, grace only crossing over and relaying messages to these sacramental guards.

It is in 'The Sap,' his most detailed investigation of 'real presence,' that Vaughan suggests what to my knowledge is a unique if but allegorical explanation of the commerce between soul and sacramental species. Again, in keeping with the Neoplatonic idea that all things have a purpose or final cause toward which they naturally tend, in 'The Sap' God 'did something Infuse' (9) in man, the otherwise 'sapless Blossom' (1) that impels an incessant 'growth and stretch for heav'n' (6). This 'something,' counterpart to Christ's 'sacred bloud' which is 'By wil our sap, and Cordial' (26–7), is a 'powerful, rare dew, / Which only grief and love extract' and with which one is to 'wash your vessel wel' in preparation for receiving 'This balm for souls that ake' (40–4). Nowhere in Herbert or Donne is there anything like this correspondence between external and internal sacramental balms, dews, or saps. Vaughan quite deliberately assigns to the devotional, pre-ingestive reflection a sacramental status approaching if not equal to that which traditionally is derived from without. The internal 'rare dew' is perhaps only metaphorically sacramental, its tenor the obligatory Pauline examination. But according to the logic of that metaphor, the internal has anticipated and thus obviated the need for a regenerative power hitherto derived from an external, objective source. More than a mere disintegration of vehicle and tenor, 'The Sap' documents a sacramental operation in which inside and outside have become but equally ephemeral reflections of one another. Despite the occult imagery pervading Vaughan's poetry, his sacramental views on close inspection would seem actually to have divested the Eucharist of its traditional magic.

Though both were royalist in politics, Vaughan and Crashaw represent very different religious tendencies. The sacramental dimension of Vaughan's verse is subordinated to an internal, mystical experience, whereas Crashaw's inward forays are subsumed always by their ceremonial contexts. Though apparently fighting on the king's side when war broke out in the following decade and when Crashaw was associating with English exiles in Paris, Vaughan did not publish his religious verse, *Silex Scintillans*, until after the defeat of the royalist cause. The inward, mystical character of the poetry, then, may have been in part a reaction not unlike Milton's own turn toward a 'paradise within ... happier far'[4] – though for very different reasons. Vaughan's poetic interiority may represent after all not merely royalist disappointment but rather a genuine distrust of sensory experience and a deliberate if muted diminution of sacrament and ceremony.

The fault line which had always plagued the English church's efforts to establish a definitive confessional identity became even more pronounced both during and after the Laudian archbishopric, when the rise of such sectarian movements as the Fifth Monarchy and the Quakers placed ever greater emphasis on psychological experientialism and thus eschewed traditional ceremonial forms. As this book has sought to demonstrate, however, such differences existed *within* the religious establishment long before the 1641 abolition of episcopacy. The difference in religious sensibility between Crashaw and Vaughan was much more polarized in the 1650s than in the 1620s, even if both poets can be said to have regretted the demise of the English church as a unified state institution. But if pre–Civil War clergy such as Donne and Herbert articulated a vision of the church in which inward searches and outward forms are wholly compatible and equally necessary aspects of the devotional life, they did so evidently in response to the shifting political fortunes of various positions on the ideological spectrum. It is also evident, however, that an examination of Stuart religious politics provides only a partial explanation of the relationship in these poets between internal and ceremonial pieties. It is the paradoxical nature of the Incarnation itself that lay at the heart of disputes over the extent to which and in what manner, precisely, the eternal Logos is made humanly manifest. The problem of reconciling the somatic and extracorporeal elements of the incarnational paradox was necessarily extended to include the Eucharist, both in its theological and in its institutional and political aspects. Though ideally resting on that paradox rather than on some specific doctrinal formula, Donne's and Herbert's sacramental poetics were far from immune to the human desire to understand and to articulate what in the final analysis must elude even the most generous of linguistic phenomena.

The *hoc meum corpus est*, despite the relentless pursuit of scholastic rationality to explain it, of Reformation ideology to metaphorize, and

Christian Neoplatonism to mystify it, persisted throughout as the histori-cal reminder of that most scandalous of Christian claims – that the Word has become flesh and dwelt among us. John Donne and George Herbert forged a distinctive sacramental poetics at a time when the Eucharist, despite its potential for uniting disparate Christian faiths around a shared ceremonial practice, was just as likely to be the cause of febrile and very often vicious and even deadly religious dispute. Sacrament's cultural centrality in the later sixteenth and early seventeenth centuries, evident not only in religious verse and sermon but also in the numerous eucha-ristic conceits of Donne's profane lyrics, was perhaps an effect of its conceptual applicability to analogous contemporary spheres of inquiry and, for this reason, all the more susceptible of provoking debate. It is not too difficult, for example, to see the relevance of sacrament for early Stuart ideas about kingship as discussed in chapter 1, for in both cases the issue was one of determining the locus of divine authority and the proper extent of its secular application. Moreover, the degree to which the communication of grace was an individual relative to a corporate transaction, a private rather than public celebration, might register also different beliefs about individual autonomy vis-à-vis political obligation and social responsibility.

Such issues had been important long before Charles I fled London in October of 1641. But they resonate also in our own era when notions of globalization are confronted with the realities of entrenched national-isms and when the cultural triumph of Western individualism would do well to yield to more sober contemplation of the latter's social and political limitations. Just as a nostalgic return to some ideal community of like-minded persons united by the ties of church and sacrament is no solution to present concerns, neither is there any evidence to suggest that such a community ever existed in the past. From the national church to the relatively insular world of Herbert's *Temple* devout, the religious sphere is never immune to ideological tension. The need to discover peaceful means of coexistence, as pressing now as ever, was one with which in its own way the religious discourse of the seventeenth century was entirely familiar. The otherwise idiosyncratic voices of such poets as Donne and Herbert shared a concern deliberately to articulate an institutional individual, not in order to demur at, erase, attenuate, or control the vast psychological space of a modern interiority, but rather to cultivate that emerging consciousness as a familiar if evolving reflec-tion of the world it would inhabit. Their efforts exemplify what Kevin Sharpe describes as the 'quest for public order' that is also 'a search for personal integrity, for an external unity that might conjoin the lonely soul to god as well as unite the subjects of the state' as one 'commonweal.'[5] The Eucharist became an appropriate topos on which to explore this juncture of imagined and 'real' worlds, the sacramental intersection of the divine with the religious poet's daily bread, the human rendered *sub specie aeternitatis.*

Notes

Prologue

1 Watt, ix–x; Joyce, 1.
2 Martz, 9.
3 Ibid., 127–8, 299. In *A Reading of George Herbert*, Rosemond Tuve anticipated Martz, documenting in detail Herbert's debt to the Roman Catholic tradition informing medieval liturgy, devotional manuals, and verse.
4 Martz, 174–5.
5 Lake defines 'avant-garde conformity' as a style of divinity that went beyond a traditionally adiaphoric view of ceremonies, envisioning for sacraments and their priestly administration a central role in religious life. This emphasis, moreover, was deliberately opposed to a moderate puritan piety that granted at least equal importance to the word, preaching, and the predestinarian separation of a godly elect from the ungodly ('Andrewes and Buckeridge,' 113–14).
6 M. Ross, 23.
7 Strier, 47. William Halewood maintains a rigid opposition between sacramental formalism and the internalized spirituality symptomatic of puritan doctrine and practice (65–73). According to Lewalski, the void left by this suspicion of sacramental divinity is filled by a word-centred piety that urges the sermon as a preparation for meditation (*Protestant Poetics*, 155–6). Even Stanley Fish, who could hardly be said to harbour a *confessional* bias, nevertheless stresses the priority in Herbert's sacramentalism of Prayer Book calls to self-examination (*Living Temple*, 111). Earlier in Fish's oeuvre, of course, it is the human-will-denying sovereignty of Calvin's deity that makes of *The Temple* a self-consuming artifact, and of external poetic form that which is only 'mended or completed or given meaning by God' (*Self-Consuming*

Artifacts, 203). In keeping with current historiography the term 'Reform' here refers to Calvinist theology (Milton, 8 and n14; see also J. Davies, 298).

8 Veith, 218.
9 Hodgkins, 20.
10 Ibid., 24–31.
11 Doerksen, 21.
12 Ibid., 97, 139.
13 For a concise overview of these issues, see Lake and Questier, ix–xx.
14 Guibbory, *Ceremony*, 55.
15 Clarke, 115–16; Targoff, *Common Prayer*, 97.
16 Young, 82–3.
17 Ibid., 122.
18 Asals, 56.
19 Young, 133–4.
20 *Institutes*, 4.17.3, 4.17.10. All *Institutes* references indicate book, chapter, and part in the Battle/McNeill edition.
21 Young, 128.
22 Anderson, 27–47.
23 Rubin, 288, 334.
24 On Donne's Roman Catholic heritage, see Flynn, 54–79.

Introduction: The Eucharist and the English Reformation

1 Schillebeeckx, 65–9.
2 Rubin, 14–16. See also Sheedy, 102–7, and Chauvet, 293.
3 Aquinas, 119. Selected Latin insertions are from the original included in the Blackfriars edition.
4 Ibid., 59.
5 Ibid., 109.
6 Ibid., 75.
7 Aristotle, 656–7. In the *Metaphysics* Aristotle distinguishes accident from substance, the latter corresponding to the essence of a thing, the former to its sensible attributes. Thus, for example, 'This is the distinction between substance and accident – white is accidental to man, because though he is white, whiteness is not his essence' (Aristotle, 1590). The philosopher distinguishes between 'two senses' of the term substance: 'the ultimate substratum, which is no longer predicated of anything else,' and that which is a 'this,' the 'shape or form of each thing.' It is also in this discussion that Aristotle avers all things to be 'in an accidental sense' and 'by their own nature' (1606–7). The difference between accident proper and the second

sense of substance, then, would seem to be that whereas the former refers to attributes shared by distinct entities, the latter refers to the same as manifested by the form or appearance of one entity specifically. Accident and substance might thus be said to correspond to Aristotelian form and matter (the latter 'ultimate' as distinct from 'proximate' matter [1605–6]) or even form and essence – at least as concerns St Thomas's discussion of sacrament.

8 Aquinas, 117.

9 Rubin, 32–5; 324–6.

10 Luther, 21, 29–30.

11 Ibid., 33.

12 Ibid., 105–7, 110, 127.

13 Ibid., 306–7.

14 Ibid., 300.

15 Zwingli, 198.

16 Ibid., 224.

17 Cited in Stephens, 81–2.

18 Ibid., 105.

19 *Institutes*, 4.17.5.

20 Ibid., 4.17.6.

21 Ibid., 4.17.10.

22 *Corpus Reformatorum*, 49:489 (cited in McDonnell, 231).

23 *Institutes*, 4.14.1.

24 Ibid., 4.17.3. For Calvin, Augustine, and seal, see McDonnell, 286.

25 *Institutes*, 4.17.14.

26 Ibid., 4.17.15.

27 Ibid., 4.17.16.

28 Ibid., 4.17.31.

29 Anderson, 40–1.

30 Ridley, 274.

31 Ibid., 175.

32 Ibid., 202.

33 Ridley, 213; Cranmer, 127. Ridley distinguishes between two definitions. The first, which he opposes, is that of 'the real and corporal substance.' The other, which he approves, is 'secundum rem aliquam quae ad corpus Christi pertinet, i.e., according to something that appertaineth to Christ's body' (213). On the sun metaphor, see Ridley, 13; Calvin, *Institutes*, 4.17.8 (cited in Anderson, 44); Donne, *Sermons*, 7.296.

34 Cranmer, 89.

35 Ibid., 131.

36 Ibid., 134.
37 Anderson, 38.
38 Aquinas, 185.
39 Hooker, 231–2.
40 Ibid., 334–5.
41 Ibid., 341.
42 Ibid., 343.
43 Rubin, 34–77.
44 Ibid., 142, 15, 169.
45 Ibid., 188.
46 Ibid., 272–3.
47 Duffy, 111–12.
48 Ibid., 118–19.
49 Rubin, 150.
50 Duffy, 122–3.
51 Ibid., 392, 421.
52 Luther responded in *Contra Henricum Regem Angliae*, notes Robert C. Croken, by denouncing what he saw as the Mass's stress on human effort and word rather than on receiving the gifts signified by bread and wine. While Henry's authorship of the *Assertio* is doubtful, Leo apparently thought otherwise (Croken, 36 and n11).
53 Duffy, 388.
54 Ibid., 395, 407, 410–12.
55 Ibid., 431, 446–7.
56 Ibid., 399–401.
57 Ibid., 410–11.
58 Ibid., 424.
59 Whiting, 186.
60 Duffy, 428–9, 432–3.
61 Ibid., 442.
62 Ibid., 450–2.
63 Ibid., 465–70.
64 Cressy and Ferrell, 48.
65 Duffy, 474.
66 Ibid., 531.
67 Ibid., 540–2.
68 Cressy and Ferrell, 47.
69 Ibid., 59.
70 Ibid., 66.
71 *Institutes*, 4.14.15.

72 Cressy and Ferrell, 67.

73 Russell, *Causes*, 87.

74 Cressy and Ferrell, 84.

75 Hodgkins, 27.

1. Secular Verse of the Religious Man

1 DiPasquale, 147–54.

2 Rubin, 288.

3 De Saussure, 8–9.

4 Chauvet, 121.

5 Mazzola, 3.

6 Poems are cited from Donne, *Complete English Poems*, ed. C.A. Patrides. For an early and eloquent account of the interpenetration of divine and secular loves in Donne, see Colie, 129–35. Indeed, it would appear that Thomas Docherty's delight in the poststructuralist witticism 'res-erection,' mentioned three times on one page alone (135), is derived from Colie's much earlier (and less giddy) observation that in Donne 'erection becomes a symbol for resurrection' (132).

7 DiPasquale, 164.

8 Ibid., 169–70. Eleanor McNees, in her Anglican reading, similarly argues that 'Twicknam Garden' is one of several poems which 'reinforce Donne's complaint that Roman Catholics emphasize miracles over faith' (*Eucharistic Poetry*, 45). Such observations suggest polemical seriousness for a poem whose appropriation of religious language is meant merely to ridicule the speakers' pretensions: the application of the Roman Catholic language of sacrament to the lovers' posturings creates a satirical effect, a deliberate incongruity pointing to the actual gap between such language and its relatively trivial referent.

9 The sacrament, writes Calvin, 'is turned into a deadly poison for all those whose faith it does not nourish and strengthen, and whom it does not arouse to thanksgiving and to love' (*Institutes*, 4.17.40).

10 The term 'transubstantiation' was common among alchemical as well as less recondite discourses. The *OED*, for example, cites the following: '1594 Plat *Jewell-ho*. iii. 65 The Vintners practising ... sometimes even real transubstantiations, of white wine into Claret.' Its proximity in the poem to 'distill,' 'dew,' and 'manna' would have suggested to a contemporary reader both the term's sacred and profane senses.

11 Cited in Frye, *Words*, 226.

12 For an eucharistic reading of 'The Flea,' see DiPasquale, 173–86.

13 Collinson, *Religion of Protestants*, 82.

14 DiPasquale, 161.

15 Patrides' gloss is cautious: 'possibly Christ?' (Donne, *Poems*, 112n18). John Shawcross argues for the poem's fear of a mis-devotion enamoured more of things – relics – than of God. He suggests King David for 'something else,' a sinner who finds grace in the relic's miraculous powers (58–9). Shawcross thus approaches my sacramental reading – relic as means of grace – but Patrides' hunch, albeit reluctant, seems to me more plausible.

16 *Birthpangs*, 53.

17 Shklovsky, 16–29.

18 The phrase is C.W. Dugmore's description of the sacramental attitude of Stuart divines who eschewed theological accuracy for religious wonder (61n3).

19 Marx, 167.

20 Foucault, 169, 172.

21 Ibid., 181.

22 Halpern, 145–6.

23 DiPasquale, 226.

24 Ibid., 234–5.

25 Donne, *Letters*, xix.

26 DiPasquale, 233.

27 Tilman, notes Helen Gardner, was appointed deacon in 1618, but only after having expressed considerable reluctance to take orders (Donne, *Divine Poems*, 639 and Appendix D).

28 It was not uncommon among Jacobean and Caroline divines to treat Ordination as a sacrament, even if only Baptism and Holy Communion held offical sanction (Milton, 475–9).

29 Milton, 56–7.

30 Baumlin, 369.

31 McCullough, 16–17.

32 Cressy and Ferrell, 67.

33 Lake, 'Andrewes and Buckeridge,' 113–14.

34 Hester, *Kinde Pitty*, 93–5.

35 DiPasquale, 1.

36 Carr and Lady Howard were soon to be convicted for the poisoning of Sir Thomas Overbury, who, as secretary to Somerset, had been outspoken in his opposition to the marriage, which followed Howard's all too recent divorce from the earl of Essex. Annabel Patterson has pointed out that Donne's subsequent appointment to Overbury's old post may thus be related to Idios's reluctant courtiership, and perhaps provides the background for a reference in 'Satyre IV' to one 'who by poyson / Hasts to an

Offices reversion' (101–2). If that poem can thus be dated as roughly contemporary with the Overbury scandal, it may provide some insight into Donne's thoughts at a time when his vocational destiny was still uncertain but about to be decided (Patterson, 'All Donne,' 51–2). Patrides notes John Shawcross's dating of the satires in the 1590s but allows that several, including 'Satyre IV,' may have been composed much later (Donne, *Poems*, 213).

37 Calvin, *Institutes*, 4.17.10.
38 Patterson, 'All Donne,' 52.
39 Carey, 106, 14.
40 *Coterie Poet*, 253.
41 *Manuscript*, 247–56.

2. Sacrament and Grace

1 Herbert, *Works*, 259.
2 *Institutes*, 4.14.15.
3 Luther, 26.
4 Rubin, 66.
5 *Institutes*, 4.17.40.
6 Tyacke, 'Puritanism,' 65.
7 Lake, 'Calvinism,' 59.
8 Ibid., 66.
9 Tyacke, *Anti-Calvinists*, 5–6. See also Russell, *Unrevolutionary*, 202.
10 Kendall, 141–50. See also Lake, 'Calvinism,' 39–40.
11 Lake, *Anglicans*, 155–7.
12 Lake, 'Calvinism,' 42.
13 Hooker, 246–7.
14 Ibid., 242.
15 *Religion of Protestants*, 82. Collinson and others (Milton, 395–407, Sommerville, 208) agree that while there often was vehement disagreement over matters of church government and the externals of ceremonial worship, doctrinal Calvinism provided, for a time, a confessional identity of sorts. Nicholas Tyacke finds that 'puritan' as a derogatory label did not become associated specifically with doctrinal Calvinism and predestinarian thought until the 1620s when the rise of Arminianism inaugurated a process that eventually rendered heterodox what hitherto had been the Reform core of English religious orthodoxy. Prior to this time, conformist and nonconformist alike shared a doctrinally Calvinist heritage, so that the majority of conformist divines, whether inclining to a sacrament-centred ministry or one that emphasized preaching and a private lay piety, may be called

'Calvinist episcopalians' ('Puritanism,' 55–6, 68). Lake observes that while an anti-Calvinist element had always existed, the question is one of 'Calvinist hegemony.' Distaste for Reform orthodoxy did not prevent participation in Jacobean ecclesiastical life, nor, for that matter, opportunity for preferment. The relative silence of such individuals, however, is 'evidence of the extent to which Calvinism had established itself in control of the crucial cultural media of the day' ('Calvinism,' 34).

16 Kendall, 8, 79n6. The semantic ambiguity of 'experimental,' Kendall observes, is actually a useful polysemy, for it suggests both 'experience' and 'hypothesis,' each an important element in the practical application of predestinarian theology (9).

17 Ibid., 109.

18 Ibid., 146–7.

19 Ibid., 149. For Calvin, Beza, and Perkins on temporary faith, see Kendall, 21–5, 36, and 67–75. For Beza and Perkins on the two graces, see 34–5 and 64–5.

20 *Institutes*, 3.24.14.

21 Ibid., 3.24.4, 3.24.6, 3.24.7.

22 Kendall, 24. Calvin's answer to the objection that even the very elect could suspect that their faith is but the temporary, ineffectual faith of the reprobate is merely to assert that 'only in the elect does that confidence flourish which Paul extols, that they loudly proclaim Abba, Father' (*Commentaries*, Luke 17.13; cited in Kendall, 23).

23 Oliver, 141.

24 Aers and Kress, 66–7. Paul Sellin's division of *Holy Sonnets* into 'poems of Assurance' and 'poems of Angst' ('Mimetic Poetry,' 163–4) is closer to the mark, though such impulses, as we shall see, inhabit single poems as well. Peter Ivor Kaufman gets it right in opposing those, like Oliver, who find in *Holy Sonnets* 'the speaker's or poet's uneasiness with Calvinism' (157). Donne's is a 'deliberation *as* devotion,' the 'English Calvinist construction' of religious subjectivity (1). For early Calvinist readings of *Holy Sonnets*, see Halewood, 80–5, and Lewalski, *Protestant Poetics*, 264–82.

25 Collinson, *Birthpangs*, 121–5. Donne may be far from the Cartesian dualism of Marvell's 'Dialogue between the Soul and Body,' but that poem's ironic conclusion suggests an angst not unlike that of Donne's tortured penitents:

What but a soul could have the wit
To build me up for sin so fit?
So architects do square and hew,
Green trees that in the forest grew. (41–4)

26 Concerned with countering the critical dominance of protestant poetics, R.V. Young nowhere in his discussion of *La Corona* (90–2) considers 'Crucifying' and 'Resurrection,' sonnets which deal directly with the mutual relevance of grace and sacrament, as do 'Oh my black Soule,' 'At the round earths imagin'd corners,' and 'Wilt thou love God,' poems also neglected by Young.

27 DiPasquale, 76–9. Patrick O'Connell notes the Pelagian tendency of the first sonnet in the sequence (119–30), but fails to recognize a possible refutation of the same here. Elsewhere, DiPasquale is careful to note Donne's theological and thus confessional complexity. His ideas about the Eucharist are 'distinctly his own,' combining 'Calvinist formulations and Catholic-sounding language' (10). However, though DiPasquale objects to narrowly Calvinist readings of *La Corona* and implies for the poems a *via media* that is 'neither strictly Roman nor strictly Calvinist but distinctively English' (59–60), her description of that middle road as emphasizing 'reception rather than consecration, Eucharistic *experience* rather than priestly *opus*' (77) is, as Christopher Hodgkins has said of Herbert, 'very nearly Calvinist. Very, very nearly' (20).

28 A similar strategy informs the close of the final poem, 'if' qualifying the suppliant tone of the sequence's first and final lines, the crown's connecting clasp: 'if thy holy Spirit, my Muse did raise, / *Deigne at my hands this crown of prayer and praise*' (13–14).

29 Stachniewski, 273–4.

30 Nardo, 158.

31 Corthell, 147–9.

32 Both Oliver (74) and DiPasquale (32) recognize the baptismal but not the eucharistic significance of 'dew'd.'

33 Oliver, 80.

34 Ibid., 90, 117.

35 Tyacke, *Anti-Calvinists*, 5–6. For discussion of the contradictory aspects of Calvin's predestinarian theology, see Stachniewski, 20–6.

36 Patrides notes that in at least one manuscript 'busie' is 'buy' and 'she' is 'he' (Donne, *Poems*, 454n44). This would suggest Jesus himself as sole mediator, but the church's role as visible manifestation of Jesus' authority is reinforced by reference to 'this day' – the temporal coincidence of Annunciation and Passion afforded in line 23 by 'the Church, Gods Court of faculties.'

37 Gosse, 32–4 (cited in Lewalski, *Protestant Poetics*, 260).

38 DiPasquale, 51.

39 Ridley, 239. See also Hooker, 208.

40 Ferry, 227.

3. Eating the Word

1 *Anatomy*, 58. Opposing the secular poems, with their full integration of erotic and spiritual loves, to the divine, which allow disintegration of the same, Achsah Guibbory insists on the noncorporeal use of 'seale' as support for a Protestant reading of this poem's sacramental features ('Sacramental Love,' 211). To the extent that the term here is evocative of *Marriage*, however, it suggests not the Calvinist Church of England so much as the Roman church, for which Marriage remained an official sacrament. Marriage, writes Guibbory, is 'constituted by the agreement between loving partners rather than by any officiating priest' (205). The private, noninstitutional, 'priestless' characteristics of Donnean love Guibbory would celebrate as Roman Catholic are, if anything, features of a Reformation sensibility.

2 McNees, 'Anglican Doctrine,' 94–114.

3 Milton, 5.

4 Ibid., 470–5, 407–24. In this respect such divines reflected Calvin's own reluctance to make predestination central to Protestant doctrine. In 'The right and wrong way to attain certainty of election,' from the section on predestination in which Book 3 of the *Institutes* culminates, Calvin writes, 'Satan has no more grievous or dangerous temptation to dishearten believers than when he unsettles them with doubt about their election, while at the same time he arouses them with a wicked desire to seek it outside the way.' Man seeks 'outside the way' when he 'attempts to break into the inner recesses of divine wisdom, and tries to penetrate even to highest eternity, in order to find out what decision has been made concerning himself at God's judgment seat.' And yet, as we have seen, Calvin knew that 'almost all of us' are inclined to do precisely this (3.24.4). Christopher Hodgkins calls English obsession with speculative predestination 'neo-Calvinism' and blames its popularity on a shift in theological emphasis first promulgated by Theodore Beza and in England by William Perkins. While Calvin may have disapproved of this development, as Hodgkins supposes (14–15), he was also keenly aware of having provided fuel for the fire. For a discussion of English divines' efforts to dissociate themselves from predestinarian extremism while defending Calvin and even Beza, see Milton, 407–18.

5 McCullough, 7.

6 Hodgkins, 24–33.

7 Calvin, *Institutes*, 4.17.5–6.

8 See Milton, 196–205.

9 Tyacke, *Anti-Calvinists*, 5–6.

10 Collinson, *Puritan Character*, 31. Peter Lake has demonstrated that Hooker

saw in the Eucharist an opportunity to avoid the problematic opposition of visible and invisible churches. By focusing on the atoning sacrifice and salvific efficacy for all who received it, Hooker promoted a Calvinist Christocentrism without worrying about the issue of election (Lake, 'Calvinism,' 42).

11 Milton, 8.

12 *Institutes*, 4.17.6.

13 Browne, 15.

14 *Concilii Tridentini Acta*, 7.187 (cited in Schillebeeckx, 38).

15 McNees, 'Anglican Doctrine,' 103; DiPasquale, 80–1. DiPasquale does acknowledge for the passage the possibility of a conflation of Protestant and Roman Catholic doctrine, but only in a note, and thus does not give the observation the attention it deserves. Moreover, though she acknowledges Donne's fondness for eating metaphors with respect to sacrament and sermon, DiPasquale fails to recognize that the 1626 Christmas sermon is the most conspicuous example of that particular reconciling strategy (8 and n39, cf. Oliver, 244). Though his theological conclusions are similar to McNees's, Jeffrey Johnson's reading of sacrament in the Christmas sermon (140–1) neglects this problematic passage.

16 Young, 96–8. Nowhere in his discussion of sacrament in Donne's sermons (95–9) does Young cite that of Christmas 1626.

17 Dugmore, 61n3. See also Milton, 197–8.

18 Aquinas, 3.76.7.

19 Milton, 63–72, 471–2, 541–4.

20 Ibid., 414.

21 Johnson, 131–6, 14.

22 *Institutes*, 3.23.3.

23 Ibid., 3.24.14.

24 Scodel, 60.

25 Cosin, 96–7. I am alerted to this sermon by Tyacke, *Anti-Calvinists*, 124.

26 Cosin, 87–8, 99, 105.

27 Tyacke, *Anti-Calvinists*, 106–24; Milton, 428.

28 Tyacke, *Anti-Calvinists*, 48.

29 Ibid., 154–5.

30 Ibid., 167. For Arminian opposition to the Lambeth Articles and Dort, see Lake, 'Calvinism,' 62. It was also at York House that Cosin and others corroborated the view expressed some years earlier by the recusant Benjamin Carier, to wit, that predestination necessarily undermines sacramental efficacy and thus institutional authority (Milton, 544 and n31). As prolocutor to the 1626 Convocation Donne would have been aware of these events,

though Montagu's book, under the advice of Andrewes, was not discussed in the House because of the supposed Calvinist leanings of the bishops and clergy. The same Convocation, however, did examine a sermon preached before the king by the bishop of Gloucester, Godfrey Goodman. Questionable passages reportedly contained too carnal an emphasis on presence in the sacrament (Bald, 482). That the House remained undecided may suggest a relatively innocuous status for the passages in question; given the current controversy and Charles's demand for peace, however, they just as well may have suggested reluctance to establish a firm position on the matter and thereby risk provoking further disquiet.

31 Scodel, 64.

32 *Judgement*, E1v.

33 Tyacke, *Anti-Calvinists*, 47; see also Milton, 406. On Donne's support for the Dutch orthodox censure of Remonstrant rebellion, public endorsement of Dort policies, and general discussion of his ties with Reform luminaries, see Sellin, *So Doth*, 109–134.

34 Tyacke, *Anti-Calvinists*, 176–7.

35 Milton, 422.

36 Lake, 'Calvinism,' 65.

37 Walton, 265. Croll's phrase, of course, is 'an actual meditation in progress' (1074). Tyacke notes that by 1629 Donne was bold enough to attack, in a Paul's Cross sermon no less, those who are 'loth that Christ should spread his armes or shed his blood in such a compasse as might fall upon all' (9.119; *Anti-Calvinists*, 182). Tyacke neglects to observe, however, that by the end of the paragraph Donne resorts to the safety of the *via media* – 'And these are one sect ... that think there are men, whom *Christ cannot* save, And the other is of men that think they *can* save other men.' These latter, Donne goes on to say, are those who seek through '*sanctification*, and *holinesse of life* ... to make God more beholden to them' (9.120). Notice also that Donne condemns not those who say Christ *does not* save, but those who say he *cannot*, and is thus perhaps less dismissive of predestination per se than of a polemically motivated and false characterization of the doctrine as threatening divine sovereignty, 'the glory of God.'

It is notable that in an earlier sermon Donne had defended the more moderate King James's 1622 *Directions to Preachers*, a royal admonition sharing with Charles's proclamation of 1626 the concern that pulpits refrain from addressing predestinarian controversy (4.178). See Oliver, 253. As Jeanne Shami points out, however, Donne's was a 'generous interpretation' of James's order that did not altogether exclude the possibility of addressing doctrinal controversy (Shami, 394–5).

38 Como, 76.

39 Earlier in the sermon Donne includes as necessary preparation for receiving the sacrament hearing 'that which was said before' (7.280). The editors of the *Sermons* note that he alludes here to one preached earlier the same day, prior to the administration of the Eucharist; the present sermon likely was preached sometime in the afternoon (7.24).

40 Hooker, 161.

41 Winfried Schleiner notes Augustine's use of the term 'character' when writing of sacramental 'seals' (105), but neglects to mention its influence here.

42 Lewalski, 'Typological Symbolism,' 82.

43 Quinn, 276.

44 Shuger, *Sacred Rhetoric*, 198–9, 46, and 209.

45 Cited in ibid., 198. An early proponent of a sacramental model for the sermons, Joan Webber saw that style and subject matter are integral with Donne's beliefs (69). If perhaps too quick to assert his victory in the 'war with abstractions' (84), Webber at least recognized that for Donne the 'truce [was] not an easy one' (76).

46 Targoff, 'Performance,' 50–60.

4. Heart's Altar

1 Unless otherwise indicated, Herbert citations are from *Works*, ed. F.E. Hutchinson. 1633, B, and W refer to, respectively, the first edition printed by Thomas Buck at Cambridge, Buck's MS source transcribed by the Ferrars at Little Gidding (the Bodleian Library's Tanner 307) and supposedly based on Herbert's 'little book' (now lost), and the earlier MS Jones 28.169 now in the Williams library. For a discussion of the dating of this latter and its autograph status, see Charles, 78–87.

2 Hooker, 246–7. Hooker had little patience for puritan efforts to distinguish between the godly and ungodly in the visible church, for 'neither doth God thus binde us to dive into mens consciences, nor can theire fraude and deceipt hurte any man but them selves. To him they seeme such as they are, but of us they must be taken for such as they seeme. In the eye of God they are against Christ that are not trulie and sincerelie with him, in our eyes they must be received as with Christ that are not to outward showe against him' (354). See also Collinson, *Puritan Character*, 31.

3 Lake, 'Calvinism,' 74–5. Joseph Summers observes that Herbert 'believed as strongly in predestination and the doctrine of the Covenant of Grace as he believed in the significance and beauty of the ritual' (*Religion and Art*, 58).

4   Young, 35.

5   *Institutes*, 3.24.14.

6   Como, 66.

7   Milton, 527–8, 12. See also J. Davies, 18–45, and Lake, 'Andrewes and Buckeridge,' 113–33.

8   Young, 88–9.

9   Ibid., 122–3.

10   Herbert, *English Poems*, 17.

11   Dugmore, 61n3, 26–7. See also H. Davies, 288–91. Gene Veith recognizes that the doctrine of transubstantiation, because it abolishes the species, is actually less carnal than, say, the Lutheran schemes of ubiquity and consubstantiation (207). It should be stressed, however, that popular understanding of the Roman doctrine, fuelled by English antipopery, often was scathing toward 'breadengod' worship of any stripe, Lutheran or otherwise (Milton, 385–6; J. Davies, 292).

12   Milton cites a speech given before the 1629 parliament in which the Laudian bishop Richard Neile goes so far as to dismiss not only the Church of Rome, but also the Mass and transubstantiation (86). It is important to emphasize, however, that such vehemence among the more avant-garde divines may have been less a statement of confessional loyalty than the expedient deflection of charges of Roman sympathy (Milton, 84–91).

13   Ibid., 202–5.

14   Hooker, 342–3.

15   Richard Strier insists that eucharistic readings of 'Divinitie' are erroneous in so far as they neglect the non-conducive order of the words 'bloud' and 'wine' (47). R.V. Young rightly observes that 'take his bloud for wine' is compatible with Thomist teaching. The same applies to the final line of 'The Agonie' (Young, 117–18).

16   I do not include as part of 'The H. Communion' what in B and 1633 apparently is the poem's second half and what in the earlier W is the separate poem 'Prayer (II).' For an account of possible editorial error, see Huntley, 65–76. Allowing the two-part version authority, Elizabeth Clarke discerns a dual motion of outward form toward inward spirituality and the subsequent movement of the grace-inspired soul toward heaven (161). This outward-inward motion is apparent, it seems to me, in the poem's 'first half' alone.

17   Russell, *Causes*, 86.

18   *Institutes*, 4.14.1.

19   Young, 138.

20   *Institutes*, 4.14.17; Young, 138.

21   Robert Ellrodt avers that Herbert's sacramental doctrine as expressed in the

later 'H. Communion' was 'truly original' because it advanced simultane-
ously 'two realities, sensible and spiritual, at once distinct and conjoined'
(*Seven Poets*, 210–11). Whereas for Calvin the physical aspect of the Eucharist
was only metaphorically parallel to an essentially spiritual operation, for
Herbert the communication of grace included a very real physical dimension. But this twofold sacramentality nonetheless is clearly hierarchical:
'*Onely* thy grace,' writes Herbert, can 'get over to my soul.' Neither is
Herbert's more-than-merely-metaphorical parallel between matter and
spirit without precedent in English Protestantism. Nicholas Ridley, we have
seen, held that 'even as the mortal body is nourished by that visible bread,
so is the internal soul fed with the heavenly food of Christ's body' (274),
while Hooker could write that in receiving the sacrament 'wee are died
redd both within and without, our hunger is satisfied and our thirst for ever
quenched' (343).

22 Milton describes Laudian reform as 'the desire to transform English Protestants' perception of the relative importance of discipline vis-à-vis doctrine,
and of sacraments vis-à-vis preaching' (447).

23 That the W version was finally excluded from *The Temple* may be evidence of
Herbert's increasingly eirenic attitude (Summers, 'Anglican Traditions,' 24;
McGill, 21–2; Stewart, 54).

24 Luther, 306–7.

25 Schoenfeldt, *Bodies*, 98.

26 For an account of Herbert's increasingly sensualist view, see Ellrodt, *Poètes
Métaphysiques*, 323–41.

27 Herbert, *The Temple*, 18; Herbert, *Williams*, 15v. Though careful to avoid
narrow characterization of his devotional orientation (her chapter on the
poet is subtitled 'the art of contradiction'), Achsah Guibbory erroneously
attributes this particular bit of editorial doctoring to Herbert himself
(*Ceremony*, 47). Neither W nor B provides authority for Buck's innovation.

28 McLaughlin and Thomas, 116. See also Bienz, 82, and Doerksen, 97.

29 Clarke, 206.

30 Hester, 'Altering the Text,' 112.

31 Herbert's biographer, Amy Charles, asserts the autograph status of W (79–
80).

32 Herbert, *Works*, 488.

33 Young, 120–1. Stanley Stewart affirms Herbert's reluctance in the poem to
be specific about the mechanics of presence (54).

34 The Williams version is comparatively calm, concerned less with the poet's
reaction to life's pleasures than contemplation of the pleasures themselves
(*Williams*, 58v).

5. Sacramental Puritanism

1 *OED*, 6.a.

2 Young, 115.

3 According to Amy Charles, the subject matter and the fact that the poem is absent from W suggest a date approximating Herbert's anticipation of Ordination (140–1).

4 Though episcopacy by divine right was initially advanced by the more rigidly Calvinist conformists as a way of asserting their autonomy against the crown's own *iure divino* claims, puritan reservation increased proportional to the doctrine's association with the sacerdotal policies and practices of the more avant-garde divines (Milton, 454–6).

5 This latter is a traditional feature of medieval and Renaissance iconography. See, for example, Timoteo Viti's *Annunciation*, where the infant Christ descends on a dove over the praying Virgin (D'Ancona, 38 and fig. 21).

6 Young, 132.

7 Herbert, *Works*, 482.

8 'Contentiousnesse in a feast of Charity,' Herbert warns in *A Priest to the Temple*, 'is more scandall then any posture' (*Works*, 259). Herbert here also supports monthly, even less frequent, sacraments, 'yet at least five or six times in the year.' I am not aware of a similar warning with respect to prayer, though 'The Parson Praying' is anxious that the priest 'exacts of [the people] all possible reverence' and warns against 'any undutifull behaviour in them' (ibid., 231). William Bonnell has proposed an intimate connection between prayer and the Eucharist in 'Prayer (I)' (40), though the emphasis in that poem is on liturgical as opposed to private devotion. Terry Sherwood goes further, suggesting that Herbert's solution to eucharistic controversy is to 'mingle the identities of the Eucharist and prayer. By treating them as inextricable expressions of the same truth, he reveals a subtle grasp of both biblical sacrifice and the reformed tradition' (*Prayerful Art*, 18–19).

9 Sermon 272 (cited in Chauvet, 291–2).

10 H. Davies, 287.

11 Northrop Frye's theory of demonic parody (*Anatomy*, 147–50) has particular relevance for the Eucharist, for it is there that the identification of a ruthless, inscrutable will, with its sacrificial counterpart or *pharmakos*, is most concentrated. A similar duality surrounds the 'sweetned pill' of 'Affliction (I),' which the speaker 'took ... till I came where / I could not go away, nor persevere' (47–8). There may also be a sacramental aspect to the pill in as much as excessive confidence at the Lord's Supper might incur sickness

and even death: the poet's joy in 'naturall delights' (5) and 'a world of mirth' (12) is presumptuous, leading him to seek God 'with fiercenesse' (18) rather than appropriate caution and reverence. On the other hand, because sacraments for Herbert involve a concern to identify with Christ's sacrifice, affliction is simply an integral part of grace. But even this recognition is a consolation no sooner allowed than withdrawn:

> Yet lest perchance I should too happie be
>> In my unhappinesse,
> Turning my purge to food, thou throwest me
>> Into more sicknesses. (49–52)

12 That violence is an aspect of some of these poems is hardly surprising given the speaker's frustration at paradoxes whose relevance is often personal, not to mention the imagery conjured by the Eucharist itself. A formalized and ceremonious hymn, 'Antiphon (II)' is not shy about the violent dimension of eucharistic sacrifice:

> CHO. He our foes in pieces brake;
>> *Ang.* Him we touch;
>> *Men.* And him we take. (13–15)

The Eucharist, as Christ's body, is appropriately broken and identified with the sinners' bodies ('foes') it becomes and crucifies. Random Cloud, arguing that Herbert occasionally directs his frustration at Christ himself, goes to some pains to demonstrate that the imped wing in 'Easter Wings' is *imposed* by the speaker, not only shared, suggesting Herbert willingly advances affliction in his Lord, thus 'getting back at the Punisher' (126–34).

13 Stanwood and Asals, 179.

14 In keeping with the poem's subtle celebration of prevenient grace, 'rode' may be an ironic pun on the Middle English variant for 'cross.'

15 Harman, 81–2.

16 Wilcox, 64.

17 Guibbory, *Ceremony*, 45. Debora Shuger similarly argues that the 'confessional intimacy of the divine-human encounter in Herbert fulfils the need for a relationship not available in society' (*Habits*, 104).

18 Clarke, 193–4.

19 In his early study of sacramental literature, Ross finds that eucharistic imagery in Herbert is but 'Catholic rhetoric' as opposed to true 'Catholic dogma,' the former mere ornamental veneer, the latter absent altogether (179–80).

20 According to Walton, 'little book' was Herbert's name for the volume of poems sent from his death-bed to Nicholas Ferrar (286). The editors of the B facsimile also use the phrase to describe the no longer extant manuscript

likely received by Ferrar at Little Gidding (Herbert, *Bodleian*, xii). Amy Charles reminds us, however, that Walton knew Herbert's poems only as published and that 'any of the seventeenth-century editions was, indeed, a little book' (Charles, 182n12).

6. Poetry and Self

1 The phrase is Hegel's description, as cited by Harold Bloom, for Shakespearean character (Bloom, 6).
2 Fish, *Self-Consuming Artifacts*, 203.
3 Clarke, 123.
4 Ibid., 80.
5 *OED*, 3.b.
6 The polysemous 'veins' and its relevance for the tears/blood conceit is also a feature of 'Grief,' where the speaker as microcosm pleads with God to 'Let ev'ry vein / Suck up a river to supply mine eyes' (4–5).
7 Schoenfeldt, *Prayer and Power*, 212.
8 Vendler, 59. See also Toliver, 249.
9 Bloch, 111.
10 Young, 136.
11 Colie, 210.
12 Herbert, *English Poems*, 6. See also Guibbory, *Ceremony*, 46–50.
13 Shell, 61, my emphasis.
14 Patrides' note in Herbert, *English Poems*, 107n40. Hutchinson confirms as sacramental only the meat/rain conceit (Herbert, *Works*, 509).
15 For the Israelites crossing the Jordan, see Josh. 3–4; for Jesus' Baptism, see Matt. 3.13–17.
16 Bacon, 24.
17 Ibid., 22.
18 'Jordan (II)' is also concerned with artifice and substance, or 'trim invention' and 'plain intention' (3–5). The poet, 'as flames do work and winde, when they ascend,' weaves himself 'into the sense' (13–14). Devotional verse is thus a sacrificial offering, ascending in flames which achieve their end only in passing to ethereal vapour. The godly versifier, like Sidney's Astrophel admonished to 'look in thy heart and write,' is to replicate precisely and only the essence of love: '*There is in love a sweetness readie penn'd: / Copie out onely that, and save expense*' (17–18).
19 Fish, *Self-Consuming Artifacts*, 203. William Pahlka, similarly, avers that 'Herbert may write the words, but if they are accepted as a sacrifice on the altar and transformed into divine signs, that is none of his doing' (200).

20 *Williams*, 25v; *Bodleian*, 24r; *The Temple*, 30. Patrides and Hutchinson follow
1633 in having the three stanza's of W 's 'The Passion' follow 'Good Friday'
as continuous with the latter. It should be noted, however, that while the
'Passion' stanzas follow in B, they do so on a new verso page. It is possible
the scribe simply ran out of space in copying an authorized conflation; but
it is also possible s/he neglected to include the title for what originally was
meant to be a separate poem. Whatever Herbert's intentions, however, the
close proximity of the two poems in the later MS and first edition emphasizes their mutual relevance.

21 Something like this is suggested by Richard Todd's reader response approach to *The Temple*, in which God 'stands to the poet as the poet stands to
the reader'; both Herbert's initial 'offering' and the reader's participation
in the resulting text are 'sacramental' activities (8).

Conclusion: Sacramental Poetics

1 H. Ross, 126.
2 Elsky, 328.
3 Crashaw, 186.
4 *Paradise Lost*, 12.587.
5 Sharpe, 361.

Works Cited

Aers, David, and Gunther Kress. 'Vexatious Contraries: A Reading of Donne's Poetry.' *Literature, Language and Society in England, 1580–1680*. Ed. David Aers, Bob Hodge, and Gunther Kress. Dublin: Gill and Macmillan, 1981. 49–74.

Anderson, Judith H. 'Language and History in the Reformation: Cranmer, Gardiner, and the Words of Institution.' *Renaissance Quarterly* 54.1 (2001): 20–51.

Aquinas, St Thomas. *The Eucharistic Presence*. Ed. William Barden. London: Blackfriars, 1965. Vol. 58 of *Summa Theologiae*. 60 vols. 1964–76.

Aristotle. *The Complete Works of Aristotle*. Ed. Jonathan Barnes. 2 vols. Princeton: Princeton UP, 1991.

Asals, Heather A.R. *Equivocal Predication: George Herbert's Way to God*. Toronto: U of Toronto P, 1981.

Bacon, Francis. *Essays and New Atlantis*. Ed. Gordon S. Haight. New York: Walter J. Black, 1942.

Bald, R.C. *John Donne: A Life*. Oxford: Clarendon P, 1970.

Baumlin, James S. 'Donne's "Satyre IV": The Failure of Language and Genre.' *Texas Studies in Literature and Language* 30.3 (1988): 363–87.

Bienz, John. 'Images and Ceremonial in *The Temple*.' *Studies in English Literature* 26.1 (1986): 73–95.

Bloch, Chana. *Spelling the Word: George Herbert and the Bible*. Berkeley: U of California P, 1985.

Bonnell, William. 'The Eucharistic Substance of George Herbert's "Prayer (I)."' *George Herbert Journal* 9.2 (1986): 35–47.

Browne, Thomas. *The Works of Sir Thomas Browne*. Ed. Geoffrey Keynes. Vol. 1. Chicago: Chicago UP, 1964.

Calvin, John. *Calvin's Commentaries: Matthew, Mark and Luke*. 3 vols. Edinburgh: St Andrew P, 1972.

- *Corpus Reformatorum, Joannis Calvini Opera quae supersunt omnia.* Ed. G. Baum et al. 59 vols. Braunschweig: C.A. Schwetschke, 1893–1900.
- *Institutes of the Christian Religion.* Trans. Ford Lewis Battles. Ed. John T. McNeill. 2 vols. Philadelphia: Westminster P, 1960.

Carey, John. *John Donne: Life, Mind and Art.* London: Faber, 1981.

Charles, Amy. *A Life of George Herbert.* Ithaca, NY: Cornell UP, 1977.

Chauvet, Louis-Marie. *Symbol and Sacrament: A Sacramental Reinterpretation of Christian Existence.* Trans. S.J. Patrick Madigan and Madeleine Beaumont. Collegeville, MN: Liturgical P, 1995.

Clarke, Elizabeth. *Theory and Theology in George Herbert's Poetry: Divinitie, and Poesie, Met.* Oxford: Clarendon P, 1997.

Cloud, Random. 'Fiat ∫Lux.' *Crisis in Editing: Texts of the English Renaissance.* Ed. Randall M Leod. New York: AMS P, 1993. 61–172.

Colie, Rosalie L. *Paradoxia Epidemica: The Renaissance Tradition of Paradox.* Princeton: Princeton UP, 1966.

Collinson, Patrick. *The Birthpangs of Protestant England: Religious and Cultural Change in the Sixteenth and Seventeenth Centuries.* London: Macmillan, 1988.
- *The Puritan Character: Polemics and Polarities in Early Seventeenth-Century Culture.* Los Angeles: William Andrews Clark, 1989.
- *The Religion of Protestants: The Church in English Society 1559–1625.* Oxford: Clarendon P, 1982.

Como, David. 'Puritans, Predestination and the Construction of Orthodoxy in Early Seventeenth-Century England.' *Conformity and Orthodoxy in the English Church, c.1560–1660.* Ed. Peter Lake and Michael Questier. Woodbridge, Suffolk: Boydell P, 2000.

Corthell, Ronald. *Ideology and Desire in Renaissance Poetry: The Subject of Donne.* Detroit: Wayne State UP, 1997.

Cosin, John. *Works.* Vol.1. Oxford: John Henry Parker, 1843.

Cranmer, Thomas. *The Works of Thomas Cranmer.* Ed. John Edmund Cox. Vol. 1. Cambridge: Cambridge UP, 1844.

Crashaw, Richard. *The Complete Poetry of Richard Crashaw.* Ed. George Walton Williams. New York: Doubleday, 1970.

Cressy, David, and Lori Anne Ferrell, eds. *Religion and Society in Early Modern England: A Sourcebook.* London: Routledge, 1996.

Croken, Robert C. *Luther's First Font: The Eucharist as Sacrifice.* Ottawa: U of Ottawa P, 1990.

Croll, Morris W. 'The Baroque Style in Prose.' *Seventeenth Century Prose and Poetry.* Ed. A.M. Witherspoon and F.J. Warnke. 2nd ed. Fort Worth, TX: Harcourt Brace Jovanovich, 1982. 1065–77.

D'Ancona, Mirella Levi. *The Iconography of the Immaculate Conception in the Middle Ages and the Early Renaissance.* New York: College Art Association of America, 1957.

Davies, Horton. *Worship and Theology in England.* Vol. 2. Princeton: Princeton UP, 1970–5.

Davies, Julian. *The Caroline Captivity of the Church: Charles I and the Remoulding of Anglicanism 1625–1641.* Oxford: Clarendon P, 1992.

De Saussure, Ferdinand. 'The Object of Study.' *Modern Criticism and Theory.* Ed. David Lodge. New York: Longman, 1988. 2–9.

DiPasquale, Theresa M. *Literature and Sacrament: The Sacred and the Secular in John Donne.* Pittsburgh: Duquesne UP, 1999.

Docherty, Thomas. *John Donne Undone.* London: Methuen, 1986.

Doerksen, Daniel W. *Conforming to the Word: Herbert, Donne, and the English Church Before Laud.* Lewisburg, PA: Bucknell UP, 1997.

Donne, John. *The Complete English Poems of John Donne.* Ed. C.A. Patrides. London: J.M. Dent & Sons, 1989.

– *John Donne: The Divine Poems.* Ed. Helen Gardner. 2nd ed. Oxford: Clarendon P, 1978.

– *Letters to Severall Persons of Honour.* 1651. Ed. M. Thomas Hester. Facs. rpt. Delmar, NY: Scholar P, 1977.

– *The Sermons of John Donne.* Ed. Evelyn M. Simpson and George R. Potter. 10 vols. Berkeley: U of California P, 1953–62.

Duffy, Eamon. *The Stripping of the Altars: Traditional Religion in England c.1400– c.1580.* New Haven: Yale UP, 1992.

Dugmore, C.W. *Eucharistic Doctrine in England from Hooker to Waterland: Being the Norrisian Prize Essay in the University of Cambridge for the Year 1940.* London: Society for Promoting Christian Knowledge, 1942.

Ellrodt, Robert. *Les poètes métaphysiques anglais: John Donne et les poètes de la tradition chrétienne.* Vol. 1. Paris: J. Corti, 1960.

– *Seven Metaphysical Poets: A Structural Study of the Unchanging Self.* Oxford: Oxford UP, 2000.

Elsky, Martin. 'The Sacramental Frame of George Herbert's "The Church" and the Shape of Spiritual Autobiography.' *Journal of English and Germanic Philology* 83 (1984): 313–29.

Ferry, Anne. *The 'Inward' Language: Sonnets of Wyatt, Sidney, Shakespeare, Donne.* Chicago: U of Chicago P, 1983.

Fish, Stanley. *The Living Temple: George Herbert and Catechizing.* Los Angeles: U of California P, 1978.

– *Self-Consuming Artifacts: The Experience of Seventeenth-Century Literature.* Los Angeles: U of California P, 1972.

Flynn, Dennis. *John Donne and the Ancient Catholic Nobility.* Bloomington, IN: Indiana UP, 1995.

Foucault, Michel. *The Order of Things: An Archaeology of the Human Sciences.* 1970. New York: Vintage P, 1973.

Frye, Northrop. *Anatomy of Criticism.* 1957. New York: Atheneum, 1966.

– *Words with Power: Being a Second Study of the Bible and Literature.* Toronto: Penguin, 1992.

Gosse, Edmund, ed. *The Life and Letters of John Donne.* Rev. ed. Gloucester, MA: P. Smith, 1959.

Guibbory, Achsah. *Ceremony and Community from Herbert to Milton: Literature, Religion, and Cultural Conflict in Seventeenth-Century England.* Cambridge: Cambridge UP, 1998.

– 'Fear of "loving more": Death and the Loss of Sacramental Love.' *John Donne's 'desire of more': The Subject of Anne More Donne in His Poetry.* Ed. M. Thomas Hester. Newark, DE: U of Delaware P, 1996. 204–27.

Halewood, William. *The Poetry of Grace: Reformation Themes and Structures in Seventeenth-Century Poetry.* New Haven: Yale UP, 1970.

Halpern, Richard. *The Poetics of Private Accumulation: English Renaissance Culture and the Genealogy of Capital.* Ithaca, NY: Cornell UP, 1991.

Harman, Barbara Leah. *Costly Monuments: Representations of the Self in George Herbert's Poetry.* Cambridge, MA: Harvard UP, 1982.

Herbert, George. *The Bodleian Manuscript of George Herbert's Poems: A Facsimile of Tanner 307.* Ed. Amy M. Charles and Mario A. Di Cesare. New York: Scholars' Facsimiles & Reprints, 1984.

– *The English Poems of George Herbert.* Ed. C.A. Patrides. London: J.M. Dent & Sons, 1988.

– *George Herbert The Temple: A Diplomatic Edition of the Bodleian Manuscript (Tanner 307).* Ed. Mario A. Di Cesare. Binghamton, NY: Medieval and Renaissance Texts Society, 1995.

– *George Herbert: The Temple.* 1633. Menston, Yorkshire: Scolar P, 1968.

– *The Williams Manuscript of George Herbert's Poems.* Ed. Amy M. Charles. Delmar, NY: Scholars' Facsimiles & Reprints, 1977.

– *The Works of George Herbert.* Ed. F.E. Hutchinson. Oxford: Clarendon P, 1941.

Hester, M. Thomas. 'Altering the Text of the Self: The Shapes of "The Altar."' *A Fine Tuning: Studies of the Religious Poetry of Herbert and Milton.* Ed. Mary A. Maleski. Binghamton, NY: Medieval & Renaissance Texts & Studies, 1989. 95–116.

– *Kinde Pitty and Brave Scorn: John Donne's* Satyres. Durham, NC: Duke UP, 1982.

Hodgkins, Christopher. *Authority, Church, and Society in George Herbert: Return to the Middle Way.* Columbia: U of Missouri P, 1993.

Hooker, Richard. *The Folger Library Edition of the Works of Richard Hooker*. Vol. 2. Ed. W. Speed Hill. Cambridge, MA: Harvard UP, 1977.

Huntley, Frank L. 'What Happened to Two of Herbert's Poems?' *Essays in Persuasion: On Seventeenth-Century Literature*. Chicago: U of Chicago P, 1981. 65–76.

Johnson, Jeffrey. *The Theology of John Donne*. Cambridge: D. S. Brewer, 1999.

Jonson, Ben. *Bartholomew Fair*. Ed. E.A. Horsman. London: Revels, 1960.

Joyce, James. *Ulysses*. 1922. Ed. Declan Kiberd. London: Penguin, 1992.

The Judgement of the Synode Holden at Dort, London 1619. Facs. rpt. Amsterdam: Theatrum Orbis Terrarum, 1974.

Kaufman, Peter Ivor. *Prayer, Despair and Drama: Elizabethan Introspection*. Chicago: U of Illinois P, 1996.

Kendall, R.T. *Calvin and English Calvinism to 1649*. Oxford: Oxford UP, 1979.

Lake, Peter. *Anglicans and Puritans? Presbyterian and English Conformist Thought from Whitgift to Hooker*. London: Allen & Unwin, 1988.

– 'Calvinism and the English Church.' *Past and Present* 114 (1987): 32–76.

– 'Lancelot Andrewes, John Buckeridge and Avant-Garde Conformity at the Court of James I.' *The Mental World of the Jacobean Court*. Ed. L. Levy Peck. Cambridge: Cambridge UP, 1991. 113–33.

Lake, Peter, and Michael Questier, eds. *Conformity and Orthodoxy in the English Church, c.1560–1660*. Woodbridge, Suffolk: Boydell P, 2000.

Lewalski, Barbara K. *Protestant Poetics and the Seventeenth-Century Religious Lyric*. Princeton: Princeton UP, 1979.

– 'Typological Symbolism and the "Progress of the Soul."' *Literary Uses of Typology from the Late Middle Ages to the Present*. Ed. Earl Miner. Princeton: Princeton UP, 1977. 79–114.

Luther, Martin. *Luther's Works*. Gen. ed. Helmut T. Lehmann. Vol. 38. Philadelphia: Fortress P, 1971.

Marotti, Arthur F. *John Donne, Coterie Poet*. Madison: U of Wisconsin P, 1986.

– *Manuscript, Print, and the English Renaissance Lyric*. Ithaca, NY: Cornell UP, 1995.

Martz, Louis L. *The Poetry of Meditation: A Study in English Religious Literature of the Seventeenth Century*. New Haven: Yale UP, 1954.

Marvell, Andrew. *The Complete Poems*. Ed. Elizabeth Story Donno. London: Penguin, 1972.

Marx, Karl. 'Economic and Philosophical Manuscripts.' Trans. T.B. Bottomore. *Marx's Concept of Man*. Ed. Erich Fromm. New York: Continuum, 1966. 85–196.

Mazzola, Elizabeth. *The Pathology of the English Renaissance: Sacred Remains and Holy Ghosts*. Leiden: Brill, 1998.

McCullough, Peter E. *Sermons at Court: Politics and Religion in Elizabethan and Jacobean Preaching.* Cambridge: Cambridge UP, 1998.

McDonnell, Kilian. *John Calvin, the Church, and the Eucharist.* Princeton: Princeton UP, 1967.

McGill, William J., Jr. 'George Herbert's View of the Eucharist.' *Lock Haven Review* 8 (1966): 16–24.

McLaughlin, Elizabeth, and Gail Thomas. 'Communion in *The Temple.' Studies in English Literature* 15.1 (1975): 111–24.

McNees, Eleanor. *Eucharistic Poetry: The Search for Presence in the Writings of John Donne, Gerard Manley Hopkins, Dylan Thomas, and Geoffrey Hill.* Lewisburg, PA: Bucknell UP, 1992.

– 'John Donne and the Anglican Doctrine of the Eucharist.' *Texas Studies in Literature and Language* 29.1 (1987): 94–114.

Milton, Anthony. *Catholic and Reformed: The Roman and Protestant Churches in English Protestant Thought.* Cambridge: Cambridge UP, 1995.

Milton, John. *Paradise Lost.* Ed. Scott Elledge. 2nd ed. New York: Norton, 1993.

Nardo, Anna K. 'John Donne at Play in Between.' *The Eagle and the Dove: Reassessing John Donne.* Ed. Claude J. Summers and Ted-Larry Pebworth. Columbia: U of Missouri P, 1986. 157–65.

O'Connell, Patrick F. '"La Corona": Donne's *Ars Poetica Sacra.' The Eagle and the Dove: Reassessing John Donne.* Ed. Claude J. Summers and Ted-Larry Pebworth. Columbia: University of Missouri P, 1986. 119–30.

Oliver, P.M. *Donne's Religious Writing: A Discourse of Feigned Devotion.* London: Longman, 1997.

Pahlka, William H. *Saint Augustine's Meter and George Herbert's Will.* Kent, OH: Kent State UP, 1987.

Patterson, Annabel. 'All Donne.' *Soliciting Interpretation: Literary Theory and Seventeenth-Century English Poetry.* Ed. Elizabeth D. Harvey and Katherine Eisaman Maus. Chicago: U of Chicago P, 1990. 37–67.

– *Censorship and Interpretation: The Conditions of Writing and Reading in Early Modern England.* Madison, WI: U of Wisconsin P, 1984.

Quinn, Dennis. 'John Donne's Principles of Biblical Exegesis.' *Journal of English and Germanic Philology* 61 (1962): 313–29.

Reeves, Troy. *Index to the Sermons of John Donne.* 3 vols. Salzburg: Institut fur Anglistik und Amerikanistik, 1979–81.

Ridley, Nicholas. *The Works of Nicholas Ridley.* Ed. Henry Christmas. Cambridge: Parker Society, 1841.

Ross, Heather. 'Meating God: Herbert's Poetry and the Discourse of Appetite.'

George Herbert: Sacred and Profane. Ed. Helen Wilcox and Richard Todd. Amsterdam: Vrije Universiteit P, 1995. 121–6.

Ross, Malcolm Mackenzie. *Poetry and Dogma: The Transfiguration of Eucharistic Symbols in Seventeenth-Century English Poetry.* New Brunswick, NJ: Rutgers UP, 1954.

Rubin, Miri. *Corpus Christi: The Eucharist in Late Medieval Culture.* Cambridge: Cambridge UP, 1991.

Russell, Conrad. *The Causes of the English Civil War.* Oxford: Clarendon P, 1990.

– *Unrevolutionary England, 1603–1642.* London: Hambleton P, 1990.

Schillebeeckx, E. *The Eucharist.* Trans. N.D. Smith. New York: Sheed and Ward, 1968.

Schleiner, Winfried. *The Imagery of John Donne's Sermons.* Providence, RI: Brown UP, 1970.

Schoenfeldt, Michael C. *Bodies and Selves in Early Modern England: Physiology and Inwardness in Spenser, Shakespeare, Herbert, and Milton.* Cambridge: Cambridge UP, 1999.

– *Prayer and Power: George Herbert and Renaissance Courtship.* Chicago: U of Chicago P, 1991.

Scodel, Joshua. 'John Donne and the Religious Politics of the Mean.' *John Donne's Religious Imagination: Essays in Honour of John T. Shawcross.* Ed. Raymond-Jean Frontain and Frances M. Malpezzi. Conway, AR: U of Central Arkansas P, 1995. 45–80.

The Second Shepherd's Pageant. Everyman and Medieval Miracle Plays. Ed. A.C. Cawley. London: J.M. Dent & Sons, 1981. 81–108.

Sellin, Paul R. 'The Mimetic Poetry of Jack and John Donne: A Field Theory for the Amorous and the Divine.' *Sacred and Profane: Secular and Devotional Interplay in Early Modern British Literature.* Ed. Helen Wilcox, Richard Todd, and Alasdair MacDonald. Amsterdam: Vrije Universiteit P, 1996. 163–72.

– *So Doth, So Is Religion: John Donne and Diplomatic Contexts in the Reformed Netherlands, 1619–1620.* Columbia: U of Missouri P, 1988.

Shakespeare, William. *The Riverside Shakespeare.* Ed. G. Blakemore Evans et al. Boston: Houghton Mifflin, 1974.

Shami, Jeanne. 'Donne's *Sermons* and the Absolutist Politics of Quotation.' *John Donne's Religious Imagination: Essays in Honour of John T. Shawcross.* Ed. Raymond-Jean Frontain and Frances M. Malpezzi. Conway, AR: U of Central Arkansas P, 1995. 380–412.

Sharpe, Kevin. *Remapping Early Modern England: The Culture of Seventeenth-Century Politics.* Cambridge: Cambridge UP, 2000.

Shawcross, John T. 'Poetry, Personal and Impersonal: The Case of Donne.'

The Eagle and the Dove: Reassessing John Donne. Ed. Claude J. Summers and Ted-Larry Pebworth. Columbia: U of Missouri P, 1986. 53–66.

Sheedy, Charles E. *The Eucharistic Controversy of the Eleventh Century.* Washington: Catholic UP, 1947.

Shell, Alison. *Catholicism, Controversy and the English Literary Imagination.* Cambridge: Cambridge UP, 1999.

Sherwood, Terry G. *Fulfilling the Circle: A Study of John Donne's Thought.* Toronto: U of Toronto P, 1984.

– *Herbert's Prayerful Art.* Toronto: U of Toronto P, 1989.

Shklovsky, Victor. 'Art as Technique.' *Modern Criticism and Theory.* Ed. David Lodge. New York: Longman, 1988. 16–30.

Shuger, Debora K. *Habits of Thought in the English Renaissance: Religion, Politics, and the Dominant Culture.* Los Angeles: U of California P, 1990.

– *Sacred Rhetoric: The Christian Grand Style in the English Renaissance.* Princeton: Princeton UP, 1988.

Singleton, Marion White. *God's Courtier: Configuring a Different Grace in George Herbert's* Temple. Cambridge: Cambridge UP, 1987.

Sommerville, J.P. *Politics and Ideology in England, 1603–40.* London: Longman, 1986.

Southwell, Robert. *The Poems of Robert Southwell, S.J.* Ed. James H. McDonald and Nancy Pollard Brown. Oxford: Clarendon P, 1967.

Spenser, Edmund. *The Works of Edmund Spenser.* Ed. Tim Cook. Hertfordshire: Wordsworth Editions, 1995.

Stachniewski, John. *The Persecutory Imagination: English Puritanism and the Literature of Religious Despair.* Oxford: Clarendon P, 1991.

Stanwood, P.G., and Heather Ross Asals, eds. *John Donne and the Theology of Language.* Columbia: U of Missouri P, 1986.

Stephens, W.P. *Zwingli: An Introduction to His Thought.* Oxford: Clarendon P, 1994.

Stewart, Stanley. *George Herbert.* Boston: Twayne, 1986.

Strier, Richard. *Love Known: Theology and Experience in George Herbert's Poetry.* Chicago: U of Chicago P, 1983.

Summers, Joseph H. 'George Herbert and Anglican Traditions.' *George Herbert Journal* 16.1 (1993): 21–39.

– *George Herbert: His Religion and Art.* Binghamton, NY: Medieval & Renaissance Texts & Studies, 1981.

Targoff, Ramie. *Common Prayer: The Language of Public Devotion in Early Modern England.* Chicago: U of Chicago P, 2001.

– 'The Performance of Prayer: Sincerity and Theatricality in Early Modern England.' *Representations* 60 (1997): 49–69.

Todd, Richard. *The Opacity of Signs: Acts of Interpretation in George Herbert's* The
  Temple. Columbia: U of Missouri P, 1986.
Toliver, Harold. *George Herbert's Christian Narrative*. University Park, PA: Pennsyl-
  vania State UP, 1993.
Tuve, Rosemond. *A Reading of George Herbert*. Chicago: U of Chicago P, 1952.
Tyacke, Nicholas. *Anti-Calvinists: The Rise of English Arminianism c.1590–1640*.
  Oxford: Clarendon P, 1987.
– 'Puritanism, Arminianism and Counter-Revolution.' 1973. Reprinted and
  abridged in *Reformation to Revolution: Politics and Religion in Early Modern
  England*. Ed. Margot Todd. London: Routledge, 1995. 53–70.
Vaughan, Henry. *The Works of Henry Vaughan*. Ed. L.C. Martin. 2nd ed. Oxford:
  Clarendon P, 1957.
Veith, Gene Edward, Jr. *Reformation Spirituality: The Religion of George Herbert*.
  Lewisburg, PA: Bucknell UP, 1985.
Vendler, Helen. *The Poetry of George Herbert*. Cambridge, MA: Harvard UP, 1975.
Walton, Izaak. 'The Life of Dr. John Donne' and 'The Life of Mr. George
  Herbert.' *Seventeenth Century Prose and Poetry*. Ed. A.M. Witherspoon and F.J.
  Warnke. 2nd ed. Fort Worth, TX: Harcourt Brace Jovanovich, 1982. 250–88.
Watt, Stephen. 'Introduction.' *Dubliners*. 1914. New York: Simon & Schuster,
  1998.
Webber, Joan. *Contrary Music: The Prose Style of John Donne*. Madison, WI: U of
  Wisconsin P, 1963.
Whiting, Robert. *The Blind Devotion of the People: Popular Religion and the English
  Reformation*. Cambridge: Cambridge UP, 1989.
Wilcox, Helen. '"Heaven's Lidger Here": Herbert's *Temple* and Seventeenth-
  Century Devotion.' *Images of Belief in Literature*. Ed. David Jasper. London:
  Macmillan, 1984. 153–68.
Young, R.V. *Doctrine and Devotion in Seventeenth-Century Poetry: Studies in Donne,
  Herbert, Crashaw, and Vaughan*. Cambridge: D.S. Brewer, 2000.
Zwingli, Huldreich. *Zwingli and Bullinger*. Trans. G.W. Bromiley. London:
  Students' Christian Movement P, 1953.

Index